Early 20th Century German Fiction

The German Library: Volume 67

Volkmar Sander, General Editor

A. Döblin, L. Feuchtwanger,
A. Seghers, A. Zweig

EARLY 20TH CENTURY GERMAN FICTION

Edited by Alexander Stephan

CONTINUUM
NEW YORK · LONDON

2003

The Continuum International Publishing Group Inc
370 Lexington Avenue, New York, NY 10017

The Continuum International Publishing Group Ltd
The Tower Building, 11 York Road, London SE1 7NX

The German Library
is published in cooperation with Deutsches Haus,
New York University.
This volume has been supported by Inter Nationes.

Printed in the United States of America

Library of Congress Cataloging-in-Publication Data

Early 20th century German fiction / edited by Alexander Stephan.
    p.   cm. — (The German library ; v. 67)
   ISBN 0-8264-1454-0 (alk. paper) — ISBN 0-8264-1455-9 (pbk. : alk.
paper).
   1. German literature—20th century—Translations into English.   I.
Title: Early twentieth century German fiction.   II. Stephan, Alexander,
1946–   III. Series.
PT1113.E27   2002
833′.91208—dc21   2002152870

Acknowledgments will be found on page 261,
which constitutes an extension of the copyright page.

Contents

Introduction

The lives and works of the four authors presented in this volume—
Arnold Zweig (1887–1968), Alfred Döblin (1878–1957), Lion
Feuchtwanger (1884–1958) and Anna Seghers (1900–1983)—were
shaped by the problematic transition from the relatively closed
nineteenth-century society to the modern world of the twentieth
century.

They were able to free themselves, but slowly and with difficulty,
from the narrow authoritarian society of Kaiser Wilhelm's Germany, which had dominated their upbringing at home and school
and which, in some cases, moved them to join the patriotic cause of
the Prussian militarists in 1914. Their Jewish descent made them
outsiders who—except for Anna Seghers—reflected all their lives
on the issues of assimilation, persecution, Zionism, Palestine, and
the untapped potential of the Jews of Eastern Europe. Seeking alter-
natives to the oppressive atmosphere in which they were reared,
they allied themselves after 1917–18 with an idealized socialism,
often without the necessary ideological foundation, or joined the
Communist Party. Their political choices (once again with the exception of the somewhat younger Anna Seghers) were encouraged
by their direct or indirect experience of World War I with its anonymous mechanized mass battles in which the individual was made
to seem unimportant. All four writers had reasoned their way to
republican sympathies, and took a more or less positive view of the
Weimar Republic. When the Nazis came to power in Germany in
1933, they were all exiled, disenfranchised, and deprived of their
citizenship as Jews, left-wingers, and pacifists. And when they
themselves, or their books, were allowed to return in 1945, they
were caught between the camps of the East and West in the cold

war, which brought its own set of prejudices and exclusions. Döblin, who left his exile in California in 1946 to work as a cultural officer for the French army of occupation, soon turned his back on his country for a second time, disappointed by the lack of response to his writings and by the restoration of conservative forces in West Germany. Anna Seghers and Arnold Zweig settled in the German Democratic Republic and thereafter were ignored in West Germany or defamed as "state poets." Feuchtwanger, still suspected of being a Communist fellow-traveler, continued to live under FBI surveillance in his political asylum of Pacific Palisades, California, and did not dare to visit Germany because he feared that he would not be allowed to reenter the United States.

Like their lives, the writings of the four authors also show more common features than differences. The German Enlightenment, Nietzsche and Freud, and, in some cases, Marx and Lenin, shaped their basic worldviews. Arnold Zweig, whose reputation in Germany is linked primarily to *The Case of Sergeant Grischa (Der Streit um den Sergeanten Grischa),* and Lion Feuchtwanger, who gained a large-international audience with popularly written historical novels like *Jew Süss (Jud Süss),* are firmly entrenched in the realistic style of the nineteenth century. Anna Seghers tacitly experimented with modernist formal innovations in *The Seventh Cross (Das siebte Kreuz)* and "The Excursion of the Dead Girls" *(Der Ausflug der toten Mädchen),* only to be met with criticism from dogmatic fellow Communists of the Socialist Realist school who remained fixated on the models of Tolstoy and Balzac. Even the works of Döblin, whose story "The Murder of a Buttercup" *(Die Ermordung einer Butterblume)* and urban-set novel *Berlin Alexanderplatz (Berlin Alexanderplatz)* rank among the classics of Expressionism, are not systematically modernist in either form or content. None of the four authors generated literature of major international stature such as James Joyce, Franz Kafka, or Marcel Proust produced in the same period. Their themes and characters do not in many ways transcend the confines of German culture and history, and for the most part they do not break new ground stylistically. Yet, Arnold Zweig, Alfred Döblin, Lion Feuchtwanger, and Anna Seghers do hold a central place in early twentieth-century German literature in that their works reflect the birth of modernism, which in Germany as elsewhere is characterized by the loss of ideological certainty, by the living conditions of anonymous metropolises, a technology that threatens nature, savage world wars, revolutions, political terror, and racial persecution.

ARNOLD ZWEIG

Arnold Zweig, like Döblin, is among the sizable group of artists and intellectuals who greeted the outbreak of World War I in 1914 with relative enthusiasm. Two years later, Zweig was transferred out of the hell of Verdun to headquarters on the quieter Eastern front, where he served as a press officer and read Henri Barbusse's antimilitarist novel *Under Fire (Le Feu),* becoming a lifelong pacifist. The way that German officers traded for power and influence in the occupied Polish and Russian territories destroyed his faith in the morality and honor of the Prussian bureaucracy. Hearing a report of the senseless execution of a simple Russian prisoner—a man accused of being a Bolshevist agent, who was put to death as a lesson to German troops growing unruly as they observed the revolution taking place in Russia—Zweig felt moved to write the antiwar novel published in 1927 under the title *The Case of Sergeant Grischa.* Moreover Zweig, the son of a Jewish grain merchant and harness maker from Glogau in Silesia, met with Eastern European Jews during his stay in Poland and Lithuania, and became a cultural Zionist, having been already stirred by the fate of Eastern Jews in tsarist Russia to write a short narrative called "Pogrom" *(Episode aus Zarenland),* which was published in 1912.

The Case of Sergeant Grischa is among the German novels that treat the horrors of World War I from a postwar point of view. Unlike Erich Maria Remarque and Ernst Jünger, who describe from opposite points of view the heavily armed battles of this first major technological war in human history, Zweig aims to expose in a realistic and three-dimensional form the cold mechanics of the Prussian military bureaucracy, and to show how the individual is swallowed up in the anonymity of modern life. Grigori Iljitsch Paprotkin, known as Grischa, the protagonist, is anything but a war hero. Homesickness drives him to escape from a German POW camp in the spring of 1917, shortly before hostilities end on the Eastern front. Beginning a relationship with Babka, the woman leader of a partisan group, he is advised by her to avoid imminent capture by assuming the identity of a Russian deserter called Bjuschew, and so gets caught in the fatal legal machinery of the Prussian military. Recaptured by the Germans, he is sentenced to death as a spy, and neither General von Lychow, a Prussian officer of the old school, von Lychow's nephew Winfried, Posnanski, a Jewish military magistrate, nor the Jewish writer Bertin can save him despite his having been proved innocent. After lengthy proceedings, von Lychow's superior Schieffenzahn, a pragmatic, authoritarian man modeled on the real-life figure of General Ludendorff, bypasses the traditional rules by ordering the sentence to be carried out, justifying his action by saying that "the State creates justice, the individual is a louse" (p. 37).

Zweig worked the events of the Russian Revolution into the background of his *Grischa* novel but they play a rather marginal role considering that socialism became a part of his life in 1917, and remained with him through his final years in the GDR. He had close associations with Martin Buber and, later, Sigmund Freud, and was equally inspired by ideas that also appear, in one form or another, in the work of Alfred Döblin, Lion Feuchtwanger, and Anna Seghers: the theme of cyclical return, represented in the birth of Grischa's and Babka's daughter, images of an archaic mother figure, references to the Bible and to Jewish culture, the instinctive wisdom of the common people, and, as an opening theme of the novel, the picture of the "little planet Tellus" reeling through the dark reaches of space.

ALFRED DÖBLIN

When in 1910 Alfred Döblin published his story "The Murder of a Buttercup," which he had written in 1904–5, the contemporary literary critics at once agreed that it had achieved the transition from Impressionism to Expressionism. Döblin, it was claimed, presented feelings and moods in a new hard cinematographic language that could shift at any time into the visionary, grotesque, ominous, cosmic. Edgar Allan Poe was the suggested model for the images of murder, decay, guilt, and megalomania; Sigmund Freud inspired the depiction of unraveling emotions, and the various taboo forms of a misogynistic, sadomasochistic sexuality, which in this story were still shown in latent guise but which became overt in *Berlin Alexanderplatz.*

"The Murder of a Buttercup" is rooted in Döblin's difficult relationship with women and sexuality. But it also forms part of that literature chiefly represented by Thomas and Heinrich Mann, which critiques the authoritarian yet insecure middle class of Kaiser Wilhelm's Germany. And those passages in which it shifts into the grotesque resemble the parables written soon after by Franz Kafka, showing an absurd world in which the quest for order, self-control, and lawfulness ends again and again in chaotic, uncontrolled fits of anxiety, madness, impotence, and despair.

The story of the death of a buttercup was among the works that began the Expressionist decade, but the heyday of Expressionism was already a distant memory by 1929 when Döblin published the novel *Berlin Alexanderplatz,* a masterpiece of modern literature that was at once greeted as the preeminent classic of Expressionist prose. The metropolis as misanthropic Moloch; the submergence of the individual in the faceless "crowds" (p. 69); the at-once fascinating and threatening aspects of technology (here represented by the electric tram, the cinema, the steam-operated pile driver, and automobile traffic); the hope for a new improved man; and the rapid shift between interior monologue, collages of quotations, a montage of fragmentary details, and an editing technique derived from film cutting—all these themes and forms were integral to the arsenal of world literature since the start of World War I: though in Germany, they had not previously been deployed in so magisterial a novel.

Döblin admits to having been influenced, if only marginally, by John Dos Passos's *Manhattan Transfer* and James Joyce's *Ulysses,* which were published in Germany while he worked on *Berlin Alexanderplatz,* and perhaps by Upton Sinclair's *The Jungle,* which had been reprinted twice in German translation in the early 1920s. In any case, the "Americanization" of Weimar culture has marked the novel in ways that can hardly be overlooked. The portrait of metropolitan Berlin is characterized by a hectic pace and an American beat. Franz Biberkopf, the antihero who lives in the underworld of criminals, prostitutes, and pimps, gives scarcely a thought to his class allegiance (the principal theme of Communist criticism of the book). A practicing physician, Döblin writes openly about homosexuality, transvestites, lesbianism, and magazines like "*The Unmarried*" (p. 82). The "happy end" that the author devises for Biberkopf, whom circumstances have driven to the brink of madness and death, may be meant ironically, but in any case has the unnatural quality of the endings of so many Hollywood films.

Like Bertolt Brecht in the didactic plays that were being written around the same time as *Berlin Alexanderplatz,* Döblin uses running synopses of the plot to focus the reader's attention on the process rather than the outcome of the "story of Franz Biberkopf." But unlike the dramatist Brecht, analyzing society with a keen intellect trained by Marxism, Döblin does not aim to change the world by political means. Instead, the beginning and ending of the book speak of "fate" (pp. 68, 102), "hell-fire" blazes from people's eyes in the periods of dream and delusion experienced by "Franzeken" (p. 97); the surface of reality is ruptured by symbolic, metaphysical and religious references to fundamental human situations; animals and people are sacrificed to Death and the mythical "whore of Babylon" (p. 102); and the themes of nature mysticism are juxtaposed with the technology that is overrunning everything. The prison from which Biberkopf is released at the start of the story, the madhouse in which he vanishes, suffering from "psychic trauma" (p. 104), near the conclusion, and the insane world of Berlin between Alexanderplatz and Rosenthalerplatz, lose their boundaries and blur into one. Even the model of the Bildungsroman, which is part of the stock-in-trade of German literature, no longer applies, because it remains an open question what Biberkopf learns from his passage through the big city, or whether he learns anything at all.

The brief "report about the first hours and days of a new man," which Döblin appends to the long "fall of Franz Biberkopf," provides anything but the sort of concrete portrait of the "new man" (p. 101) that might encourage readers to imitation. Admittedly the prisoner, just released for the second time, does at least for a moment see the roofs of the houses holding steady, which at the beginning were threatening to fall on his head in the true Expressionist manner. And the "unaccountable . . . fate" (p. 68) that has enmeshed Biberkopf in a deadly struggle for 400 pages seems to have been drummed out of the city where "there are many things to make a man well, if only his heart keeps well" (p. 107). However, the identity of those "others" (p. 111) to whom the "new Biber-kopf" (p. 94) will listen from now on, is not stated—again this is typical of Expressionism—nor is the political makeup of the troops marching into the next war with "right and left and right and left" (p. 113) who appear in the last scene. Only one thing is certain: regardless of whether or how Franz Biberkopf has changed in the course of the story, the lumpen proletariat and the pace of the modern metropolis continue to set the tone for the Alexanderplatz in Berlin.

LION FEUCHTWANGER

Unlike Alfred Döblin, Lion Feuchtwanger did not make his name with a formally experimental book about contemporary themes such as the loss of individuality within mass society and the big city as demon, but rather in a long series of historical novels. Three features are central to his work: the depiction of Jewish history from its Biblical beginnings to the contemporary persecution by the Third Reich; a clear-cut link between carefully researched historical events and things that were happening in his own time; and a readable style, deliberately blended with elements of popular fiction, by which he sought to reach as wide a public as possible.

The first of Feuchtwanger's novels to sell in large numbers around the world was *Jew Süss,* published in 1925. It tells the story of financial genius Joseph Süss Oppenheimer, who in the early eighteenth century, while serving as a minister to Duke Karl Alexander von Württemberg, amasses vast wealth and political influence in a short period of time. But Süss Oppenheimer goes too far in his appetite for power: nouveau riche, vain, and as brutal as his master, albeit more subtle in his methods, he earns the wrath of the Protestant assembly when he supports the Catholic duke's preparations for a coup d'état. The prelate Weissensee, whose daughter, Magdalen Sybille, is delivered by Süss into the hands of the lecherous Karl Alexander, takes revenge by bringing Süss's carefully protected child, Naemi, to the duke. The nobelman tries to rape the innocent girl and drives her to her death. Süss Oppenheimer even earns the enmity of the gullible Professor Harpprecht, who is concerned about the welfare of his decaying homeland, when he arranges for

Harpprecht's nephew Michael, a supporter of democracy, to be sent into exile. Süss, as a Jew, is blamed for his own hubris and the mistakes of his overlord, and is finally executed before a cheering mob. Freed of his drive for power, this man who had lived for power chooses not to avail himself of the opportunity to save his life on the grounds that he is only half Jewish. Instead, realizing in the face of death that assimilation has availed him nothing, he recalls his Jewish heritage.

Anti-Semitism, persecution, and assimilation are also the themes of Feuchtwanger's novel *The Oppermanns,* published when he was already living in exile. But in this case the themes are based in the contemporary world, at the time the Nazis seized power in 1933. The book was written at high speed and rapidly translated into a number of languages. Once again, its protagonist is a successful Jewish businessman, the furniture dealer Gustav Oppermann, who at the age of fifty, rather than expanding his business, prefers instead to write a biography of the Enlightenment thinker and dramatist G. E. Lessing. But then the Nazi teacher, Bernd Vogelsang, drives Oppermann's nephew to suicide for having written a paper critical of Armenius the Cheruscan, a figure revered by the Nazis, and storm troopers loot Gustav's home in Berlin. While he is in exile in Bern, his former secretary and now a resistance fighter, Klaus Frischlin, sends him a report about Nazi atrocities in the concentration camps, whereupon Gustav decides—just the opposite of Süss Oppenheimer—to give up his contemplative life and join the resistance struggle in Germany. Politically naive and inexperienced in the work of conspiracy, however, he is quickly caught by the Gestapo and so badly abused in a concentration camp that he dies after his release.

The German version of the novel ends with a short account of the rescue of the dying Gustav Oppermann from the camp and his final conversation with Frischlin about the meaning of his role in the struggle of the underground movement against the Nazis—a movement that is never assigned any specific political identification. A different and less harsh conclusion was written for the English translation published in New York at almost the same time. Instead of ending in a sanatorium in Bohemia, the dying Gustav, cared for by a representative of the still-undefined anti-Nazi resistance, gazes out onto the Mediterranean while listening to records of "East-Jewish songs",* receives visits from relatives, dictates his memoirs to Frischlin, and is comforted with the words: "They will not crush us. . . . Neither us, nor our children, nor the Socialists, nor the Jews, nor the spirit of reason."†

ANNA SEGHERS

A barbarous concentration camp built by the Nazis in the spring of 1933 to intimidate and reeducate their political opponents is also central to Anna Seghers's celebrated novel *The Seventh Cross,* except that this time one of the prisoners, Georg Heisler, manages to escape from the camp.

Seghers was in exile in France by the end of the 1930s when she wrote the story of Heisler and his six fellow escapees, who are recaptured and hanged on crosses in the Westhofen concentration camp. The war and Seghers's flight delayed printing of the first edition in English translation until 1942, when it was published by the Boston firm Little, Brown. It became an instant best-seller in the United States, being distributed by the Book-of-the-Month-Club, reprinted in magazines, turned into a comic strip, made into special editions for the blind and for members of the armed services, and formed the basis for an MGM film starring Spencer Tracy. Four aspects of the work led to this success. First, Americans were able to identify with the suspensefully told chase plot, which was very familiar from cops-and-robbers stories. Second, Seghers uses the tales of the seven escapees to show a cross-section of Germany in the mid-1930s, broadening the cast of characters from murderous Nazis to selfless resistance fighters and examining the question: Are Nazis and Germans identical? Third, though a practicing Communist, she managed to free herself to a large degree from the Socialist Realist style that was then dominant among Communist writers, and was able to give her novel a relatively modern form using techniques akin to montage and filmlike editing. Finally, whereas the struggle between good and evil normally did not transcend the level of political propaganda in other novels of the resistance, she raised

*Lion Feuchtwanger, *The Oppermanns,* New York: Viking 1934, p. 399.
†Ibid., p. 405.

this fight to a universal human plane where it was no longer necessary to distinguish between Communists, Social Democrats, Jews, and Christians.

Like Döblin in *Berlin Alexanderplatz,* Anna Seghers reveals the fate of the fugitive Georg Heisler at the outset, in a prefatory passage that is resumed at the conclusion of the novel, and thus focuses the reader's attention on the diverse people and experiences Heisler encounters along his way through southwestern Germany: the power of everyday life among farmers and industrial workers; the confrontation with the Christian religion during a night in Mainz Cathedral; the cautious building of solidarity between the political fugitive (presumably a Communist although it is never explicitly stated) and a Jewish doctor; the almost mythical qualities of the resistance fighter Ernst Wallau, murdered in the concentration camp, whose character emerges, in part, in imaginary dialogues with Heisler; and the story of Heisler's former girlfriend Leni, who offers no help, and that of the Roeder family, who are politically naive but supportive on a human level.

At the conclusion of *The Seventh Cross,* Anna Seghers has her hero—who is by no means shown only in a positive light—leave Mainz on a ship headed for the Dutch border, without revealing to the reader whether or not he finally succeeds in escaping. Mainz, Seghers's native city, also lies at the center of a story that she wrote in 1943–44 while in exile in Mexico, and that was first translated into English by the FBI in the course of their surveillance of her: "Excursion of the Dead Girls." This time, the plot concerns not an escape from Mainz but just the opposite: an imaginary return home by the exile who, while staying in a remote, exotic village in Mexico, remembers an outing that she and her class had made in the long-distant past. This recollection is marked by feelings of loss, mourning, and homesickness, for the house to which the female narrator returns in her thoughts was destroyed in the World War II bombing of Mainz, and many of her schoolmates and teachers had been killed in the war or as victims of the Nazis.

The tale of the dead girls' excursion is an early example of the "grief work" that German literature did not begin to address seriously until fifteen or twenty years later. It is also a minor gem of the literature of women, which depicts its story in autobiographical form but without sentimentality; which rediscovers the great themes of history in commonplace events; which confesses to fear, weariness, and loneliness without being overcome by them; and makes effective though sparing use of conjunctions, auxiliary verbs, questions, and words and expressions such as "perhaps" (p. 237), "unaware" (p. 238), and "I asked myself" (p. 254).

In 1947 Anna Seghers left Mexico, which remained alien to her despite her love for it, and achieved the homecoming that she had only dreamed about a few years earlier. However, the return to Germany was problematic for her, as it was for Arnold Zweig, Alfred Döblin, and (in the form of his books) Lion Feuchtwanger. None had the strength or opportunity to make a genuine fresh start in the country split in two by an iron curtain—although Anna Seghers, who dedicated two novels to the building of the GDR, was to some degree the exception. The emotionally and physically damaged people of postwar Germany were too foreign to them, their experiences as exiles between 1933 and 1945 had made them too different, and their energy had been used up by thirty or forty years of confrontation with a troubled time marked by contradiction and revolutionary change.

But what remains is no small achievement: the accomplished works by four authors who speak at times with anger and at times with wise restraint and serenity, as well as high artistry, of the wars and persecutions that shook the first half of the twentieth century; of the collective life and expatriation of Jews in Germany caught between assimilation and their own history; of humanity and inhumanity; senseless death and miraculous rescue.

A.S.
Translated by Jan van Heurck

ARNOLD ZWEIG

Pogrom

The ringing of shots awoke Eli Seamen. The double wings of his window, thrown wide open, with their curtains dangling in the wind like the bodies of gallows' birds, admitted the clear crack of the Browning pistols which was carried over the roofs to his bedroom. He sat: the sky above the city was touched with the red either of a conflagration or of a multitude of lights; but directly overhead the legions of the stars worked through the infinite darkness. Against the faint, distant glimmer the window cut out a hard cross right in the center of the Great Bear. Seeing the arrangement of the stars, the boy thought it must be toward eleven o'clock; they are shooting. . . . The door to his father's room was flung wide open, and Inspector Seamen strode over the threshold. "Get up, Eli," he cried, his hard voice wild with excitement. "Pogrom?" the son cried back, leaping with both legs onto the carpet; but no answer was needed.

He dressed himself with quick and trembling hands, while his father sealed a letter by the light of candle stump. The chess board still stood in the throes of the struggle, as they had left it the night before. The masterstroke had just been delivered; the figures loomed black in the candlelight, mustered with their stiff shadows on the divided board. Eli, filled with happy pride, threw one glance at it: his father, strong player that he was, had been compelled to yield in astonishment before that last triumphant move. . . . But in an instant he was pulled back into the present; while he laced his shoes hastily the thought occurred to him—and it gave him a sense of satisfaction—that things were going badly now for his enemies, those Jewish young boys who threw cakes of mud after him and shouted that he was desecrating the Sabbath and eating uncleanliness; and he felt that it served them right, for they were many, and yet never attacked him singly. "Well, are you ready? Not yet." The inspector, his fur cap on his head, raged up and down in the doorway, stamping in his high boots. He blew impatiently into his thick black beard: "Are you afraid?" And suddenly—he had never thought of this before—Eli realized that he too might be assaulted, for the band could not know that he and his father lived in a state of enmity with the others. But he forgot it again on the spot. "No, no," he answered, angrily. "Here I am. Let's go."

The father locked the letter in the writing desk. "We must see. . . . We must help them out there. . . ."

Then he turned his face on his son and examined the sixteen year old boy closely, as if he were a piece of merchandise which had just been delivered; no, he was not afraid.

"Listen, Eli. It's possible that something might happen over there . . . to me too . . . you understand: and if I'm no longer here tomorrow—" "Father!" the boy cried, and his eyes became two black holes. "Anything can happen. In that case, listen—you return to Germany, at once . . ." "Father!" "And then study something decent, see? Engineering." "Oh, please, please, stop," the boy cried in a dying voice, and with both hands he seized his father's arm. "In case you might need it—you're big enough—here!" He thrust the flat pistol toward him. Eli seized the pistol in a strong grasp, though his hands shivered. "Will the police help us, father?" But the inspector had already rushed through the door, in one hand his Browning, and in another a formidable stick, leather on the outside but iron within. His steps sounded down the corridor; hastily the boy snatched his mountain-climbing stick from the corner—a yellow oaken staff pointed with metal at the end. Beyond the outer door he found his father, clearly undetermined. "As a matter of fact, I ought to leave you here. What should you be doing over there . . . ?"

"Without you? I won't let you go alone for a single instant." "I want you to obey me," the father said. "I'll break the door open, and follow you," the powerfully built boy cried. The inspector knew his oldest son. "Well, if you must. . . . It's probably for the best," and smiling weakly he turned the key strongly in the lock.

They stumbled down the three flights of steps, and crossed the broad yard of the factory. In Eli the blood ran swiftly and joyfully:

adventure! And what an adventure! A pogrom, right on the eve of Easter Sabbath! Tomorrow songs of praise in the churches. He was not at all frightened; his finger pressed happily against the trigger of the weapon. Would he have to shoot? And would he hit his man? Surely if only his hands wouldn't tremble too much. He promised himself to get Gabriel Butterman, the red head, the thrower of stones. That man he wouldn't let escape . . . and he felt the advance happiness of envy which the whole class—and his brother Leos— would feel—when he would tell them about it. . . . He tightened his arm as though in exercise, so that the muscles rose quickly. The schoolboy of the fifth grade lifted up his face, with its arched eyebrows, and its crown of black hair, to the night air. The gatekeeper was still awake; yellow light streamed from the windows of his lodge. The inspector gave him the keys of the house and said, in Polish: "Open the door for me." "It isn't good to go out," the old man argued, while his mustaches, yellowed by smoking, wagged with his speech. "It's true, Janek. But I'll be back at one o'clock. And look after the keys for me." The door shrieked on its hinges; in the distance was heard a faint sound of shots. The father was in such a hurry that Eli was nearly left behind. The streets lay black, and deserted; only high up there were a few lighted windows. The two of them turned sharply to the right, went at a trot the whole length of the Petersburgerstrasse—blundering into pools of mud and water—straight across the Patjomkinplatz and right into the Schlusselstrasse. The noise became louder, became a wild tumult. They met people, more people, still more people. "What's the matter?" the father asked in Russian of a figure hurrying by in the dark. "They're beating the infidel Jews up, uncle, hurry up." "And the police?" "You won't find the soldiers lazy," the citizen answered, laughing contentedly, and hurried on. Eli made up his mind to shoot the soldiers even if they had killed Gabriel.

The street grew brighter in the light of the lanterns and the lamps that streamed from the houses; before long they found themselves in the midst of the crowds. They thrust their way through roughly, and when the father could not proceed fast enough he seized his son by the shoulders and thrust him into the shelter of a high house. "Where now?" the boy asked, excitedly. "Come!" They ran lightly, hastily, up two, three, four flights of steps. From the skylight, a small dirty opening, they peered out on the neighboring streets, for none of the neighboring houses were more than two or three stories high. The square frames of houses enclosed a clear picture, small in the distance, but marvelously sharp in outline. They saw flames flickering through the windows, and thickening smoke, streaked with red; they saw people running, limbs flying, men and women in knots and groups; they heard a deep roaring, the scream of high-pitched voices, single shots here and there, and through the fierce whisper and crack of conflagration dull thudding noises, as of falling beams and doors smashed open. For a single, hellish instant the horror of it beat up into his face; then suddenly the inspector pulled the son backward and thundered with him down the steps; instead of turning toward the door of the house, he went into the dark courtyard, and holding his stick in his teeth, square across his face, he climbed over the low wall into the neighboring house. Eli threw his cudgel over, leapt up, held on with his fingers, drew himself upward, lifted his legs over the obstacle, just as they did in the gymnasium, and landed on the other side almost on all fours. And now they ran noisily through the back quarters across a second courtyard and by means of a low gate again reached the street. They went swiftly along the houses on the left, through two, three small streets, without seeing a single human being, and they stood again on the Katherinestrasse, which further down, was once more filled with noise, light and smoke. They stood still for a moment, their beating hearts breathless; then they went some seventy steps slowly, easily, down to Metchnikoffstrasse, their Brownings in their hands. There they turned the corner—and something happened.

A woman came running toward them, in her underskirt; on the upper part of her body she wore a brown piece of cloth which covered her shoulders. She was out of breath, unable to utter a sound, her fleshy face distorted with the terror of death; she held her young daughter by the hand; the child had not even a cloth to cover her, her hair hung loose around her face, and the bare feet, scarcely able to keep the pace up, seemed only to be falling forwards. The woman's mouth was wide open, showing all the teeth, and her free hand was pressed against her left breast. Three young ones followed her—with just a short stretch of pavement between her and them; and on that short stretch a young boy, perhaps nine years old, stumbled horribly along, unable to catch up with his mother. . . . Eli thought he recognized Gabriel's younger brother; but at once he might be mistaken. The child reeled and fell, picked itself up, fell again, and as he rose to his feet for a second time, the first of the hooligans ran by; the second one, also running by, thrust a knife into the child's back. "Ma-a—" it cried—the sound beginning high and shrill, then sinking downward and breaking. The mother, hearing that piercing cry, turned her head, stiffened, sank on her knee, without loosening her hold on the girl. Then suddenly Eli was aware that his father, who had just been at his side, had leapt ten paces forward—and, a fiery tumult bursting out within him, he sprang after him. For a single, violent moment he was glad that his mother had long been dead, and then he saw how his father's horrible stick had whirled sideways at the skull of the first hooligan, smashing it as if it had been a clay pot, so that the man fell sideways on the stony ground; and at the same instant he saw two others put themselves on the defensive. And then the fury broke loose. He heard one shot, two shots, and he shifted his Browning to his right hand. His father leapt to the attack of the man who was shooting, but the second man was behind him, his knife uplifted. Eli felt something cold at his heart; and then he stood still, shot, shot again, again; and the knife rang on the hard pavement. A terrific excitement cried out of him: "He's hit!" He heard the piercing cry of the women behind him, the sound of heavy footsteps, a shot thundered darkly behind him, another—no Browning this time, he knew—and then he saw the face of his father turned toward him, a vivid white, with far-off eyes blazing in terrific anger: and then nothing more. He fell forward. "Father . . ." he thought, and at the same time something hammering down upon him flung him to the ground as with a lightning stroke.

The police lieutenant wiped his sabre and gave command: "Forward!" And as the policemen retreated swiftly the two women, dumb with horror, fixed a blank dead gaze on the figures lying on the ground: on the man, the youths, the boy and the child.

From The Case of Sergeant Grischa

THE PLIERS

This earth of ours, the little planet Tellus, went whirling busily through pitch-black, airless, icy space, forever swept by the waves of the uncharterd ether. In darkness made electric by her passing contact, she moved among mysterious influences, baleful or benignant. Swathed in her thick, woolly veils of air, she had now outrun that stage in her elliptical race which keeps her north-westerly parts furthest from their life-spring in the Sun; and she was turning them again towards him in the ceaseless revolutions of her course. Now the rays of the great fiery ball beat more exultantly upon the face of Europe. The atmosphere began to seethe and everywhere fierce winds rushed from the Arctic wastes to the warmer regions, where, lured by the magic of reviving light, all things awoke and blossomed. In the Northern lands life's tide was slowly rising and to her peoples came bewildering changes with the changing year.

A man stood in the thick snow, at the foot of a bare and blackened tree, that rose up slantwise in the charred forest, black against the trampled white expanse. Encased in many coverings, the man plunged his hands into the pockets of the outermost of these, and stared before him, thinking. "Butter," thinks he, "a pound and a half, two and a half pounds of meal from a farm, a loaf that I can put by, and some peas. Yes, that'll do. She can carry on for a bit with that. I'll give it to Fritzke to take with him to-morrow when he goes on leave. Perhaps I can swap my tobacco for a bit of dripping: if I throw in a mark from my pay, cookie will hand it out. Butter," thinks he, "a pound and a half." And so once more in his heavy, deliberate mind he spread out the contents of a parcel which he was planning to send to his wife, wondering whether he could not find room for yet something more.

Somewhere down in the vague depths of his inner consciousness he felt he would have like to rub his feet together, for they were rather cold; but they were enveloped in thick boots, and wrapped round with rags and the lower part of his trousers, so he let them be. His legs were embedded in the deep snow, side by side like the hind feet of an elephant. He was wearing an iron-gray cloak, with absurd red squares on the collar under his chin, and a strip of blue cloth with a number on each shoulder. And tucked closely under his arm, while he stood thinking of peas and dripping, was a long, heavy, cudgel-like object of wood, affixed to an odd-looking iron contrivance, the whole being called a rifle: with this he was able to produce cunningly directed explosions, and by their means to kill or maim other men far away from him. This man, whose ears were hidden under soft black flaps, and in whose mouth was a small pipe adapted for smoking dried leaves—a German working man—was not standing under this tree in the burnt forest for his pleasure. His thoughts were continuously driving westward, where in two or three cubical rooms in a walled house his wife and child awaited him. Here he stood, while they lay huddled in a far-off room. He yearned for them, but something had come between them, unseen but very strong: an Order: the order to watch other men. The time was winter 1917, and, more exactly, the middle of March. The inhabitants of Europe were engaged in a war which had for some time been pursued with no small determination. In the midst of a forest in these eastern marches, wrested for the time being from the so-called White Russians, stood this German soldier musing, Lance-Corporal Birkholz from Eberswalde, guarding prisoners, soldiers of these same Russians who must now labor for the Germans.

A good seventy yards away from him, on a railway line, the huge red-brown and gray-green freight-cars were being loaded up with timber. Two men were handling each car. Others dragged up on their shoulders heavy, carefully graded beams and planks, which others again, a few days before, had hewn from the dead pines whose once green and reddish brown expanses had been eaten away in many directions by the hatchets and saws of the prisoners.

Much farther than the eye could reach between the tree-trunks, a day's ride in each direction, the black pillars of this corpse of a forest stood out stark against the snow and the sky—fifty thousand acres of it. Incendiary bombs from airplanes, shells from field-guns, had each in their own time during the past summer done their work upon it faithfully. Pines and firs, birches and beeches, all alike: burnt and singed, or withered and choked from afar by the fumes of battle—all perished, and now their corpses were made to serve their turn. There was still a reek of burning from the scaling bark.

In the last car two Russians were speaking in their own language about a pair of pliers.

"Impossible," said the slighter of the two. "How can I get you such a thing? I'll have no hand in such foolery, Grischa."

The other, turning upon his friend two strangely powerful gray-blue eyes, laughed shortly.

"I've as good as got them in my pocket already, Aljoscha."

And they went on piling up the yellowish-white props, that were to serve as supports for those human caves called dug-outs and communication trenches, in a certain order in the car, the side of which hung down from its hinges. Grischa worked above and superintended the stacking of the planks; from below Aljoscha kept passing up to him the fragrant bolts of wood. They were a little shorter than a man, fully one and a half inches thick, and so grooved that they could be neatly fitted into each other.

"All I want now is a pair of pliers," persisted Grischa.

Five prisoners in a row, each with four of these props on his shoulder: they flung them down in front of the car, with the hollow clatter of dead wood, then all seven of them stood up for a moment in a group. They said nothing. Those who had carried the planks let their arms fall by their sides, and looked at the huge heap of timber.

"That'll do," said Grischa. "Go and warm yourselves, boys: time's up."

"Right you are, Grischa," answered one of them. "We'll take your word for it," and they nodded to him and went off. Further up, between the rails of the two lines that met at this point, a small field railway track and the main line, a large, fragrant fire was burning. Beside it, standing or sitting on ties, planks or stumps, were the guards and the Russian laborers with their German foremen, men of the Landsturm Army Service Corps. Iron cauldrons of coffee were hanging over the flames, and here and there a man was toasting bread on a green twig. The mighty element devoured the resinous wood with spurts and hisses and crackling leaps of flame. In front of the railway the forest fell back to left and right. Like rusted ghosts of the living, the great trunks towered above the snow, the thick, powdery, frozen March snow of western Russia on which the sun flings blue and golden light and shadows, seamed by the tracks of heavily nailed boots. From the loaded white branches moisture dripped at the contact with the sun, and froze in the circles of shadow. A remote, deep blue sky drew the men's glances upwards. "Spring's coming," said Grischa, meaningly.

"Don't you do it," Aljoscha answered in a coaxing voice. "Yes, spring is coming, and then things will be better: we shall have moss to lie on and there'll be more food. Don't be a fool, Grischa, stay here. It's madness, what you mean to do. You won't get forty miles away. The whole country is overrun with Germans—outposts, police, and all the rest of them. If you get away and they catch you again—you'll be working like a nigger for them for years after the peace."

Grischa alone had charge of the stacking of the props, and now he went about this task silently and in most unwonted fashion. No authority could possibly have ordered this waste of space: between the back of the car and its load of timber he kept a passage free, above the floor, where the shorter, heavier beams were put to steady the load, and this passage was cunningly roofed in with timber.

"Quick, Aljoscha! Before they come back!"

And Aljoscha obeyed. He knew why his friend was calling him. In this hiding-place Grischa meant to escape that night, for the car would appear fully loaded. Aljoscha did not for a moment approve of the attempt. He had set his whole heart on dissuading his friend from an undertaking that seemed to him hopeless and foolish. But he obeyed. In the whole company of prisoners, two hundred and fifty men, who for the last nine months had been employed in sawing timber at the prison camp at Navarischky, there were not two who would refuse any request or disobey any order of Sergeant Grischa Iljitsch Paprotkin, now Prisoner No. 173.

He had a jest for every man, and above all he had won the St. George's cross as far back as the siege of Przemysl: and also, every one of them knew that for his part Grischa Iljitsch would, and often did, help them in any way he could. Aljoscha, working with a passionate keenness born of his affection for his mate, began to sweat:

he was passing up one after the other of the squared pine planks to his comrade, who almost snatched them from him and handled the heavy soaking planks like matchwood. One, two: one, two: with the muffled ring of wood against wood, the roof-timbers that were to conceal the tube-like hollow fell into place. Grischa, standing on the fully laden part of the car, tested the hollow with his toe: it held. It was a neat piece of work. He had hauled up some of the planks and set them on end against the sides of the car; thus at the same time keeping out the cold and giving support to the covering timbers. Tonight he would creep into this hollow and lie there like a badger in his earth: towards morning about four o'clock an engine would draw the whole train eastward out of the forest. And eastward went his heart. A good many of these timber cars went up to the Front with the countless supply trains, and that was his goal. It was still early in the year 1917: the Russian armies, weary from countless defeats and shattering losses, had, first on their own initiative and then with the approval of the new regime, brought the War to a standstill. Strange things were happening in Petersburg: the almighty Tsar, the Little Father, Nicholas II, had abdicated to save the ancient imperial crown for his son: the Grand Duke Michael, chosen as Regent, transferred the power into the hands of that evanescent parliament, the Duma: soldiers firing on the imperial police: the red flag waving in hungry Petersburg, in Moscow, Ekaterinburg, Kronstadt, and Kazan . . . the Schlüsselburg blown up, criminals let loose, generals imprisoned, ministers hounded into exile, admirals drowned, shot, driven from the country. And in their stead, what strange new people! At that moment Russia's destinies were guided by a handful of civilians, a substantial merchant, Rodzianko, a landed proprietor, Prince Lvof, Miljukoff, a Professor, and the astute and dexterous poor man's lawyer, Kerensky.

Russia was reshaping, Russia was awaiting peace with her rifle at her feet. Firing had ceased between the German and Russian trenches: all was brotherhood. As the War must needs end soon, deserters were thronging back to their native villages and towns where, if they were lucky, their relations would still be waiting for them. But Grischa Iljitsch Paprotkin, sergeant, lived in Vologda, far away to the north-east of the vast land of Russia, and if he wanted to see his wife and children he must look for them behind the Russian front.

That was his plan. He would escape from the Germans: he could stand it no longer. With the beginning of the new year and the confirmation of all sorts of rumors, his heart had become strangely restless: slow heavy-footed thoughts had day after day fixed themselves more firmly in his head: he must get home. He had waited far too long. What with the barbed wire, the kaleidoscopic orders of the crazy Germans, so scared that they would scarcely let you breathe, and would almost have you breathe by numbers: "breathe in, breathe out, wipe your nose, now go to the latrine"—what with the cramped sleeping-quarters in the barracks, and the staring eyes of the officers—all this stifled him. He had been their prisoner for sixteen months, and he would not stand it for another day. That very night he would start on his way to Marfa Ivanovna, and his little tiny Jelisavjeta, whom he had never yet seen. As a stone falls, so his mind was set. And because he needed the pliers for his purpose, and Aljoscha was orderly to the sergeant in charge of tools, Aljoscha could easily steal them so that he could cut the wire. The latter part of the journey would be easy enough.

"Now for it, hurry up, Aljoscha," he replied inexorably to his friend's mute refusals. The thought of leaving Aljoscha made his heart a little heavy. But when the War was over they would meet again. He had thrashed it out with him a thousand times. He could not have waited if he would. In his heart was no more room for waiting. His arm thrilled with a measureless, ever fiercer impulse to beat down all before him, and hew a way out for himself; the random words of insolent corporals danced in his brain like sparks. He must go, or worse would come of it: and this Aljoscha knew. Their hands moved swiftly backward and forward and the pile of timber grew.

At last not a plank was left upon the snow. The two workmen swung their arms across their chests, cabman-fashion. Grischa jumped stiffly from the car, and pulling on the huge gray mittens, that they could not use while working, they stamped over to the fire. In the meantime, the five men who carried the wood had trotted back to their distant comrades who brought down the freshly cut timber in the small tip-wagons and trolleys of the field railway. The sawmills (and the prison camp close by), a small hutment village right in the middle of the vast desolate forest of Navarischky, stood on a little hill about three kilometers away. To protect it against aircraft, the junction of main and branch lines had been fixed at the lowest and most thickly wooded point in the forest. As far as this junction, a skillful man who knew how to slow down his lorry by thrusting a stick between the wheels, could send it thundering down the light rails without an engine. Just then, Lance-Corporal Printz, a fair-haired young rascal who, after recovering from a wound, had been drafted to the Landsturm battalion, appeared on one of these lorries . . . crashing and roaring like the Fiend.

"And you are going to bolt from the camp to-night on a thing that makes a row like that?" whispered Aljoscha maliciously to Grischa, who was stuffing his pipe with the dubious prison tobacco and held out his pouch to his friend with a meaningful gesture. Grischa dug him good-naturedly in the ribs with his elbow:

"You're a fathead, you forget the wind: as soon as the sun is down, the old trees make as much row as if I'd paid them to, as if the Devil and his grandmother were in it. I don't want you to slip me those pliers till eight o'clock. At half-past, after evening rounds, I'm off. Why don't you come, brother? Aljoscha—the two of us! We'd get through."

Aljoscha smiled. If they had not been sitting quite so near the fire, the smile would have looked more rueful still.

"I don't think so, Grischa: I don't like the looks of it."

"What doesn't your friend like the looks of?" asked Sergeant Leszinsky from the fire; he understood Russian well, knew the two as friends and favorites among the prisoners.

"The weather," answered Grischa, cheerfully. "He thinks it will rain."

Lance-Corporal Birkholz, who had sauntered up from his pine tree toward the fire—in five minutes it would be the midday interval, the field kitchen would be brought up at any moment, and he had nearly finished making up his mental parcel—Birkholz, the joiner from the Berlinerstrasse in Eberswalde, propped his rifle against a tree and held out his hands to the glow, while he sat down on a pile of planks, and the Russians moved up to make room for him. "Rain? Oh, it won't rain in a hurry, you can bet on that. Why, the way it's been blowing, evening after evening, you'd think the huts would fly away—such a row you can hardly sleep. But in the morning the sky looks as clear as mother's table-cloth on a Sunday, Russky, my boy."

Grischa put a small ember with his bare hands on the tobacco in his pipe, and puffed. Aljoscha stood beside him and smiled nervously. When he had finished speaking, nothing could be heard but the crackling and sputtering of the flames, for the words had touched the sensitive point in all of them: their longing for home. All these men, no longer young, for years now cut off from their habits and their friends, were home-sick. And while this feeling had become part of the structure of their souls, in some sense the center of their hearts' gravity, the measure of all that was within them, they noticed it themselves only from time to time. Even if the difficulties in their way had not been so insurmountable, not one of them would have contemplated making a dash for home like Odysseus, the Homecomer of the Trojan War, and let himself, like him, be whirled backward and forward in his perilous course, drawn as by a magnet, and sure in his inmost heart of his return. The most passionate soul of them all was at work in Grischa, and thus it was that what many millions of men, dressed in all manner of different clothes, and all, caught in the machinery of War at that moment, only longed to do, he did. But this measureless urge, which had been present to them all for one instant, passed over their heads like the smoke of a fire. Suddenly they all looked up: harsh trumpet-calls, like the rasping of rusty hinges were heard in the blue air. "Geese," one of them called out, and pointed to the white gleaming wedge of the great birds in flight, like a half-open pair of compasses hurtling through the air, now overhead, far above them, white and dazzling under the clouds; then speeding away over the woods—the squadrons of the spring.

"Yes, they are flying home," murmured Corporal Leszinsky.

"Eastward," said Grischa, softly, amid the significant silence of the Germans and the Russians, and in the Russian tongue. The geese were disappearing like a glittering speck against the radiant sky, and the silence round the fire was ended by a shout which came echoing from afar: the "stew-gun" (field kitchen) appeared in the shape of two large cauldrons, and was skillfully pulled up on the narrow-gauge railway.

"Fifteen!" shouted Corporal Leszinsky, the midday call of the timber workers, the welcome rallying cry to rest. All hands were stretched out toward the pots; all of them, workmen in uniform, rallying each other in the slang that reminded them of their freedom, of the time when they were not soldiers and struggled hard for their daily bread. They all ate standing. Amid the metallic clatter of the tin or aluminum pans, Aljoscha said to Grischa: "At eight, then." Grischa clapped him on the back smiling. Both knew what was meant; they did not even need to look at each other.

"What's for dinner: where's the menu?" shouted Lance-Corporal Printz, dimpling and radiant.

"Beans and bacon," answered the kitchen-corporal. "They feed you up so here, that there won't be room for you in mummy's bed when you get home."

ESCAPE!

Tempest and tumult. From the chimneys, zinc tubes with their little cowls, plumes of swirling sparks went hissing over the flat, huddled roofs of the hutment camp, black against the snow that glittered dully in the moonless night. In the corners, gangways, and recesses—darkness, compact and impenetrable, especially about those places where, from some ill-curtained window, a beam or shaft of light went questing through the storm-rent air. Over the straggling haphazard camp, sang the wind, the storm of spring, with maniac fury, in the chords of the barbed-wire fence, three or four yards high, that encircled the barracks, officers' quarters, sheds, and storehouses.

Slipping and stumbling among them on the iron surface of yesterday's thaw, which had frozen once again, came a sentry now soon to be relieved. Wrapped in a monstrous white sheepskin, his gun slung over his shoulders, muzzle downwards with the nails of his greased boots he crushed the sharp little edges and ridges of yesterday's frozen footprints. Thus staggering, and thinking of his woes, he listened to the wind that cut his cheek as it whistles by. He left his shelter, where a man might sleep in comfort, to meet his relief who should arrive at any minute. Of course, there was no sense in patrolling this place: no one was likely to bring anything into the camp. And on such a night as this no one was likely to take so much as an army loaf out of it much less his own valuable carcass. A mug's game escaping, now the War's over. This was not only the conviction of Heppke of the Landsturm, but also of nearly the whole garrison, always excepting the camp sergeant-major, who, like all his kind, would have thought he had taken leave of his senses, if he did not treat the most trivial matters of routine as solemnly as a private treats his pay-sheet.

Heppke was seething with impatience, wondering when that devil Kazmierzak, his relief, could be coming. But ever and anon he was overwhelmed by the cataract of sound which filled the air. Like a tireless torrent howled the forest gale, heaving and thrusting, piling up the snowdrifts, smiting bough on bough; till at its onslaught many a tree, made brittle by the frost, paid forfeit of its heaviest branches, booming like a cannon. No step could be heard in all this tumult; and so out of the darkness loomed Kazmierzak of the Landsturm in his black cloak, and stumbled against the sentry. "Oho," said Heppke, glad of his relief. "So you've found your legs, have you? I thought you'd got them stuck under the table playing nap."

Kazmierzak of the Landsturm, pipe in mouth against all orders, took his comrade's rifle. Heppke immediately divested himself of the heavy sentry's sheepskin, and while Kazmierzak was putting it on, he pointed out reproachfully to Heppke what he had meant to say on the way from the guard-house. "Look at those windows. You can see an inch of light everywhere; if the sergeant-major sees that, *you're* for the high jump."

Karl—he called Heppke by his Christian name—had better see they were properly darkened. Nonsense, of course: nonsense like the whole War. As if there could be airplanes in the middle of Poland, where the deadliest bombs would be droppings of wild geese. But orders are orders, duty's duty, rum's rum, and it's all sh—— together.

"Get those blighted windows darkened at once," he warned him again. "You must have been dreaming there on sentry-go, as if you didn't know Klappka and the order-book!" Klappka—that was the sergeant-major—was a choleric gentleman with an exceptional gift for exploding with fury over trivial transgressions.

"Friend," said Heppke, in an odd tone of voice. "That's not what I'm thinking. Sticking here makes me feel funny: and this blasted wind always roaring in my ears. I'm sick for home: I shall go dotty if I can't get back."

Kazmierzak said nothing. If Karl thought *that* was news to him or any other man in the army, he might put his brains in a glass case and show them in a museum. But Heppke, who had got a glimpse of his own soul, became yet more confidential. "And the songs! Listen to them singing now, those Russians; like eighteen-seventy! There's a revolution over there, Emil, mark my words there'll be peace: it'll be home, old son, me to my bench again, and the old woman in bed beside me, and the kid crawling round the table leg. Emil, we shall be hanging the old guns on every branch and trekking off home on our flat feet. Spring's here at last: just smell it coming from the forest."

Kazmierzak settled himself in his cloak, slung his rifle, an old-fashioned musket fitted with a modern lock, and opined that there was something in it; the Revolution was coming over there and that was why the Russians in the camp were singing. That was something for a sentry to think of between eight and ten, or two and four. Kazmierzak did not venture to pursue his thoughts further. He was partly Polish, as his name implied, and since the War began, experience had taught the Prussian soldiers to mistrust a Polish name—you never know, they said. The Poles were rather more closely watched than others, Alsatians excepted. And although Heppke had been his comrade and his friend, Kazmierzak was not too free with his confidences. But for the sake of company he went back with him to the guard-house, for he had two hours' sentry-go before him, and snatched at the chance of a few minutes' gossip. And Heppke was bursting with information. "All I want is to get home, and be Heppke the joiner again at Eberswalde, go to the park on a Sunday and have a beer, with the kid on a seesaw, mother knitting and having a crack with Roberta; me playing nap with Rob and Vicky—Oh God, and Rob croaked in hospital last week with spotted typhus. No, my boy, a man gets balmy walking up and down staring into the darkness, thinking—and nothing to keep up your spirits."

In the meantime Kazmierzak was preparing to deliver himself of an observation. He considered it safe to point out to his friend that peace did not seem likely for the present. America was a dark horse, Wilson had all his trumps to play, the U-boat war would tangle them up a bit, and things wouldn't be so easy.

But Heppke was too wrapped up in his own speculation.

"Emil," said he, when they had nearly reached the guard-house door, "I'll go in and have my bit of sleep; then I shan't care if it hails. And I'll dream, old boy: fancy me at forty and living on dreams. If it lasts much longer, I shall go balmy, Emil."

But Kazmierzak would have none of this escape into dreams. "'Dream, ah, dream of Paradise,' on paper sheets and sawdust, with no extra charge for bugs," he snapped out. "Perhaps we'll have peace after all. At least on our Front. But if it's only on our Front, it's no catch. They must all do like the Russkies, chuck down their rifles, and b—— off home."

This roused Heppke, who had long been of the same mind. "Us first!" he whispered, looking round him cautiously. "But we shan't risk it." And with that he opened the guard-house door, whence a waft of warm humanity rolled out into the night air; and Kazmierzak was left to his solitary task of patrolling the camp.

"Shout it out," thought he, "let 'em all hear: it's true enough, of course it should be us first, but of course we funk it. The brass hats have got us by the short hairs."

His footsteps crunched upon the frozen snow as he walked, staring at the toes of his boots, and ever in his ears echoed the song of the Russians from Hutment No. 3, near which their conversation had begun.

Where Nos. 3 and 4 met at an obtuse angle, out of the shadowy gloom now moved a figure toward the wire fence—a figure trembling at the knees with fear and excitement, fervently thankful for that song of mingled menace and despair, which drowned the hammering of his heart. The Russians were singing the song that rang through the prisons during the revolution of 1905 when the condemned were led out to death, a melody so simple and with so magical a rhythm as could only be devised by a deeply musical and enslaved people over whose heart the ploughshare of sorrow has passed. Although Grischa crawled with the utmost circumspection by the dim light of the snow, over the five or six yards in front of the first line of fence, and while he cut the wires—two, three, four, with powerful strokes of the pliers—still in his inward ear echoed the words his comrades were singing, the words of a vow never to forget the dead and always to stand by the living. When the wires were cut their loose ends sprang apart twanging and thrumming. The hole, which in a few seconds was large enough to admit, first his pack, then his bundle of blankets, and finally the man himself, lay neatly hidden in the shadow of the huts. Now there was no

going back, the escape could no longer be concealed. Soaking with
sweat, and panting with apprehension, Grischa hurried breathlessly
toward the next line of wire, in front of which he paused by the
toolsheds and breathed deeply. Now he cursed the song,—which
luckily ceased at that moment,—for it would prevent him hearing
the sentry's footsteps. He knew he was on duty then. Like all men
of his kind who are fond of a glass, Kazmierzak was strict in his
dealings with the prisoners, especially as with many of them he was
able to speak Polish. Still, Grischa felt a momentary regret that this
man—for who could say when his escape would be discovered?—
would perhaps be called to account for it. But Grischa was working
his way through the east side of the camp, and whenever an escape
had been attempted,—there had been four in the last nine
months,—the fugitives had made their way westward toward the
town, five-and-twenty miles away, where they looked for shelter
among a population bitterly hostile to the Germans. The pliers
rasped and clicked against the wires; the wind saw to it that no
sound should be heard, for here the wind blew freely; and its biting
blast almost numbed Grischa's laboring fingers.

Now for the wide and wellnigh empty space between the two
storehouses and the outermost wire fence. Showers of sparks
whirled noiselessly from the narrow chimneys of the overheated
crackling wood furnaces, and near by ticked the dynamo which
supplied the electric light. There had once been talk of setting up
arc-lamps to flood the camp with light, when the last escape cost
Sergeant-Major Busch his comfortable job. But at that time the fear
of aircraft made such a course impossible, and since in the meantime orders had been given to economize coal, this infallible safe-
guard could not be adopted. "When I'm out of it," thought
Grischa, "they'll light the place up. And these nippers will get poor
old Aljoscha into clink. But," he went on, mentally groping in all
directions through the darkness—as his thoughts moved under
their own momentum, heedless of his innermost self, which was
ever straining forward, like the hammer of a rifle at full cock—"but
perhaps he'll wangle himself out of it, or won't even be suspected."

With that he drew a deep breath, clenched his teeth, and said to
himself: "Now for it!" He tiptoed in his heavy boots across the
broad and shadowy enclosure: he was aiming for the point nearest
the edge of the forest, where the lorries stood on the field-railway.

Here a quantity of hewn timber had been piled against the wire, to put on the trucks the following day: to save time, just before they stopped for the day, the men on this work had passed the planks to one another through the wire. Thus the barrier of wire could not be seen through from either side: this would only be so, of course, until next morning, when the pile would have to be moved to make way for fresh timber. But no man of sense would look so far ahead as that. Early next morning when work was allotted and Prisoner No. 173 found missing, and all the camp in a ferment, these planks might be utterly forgotten and stay where they were till peace was made—or, for the matter of that, if the work were pressing, they might be picked up at once—God knows. From the moment when Grischa, scratching himself slightly on the wire, plunged into the dark shadows beyond, he could be sure his escape would be unnoticed till about half-past seven next morning.

The storm was writhing in the wires; Kazmierzak of the Landsturm was marching up and down. "All serene. There'll be hell with the Americans," he thought. He knew what they were after. He'd been over there, worked there, saved up his dollars, and brought them back like an idiot in 1912. He had lived on the East Side, right among the Jews, and earned good money. The Americans take hold and hang on when they once bite, like bulldogs. *They* had built the big railways, they invented skyscrapers, they made Niagara grind their turbines—they were folk worth seeing. So thinking, with the wind howling in one's ears, it was easy to pass within a couple of yards of a cut wire fence and not notice it in the dark, nor observe that it has been broken through at about the height of a man kneeling, on the innermost line of wire, near the hutments.

A man ran on tiptoe in the teeth of the wind toward the forest, from stump to stump across the clearing. What a din was in the branches! Almost as great as the turmoil in his heart. Sometimes it happened that a badly secured lorry got loose, and rolled slowly at first, then quicker and quicker, down the gentle slope between the high ground of the camp and the loading station. Wheels clattered on the rails. The frozen iron rasped and squealed. But even if there were ears to hear, who could hear this sound amid the general babel? So did the wind rage and boom and bluster in the tree-tops.

Army regulations require that loaded cars left in the forest should be guarded. But what matters when there is none to see? A warm and lighted railway shed, iron-roofed and snugly boarded, if you have two companions and plenty of tobacco, is a rare spot for playing nap in, especially as you can make tea, and your three rum rations in expert hands will yield a good supply of grog. And if you keep friends with the cook there will be no stint of sugar.

Meanwhile a man was climbing into a freight-car, easily enough, as it was open at the top. In a tube-shaped hollow encased in the resinous wood, he stretched himself full length, having first carefully pulled back over him some of the short pine planks grooved at either end; stretched himself out, and laughed aloud, and shook with that great laughter, his shirt drenched in sweat, and shivering all over, in the narrow sharp-edged coffin-like recess. It was hard lying: he could move but little. But he could laugh: and his eyes must have shone in the darkness like those of a panther which had burst its bars at last.

About half past eleven Grischa was awakened by a jolt, a noise of grinding and crashing; he started up in terror from the pack on which he had slept, wrapped in his blankets and his cloak—he had slept more serenely than for many years—and banged his head on the wood above. But he shook off his terror quicker than his pain: it was an engine backing down on to the interminable line of cars, with shrieks and whistles slowly merging into a steady clank and rumble. Once more Grischa sank down contentedly upon his wooden pillow; the train moved on, jolting and spewing forth sparks—while the firemen cursed softly at the wretched coal bricks; and the engine breasted the wind that blustered round it, as if to check its eastward course, toward Russia!

[. . .]

GOOD COUNSEL

"God will protect me," said Grischa, gravely, as he lay stretched luxuriously on the tumbled blankets of Babka's wooden bed, looking not in the least like one whom God would protect.

And Babka laughed. She had washed the soot and grime from her cheeks and deeply lined forehead, and turned her tanned face and bright eyes to gaze at this man for whose sake she had resumed the guise of a young and sturdy girl. She wore a shirt and petticoat, her feet were bare and dirty, and her firm sinewy breasts stood out under the linen fabric; and the white hair that made her look so old hung in long thin plaits against her cheeks. With a cigarette between her lips and her hands clasped behind her head, she sat on the edge of the bed and laughed at Grischa.

"Will God help you?" she repeated. "You silly soldier man. But who's going to help God?"

The dug-out, hollowed out of a sand-hill, and surrounded by birches and beech trees which had stood erect and unassailed by man for nigh two centuries, and braved the storms of spring and autumn, seemed to shiver under the hissing gusts of rain. In the left-hand corner water trickled in a yellowish stream through the leaky boards of the roof into a bucket set to catch it. From time to time the sweeping showers darkened the narrow slit of a window, which had been lifted from a country-house lavatory, to let daylight into Babka's abode.

"Why should we help God, old girl?" asked Grischa, pursuing his train of thought with imperturbable gravity. He looked a good five years younger; the loss of his long beard, which had fallen to Fedjuschka's knife, had carried him back to the days before his imprisonment. The skin beneath his eyes was no longer seamed and drawn with craving and despair, and his cheek-bones were no longer gaunt and haggard like a convict's.

"Because God's been out of this long ago, silly soldier man," she said, proceeding with her theological dissertation, as she stared into the left corner of the dug-out where the water dripped rhythmically into the bucket. "Because the Devil has shut Him up in the goatshed with the Son, and the Holy Ghost is cooing in the dove-cote, and the Devil is sprawling with his dirty soldier's boots on the red-plush chairs of Heaven's drawing-rooms. He was never so well off in his life! He does all the talking now, as any fool can see."

Grischa frowned. "Do you believe in the Devil instead of God? Why, you were properly christened and called after Holy Mother Anna, weren't you, Anna Kyrillovna?"

"That's just it. He doesn't want you to believe in him. All he wants is to do his business and leave you to yours, and he doesn't care a rap whether you believe in him or not. Do you think the Germans believe in the Devil? They crack their whips as if they did. Why, the Germans pay a visit of apology to God in church every

Sunday, because they believe nothing, and then they go their own way and do exactly as they please. As for the rest of us—the Russians believe, and the Jews believe, and so do the Poles and the Lithuanians, all believe, and believe in God, and look at them now! For three years they've been groaning under the Germans' boots. The Germans take away your money and seed corn and your last cow, and won't let you travel about in your own country, and set the police on your track everywhere, and if you get caught you're beaten with whips or rifle-butts; then they give you a bit of stamped paper to say it was all correctly done, and you can put that in your prayer book, silly soldier man: or you can do what else you like with it. But the German believes and takes this paper for his law and conscience. No, my lad," she concluded grimly, "when I was pestered with papers and police and such-like, I had as bad a time as any in the country and a bit worse, I can tell you: look at my hair, white and gray like a cat in the twilight—you don't get a head like that at twenty-four for nothing. And when I understood the game and, instead of being frightened of the police, made them frightened of me so that they wouldn't cross my path when it was getting dark, and in daylight only in twos and threes, then I was as happy as you please, though God's shut up in the goat-shed, and the Germans rule the world."

Grischa listened meditatively to the April storm roaring in the tree-tops, from which to-morrow's firewood came crashing down, and to the drumming, pattering showers with which spring washed the snow from the scarred face of good old Earth. He felt almost ill at ease in the small, cleanish, carefully boarded room, half dug-out and half hut, built entirely from the remnants of the former gun emplacement—"Tree-Cat Valley" he called it in his thoughts—which stood sheltered from wind and weather like a field-gun from the attacks of aircraft. Rather than sit and argue like this, he would have liked to go to the big sleeping-room where he had lived at first with the others, until he became the Captain's favorite. Of course he would not have sacrificed Anna Kyrillovna, his Babka, even in thought! For the first time for years he had held a woman in his arms—and such a woman!—and all the thoughts in her head, so far as they concerned himself, were good thoughts, a mother's thoughts; and years, a dreary procession of many months, had passed since he had felt such sweet reviving air about him. Like a waft from the glowing furnace of the heart, it made him happy, strong, and young once more. But what wicked talk was this—it was strange to hear such talk from a woman.

Babka broke into his thoughts. "You think it's strange to hear such talk from a woman, you silly soldier man? Do you know what the forest is? Up above, the trees stand in rows, quiet and polite, and if the Germans have had the forest for long, they stand at attention and 'Eyes Right!' when an officer passes. But underneath swarm the tangled roots; like deadly curling strands of wool, they prey upon each other every hour, and strangle each other every minute, venomous as snakes. If you scraped away a little of the earth on which we and the animals crawl, you would find yourself standing on a seething mass of roots, miles upon miles upon miles of them, and if they had voices they would howl day and night, groaning like a gang of platelayers hauling rails, and like the tree-tops now when the wind has his will with them, like a man with a maid. No, my lad, that world is not God's work, as the priest says, and the Jews read in their book. In the beginning God created heaven and earth;—that may well be so, for sometimes the earth looks pretty, and you know there is some good in it, when the sun shines on you and you lie in the forest, and the smell of the young sap makes you dizzy, and the squirrels up in the trees and the rooks sailing through the air prove that some of the job is well done: but Heaven and Earth are only half finished. You can take it from me that Somebody's meddled with it, and spat a spark into Man's brain, so that it has caught fire, and that fire has spread to every living thing. I can't think," she said after a moment, as she crushed her cigarette end against the edge of the table and threw it into the corner; and stretching out her bare arms with the unconscious grace of an animal, she added, "I can only see."

As he lay there, Grischa gazed meditatively at the cracked ceiling where the long-legged spiders slept their winter sleep. Awakened by the rain, one of these master-weavers stalked cautiously along, a little knot of living substance, as he gathered the swaying framework of his eight legs beneath him.

"Yes," he said. "You've only got to look at the pictures of Emperors and Kings and Generals—how the papers scatter them around! They're not beauties, and they don't look like saints neither. Have you seen old Schieffenzahn's face? He looks like a toad with a bird's beak"—and Grischa laughed. "But he's won three big battles. And his will is law in this country, so the German soldiers say."

Babka looked drearily across at the icon of the Virgin in the corner where it hung decked with pine branches above a red oil lamp.

"I'll tell you a tale," she went on, pursuing her swift soliloquy aloud. "There was mother and the four of us:—father, who was old but could still plough a good furrow, the two boys, and me. And over in America two more brothers collecting the dollars and sending us a good few, when times got hard: good workmen they were. One of them would sit on his steam-plough and in one day plough up half Lithuania, and the other was slitting pigs' throats in Chicago: several thousand pigs a day, one slit for each pig; they were both doing well. We had our cottage and field and potato patch and little garden and all we wanted, soldier man. Then came the War, and our boys went marching up; but the Germans weren't far off, and our men ran a trench right in front of our house. So we went away, but not very far, and a week later we came back and found things as we had left them. They hadn't used the trench, and our house was not damaged, for those sly devils, the Germans, got at us from another side. As soon as we had settled down we were swamped with orders and regulations. 'You can't do this, you mustn't do that: By Order! Prohibited!' We laughed: we're Russians although we're Lithuanians, and we thought: 'What's all this? Forbidden to carry weapons?' Not even a shot-gun, do you realize that? The hares could run over the cabbage patch and the deer over the crops, just as they pleased. 'Farmer, we want your gun,' they said. And father wrapped his gun in a cloth and kept it up in the rafters. Orders is orders, let the Devil find it if he can. Then they came along with a printed paper in our language, our Lithuanian language, which the Tsar didn't like, and also in Russian, which the Pole didn't like, saying that anyone who had a gun was to give it up, and anyone who didn't give it up and it was found, would be shot.

"'Have you ever heard such stuff?' we said. 'Give up a gun when you've got one? Why, it's madness; who's going to give you another? And to be shot for having a gun, that's just as mad, when you've not done anything.' There was a Polish landowner near by," she went on, screwing up her eyes with a grim smile, and baring her lower teeth. "Poles are obliging fellows. Bless you, they can't say No. They'll promise you anything and say nothing till they meet another man—then they'll oblige him by giving you away. That's what Poles are for! Well then, this neighbor, whose land was next to ours, always had field police billeted on him which did him no harm, and perhaps not much good either. You can't tell what's in your neighbour's head. But he knew about our gun up in the rafters. Then they fixed a time limit for all guns to be given up. But all my old father said was, 'Fear God and mind your own business.' 'A still tongue makes a wise head,' with a heap more of such proverbs that ooze out of the old folk like resin from a tree, and are just about as useful. And then one day came the head man of the village with a face on him as gray as dirty snow, and a lieutenant and six men to search the cottage. Of course they found our dollars, but the gun they carried off and the two lads with it—a boy of eighteen and another of sixteen, mere children, I tell you—and in a few weeks they brought them back. 'Anna,' said father,—he didn't kiss me, but just looked at me—'they're going to shoot us, me, Stefan, and Teodor, because we kept the gun. Good-bye! Kneel down and I'll give you my blessing. You'd better go to Peter and Nicholas in America.' I didn't cry out, I was a girl of twenty-two and wouldn't scream before the strangers. So they stood them in the trench just by our house and shot them, and they fell back into it with their faces toward the cottage—they shot them there as a warning to the neighbors. So after that they collared a heap of guns and fines from the poor neighbors—that's how my hair got white like this—and mother . . . every day she got up and cooked the dinner for her men down in the trench; they had gone there, she would say, to please themselves. Father and his sons are masters of the house, and must have their way, said she. An old woman's head is not strong like yours and mine. Every day till the day of her death she cooked a dinner of wood shavings and carried it out to the men who slept in the trench close by. Then I let the farm, when I had buried mother, in the churchyard, of course, and got the priest to consecrate the ground where the old man and the two lads were lying: everything done right and proper, with a fence round the grave and crosses on it, like we do in Lithuania, and a lily for the resurrection carved on top. And then, the day after I went, someone fired through the window of the Pole's house and hit him in the middle of his forehead. Not a bad shot, was it? So I took to the woods."

Darkness came early that afternoon. Torrent upon torrent of the spring showers stormed past the little window, and the draught from a crack in the front of the dug-out caused the light beneath the image of the Virgin to cast flickering shadows.

"Yes," answered Grischa thoughtfully. "War's a big business: once you've started it you can't control it. We've done some dirty work, too. All soldiers are the same: so are all officers. But those Germans. They've got brains in their heads like a set of pigeon-holes. If they were to catch me . . ." and drawing a deep breath, he held it for a moment in his fear.

Babka said quietly: "Make room," and lay down by him on the broad camp-bed, as a woman beside the man whom she has chosen. "Think of the summer," she said. "There's a good time coming in the forest. Hot days, days in the shade, Grischa, among the bilber-ries, good work to do and friends to help you."

Here she stopped, gazed at the ceiling, filled with tense expec-tancy.

"Any fool could stay here," said Grischa. "But it wasn't for that I gave the Germans the slip."

The young woman thrust out her broad lower jaw. "All right, go," said she. She was pale with terror and dismay: something in her was tottering—something that she had herself built up. Grischa thrust his arms firmly round her neck. Into the darkening air he spoke his fixed resolve. "Do you think I wouldn't like to stay here, Annja? Wouldn't I like to feel your arms round my neck for a long time yet? Didn't you make a man of me again, and put peace in my heart, as a man sinks a well in the earth, and the water spurts up in a fountain, washing out all the awful memories of prison? Do you think that's nothing? Wouldn't I be a hound if I thought nothing of it? But there's something pulling at me, something that wants to go home. And so I tell you straight I can't stay with you."

There was a boyish ring in his voice, piteous and imploring be-neath all the fixity of resolution.

"I shan't go yet if you'll keep me. Why shouldn't I stay here three or four weeks with you and the boys, and help you all, and then go on? . . . Then the gendarmes'll be after me again and I shall have to hide all day. And suppose they catch me!"

His anxious mind began to circle round this thought, which drew him as with the resistless power of a whirlpool.

Babka frowned darkly and said nothing. Still she stared defiantly into the empty air, where a medley of shadows clustered like the phantoms of her ruined hopes. "Will he go?" she wondered. "Will he take me with him?" So her thoughts ran on.

"Perhaps I'll have to work for them for long years after peace is made—carting earth in a wheelbarrow, clearing the soil of barbed wire, or sawing wood in their stone prisons. Wouldn't it be better to run for it, right into the gendarmes and their rifles?—one shot in the back would end it all."

She listened to his labored breath. By the deep compassion which now filled her, Babka knew the hopeless depths of her affection for this great boy, who had so struck her fancy when she first sat at his fire, this simple Simon, who called a lynx a "tree-cat," and lived alone in the woods with his knife and bow and arrows. Her breast shook with pitying laughter. She threw her arms round his neck, and bit his ear as she whispered (her breath smelling of food): "All right, go then, and I'll help you, silly soldier boy."

Her words came strangely to Grischa, who lay there propped upon his outstretched arms and gazed into her face. He saw the tears gleam in her eyes as she continued: "There's no need for everybody to know who you are. Just now there are all sorts of deserters coming through the lines, Russian soldiers that have had enough of it, and are off home to their wives and children: though, of course, their villages are on the German side, not over there in little Mother Russia. Here in the hut I've got a coat and trousers belonging to Ilja Pavlovitsch Bjuscheff, who was with me and died here though we tried hard to bring him round. He wore a bit of metal round his neck like all you soldiers, and I've kept it there in the drawer of the table. If they pinch you and your luck's out, you can just say you're Pavlovitsch Bjuscheff from Antokol, No. 5 Company, 67th Rifles, on the way home to mother: you've come through the lines, you're a deserter. They'll swallow that right enough: or at the worst, they'll clap you into a prisoner's camp again, and make enquiries. Meanwhile I'll put the old girl up to it. I know Natascha Pavlova Bjuscheff and where she lives; she'll swear to anything we ask her. What do you say to that, you silly soldier man?"

Over Grischa's round face, dark with anguish, stole an ever-broadening smile: he closed his slanting eyes, and opened them again in pride and admiration: "The Devil's not half as bad as his grandmother," he said, as he laughed aloud, "and his grandmother's an old idiot compared with a good woman that loves you," and like a swooping hawk he threw himself upon the broad, pale lips that had given him such wise counsel.

The rain spattered and poured, and drowned the lingering daylight; the red gleam of the sacred light beneath the Virgin's image shone on her tinseled robes and crown, like sparks of blood.

[. . .]

A VICTORY

Schieffenzahn rose from the table, and with a smile at the white-haired civilian opposite him, remarked:

"It's a pity, Herr van Ryjlte, that you're not a German: I should immediately put you under open arrest. What cigars! What coffee! You're corrupting our Spartan habits!"

The gray-haired Dutchman, with his ruddy, placid countenance, answered with equal courtesy:

"If I were a German, I should be patriotic enough to consider it a privilege to let you shut me up."

And they both laughed. The three officers of the Operations Division—this conversation was taking place at Brest-Litovsk—were delighted with the old gentleman's retort. They knew that Schieffenzahn's good-humor meant that he was full of bright ideas and things would go smoothly. Dr. van Ryjlte, who was more than seventy years old, sat calmly in his chair. He was waiting for the above-mentioned coffee which he had brought with him—fine strong Java coffee;—and he and his hosts each lit one of the offending cylindrical imports which he had also brought. He smiled peacefully as he looked round at the company, cracking walnuts in his bony hands, and did not betray his deep disappointment. He was a Delegate of the Red Cross who had been sent to Germany to inspect certain camps in which deported Belgian men and women had been interned, and to see their grievances redressed; he had also come to warn the great Schieffenzahn quite frankly about America. He could not get over the General's icy unbelief, his impenetrability to new ideas. "America's all bluff and humbug: they're getting above themselves." That was all he could get out of him; and indeed this was what the yellow press had incessantly dinned into its millions of readers, and the General and his grocer both believed it.

Nevertheless he had approached his task with care, and to avoid any suspicion that he was some malignant fellow, trying to paralyse the German will to victory at one of its great poles of energy, he had begun by reminding the General of how, in the year 1914, the world at large had foretold Germany's imminent defeat. "You don't know Germany," he had said to his South American business friends, when they had prophesied that she would soon be lying with her back broken under Russia's heel; and now he had come to the Germans with his message: "If you haven't been in America, you don't know what sort of bloodhounds you've got after you." The United States were not to be compared with Roumania, or Italy, he explained, although the latter had standing armies. America would cover the Front with engines of destruction, and behind each one would be a team of smart, hawk-eyed fellows all spoiling for a fight, fellows whose spirit had never been broken by a drill sergeant.

But at this point, the words died on his lips, as he observed the General's smile of polite superiority: and he said to himself, with full assurance in his heart: "With open eyes ye rush on to your destruction, and there shall be great lamentation over you." His thoughts had wandered far from the occasion and the moment; as he looked through the window to the westward, he seemed to be speaking to a multitude of assembled Germans—a vast expanse of upturned faces—who listened to the old man's hoarse entreaties. He had sunk into a deep reverie, and his fingers trembled slightly, as he held his long cigar.

Schieffenzahn, with others who shared his views, had recently contrived to baffle the Pope's peace efforts, and he now thanked the Dutchman politely for his pains. He had quite different information from America, backed by statistics and borne out by expert evidence. Herr van Ryjlte greatly underestimated the striking power of the German Army, which was the result of long training, and which had had no equal for the past half-century. Of course, he was particularly grateful for this frank and friendly expression of opinion, and if his Dutch friend wished to do a much-needed service to the nation in its hour of trial, he might use his influence to destroy the prejudice which was felt in neutral countries against the annexation of Belgium to the German Empire. Belgium itself would be much better off: she would be an independent Federal State, like Bavaria or Saxony, and a part of the greatest of the European Powers. What could she possibly want more?

Van Ryjlte's arms dropped helplessly.

"How about freedom?" he asked. "The freedom of a people?"

Schieffenzahn laughed. "Little peoples can have but little freedom. Within the German Empire, Belgium already enjoys more liberty than she did before the War. The stronger the army, the greater is the liberty it guards."

"Perfectly conclusive," agreed the Dutchman, and promised to do his best. But he meant something quite different. . . . He saw it was useless, and his hands gripped his thighs beneath the table as he resolved to sell every sort of holding he had in Germany, as quickly and quietly as possible: currency, Government loans, shares and debentures of the great Schilles works, and his credits with German firms.

"When a ship is certain to sink, a rat that did not leave it would be a fool, and deserve to drown," he reflected, grimly trying to dispel his gloom, as he put sugar in his coffee. The familiar proverb, which laid aspersions on the rat, had no doubt been invented by Insurance Companies or skippers full of whisky. For as the rat went on board of its own free will, on the assumption that the ship would float, as any reasonable ship might be expected to do, it was justified before God and the world, if it left the ship before it had to bear the consequences of the Captain's incompetence. . . . He genially apologized for his interference in matters of policy, which came very ill from a guest. "But," he added, with a faint smile, "do not consider me as a guest, but as a troublesome and unwelcome relative, who has come here with the best intentions, to warn—say, a so-in-law—against a risky business transaction."

"I like 'son-in-law,' we'll leave it at that," said Schieffenzahn with a laugh, and they sat down to talk. . . .

The city of Brest-Litovsk, beyond the railway station and the great blue-towered cathedral, lay ghost-like and silent as death at the foot of the citadel, where the Operations Section and its infrequent guests were housed in a collection of hutments and barrack-buildings. During the fighting which had led to the capture of the city, it had been gutted by fire, and was now a desert, and a habitation of ghosts. Along the gray streets the windowless facades stood up apparently undamaged, but behind them was nothing, or a mass of crumbled ruins. Broad desolate stretches traversed by roads and lined with heaps of debris from which chimneys protruded, marked the sites of wooden houses, of which only the brickwork of the fireplaces survived. Above it all the snow was drifting, for the snow had come. Since midnight it had been falling in heavy silent flakes, sometimes caught and driven by the wind, downward through the white air. The sky, yellow and lowering, gave promise of much more snow to come, when in the middle of the morning van Ryjlte had been fetched from the station in a small sleigh. He had stopped several times on the way, and in the company of the young Lieutenant who was with him, whom he immediately presented with a magnificent cigar, promising him some more as soon as he unpacked, had peered through the doorways of the stone and brick houses in this city where an Imperial garrison rubbed shoulders with an ancient and famous Jewish community. Brest, as it is called in Lithuanian, or Brisk, as the Jews have it, was the home of the Brisker Rabbinim, he reflected, and as a collector of Hebrew manuscripts, he had hoped to find much spoil. . . . Cats ran mewing up broken staircases; tall gray twisted shrubs were growing in the ground-floor rooms, and on the copings or the gutted floors of the upper stories brown weeds and grasses shivered in the wind. Everywhere warnings were posted against entering these ruined houses. Men had built them, van Ryjlte reflected, and probably men would build them up once more. In this way Corinth and Jerusalem, Alexander and Rome, had all passed and come to life again; war and peace were the ebb and flow of humanity's tide: it was good to live behind dyke, he thought.

The day had begun successfully with the Dutchman's visit, but there were some awkward hours ahead and Schieffenzahn would need all his wits about him. He clenched his fists. He wouldn't be taken in by this plausible rubbish: he would go straight on, and people in the way had better mind their toes. He stamped genially up and down the room, in the darkest corner of which was a camp-bed; there he worked and slept all the time he was at Brest. Old Lychow was the next item: "Lychow 4:30" was written in red ink on the calendar. Another of these gray-haired fools who waste the best hours of the day with their tedious importunities. Oh, these Generals! If he ever said what he thought to one of them, it would get about that that brute Schieffenzahn could not be decently polite to senior officers. It was already three o'clock, and after that strong Java coffee he could work with a will. He had first to reconsider Ober-Ost's proposal for the administration of the newly-occupied Ukrainian territories. The document was already adorned with a number of Austrian protests and counter-proposals; all the fault of that confounded Lychow, with his staff celebrations, where Count Dubna had made his drunken speeches. Thank God, the man had now definitely become a hospital case, and was being treated at Baden-Wien. But that did not affect the difficult relations between Austrians and Germans which were becoming more serious every month. A large-leaved atlas of the occupied territories was spread out with the documents on the white deal desk, the center of which was covered with green baize. There must be a way out of these difficulties, and Schieffenzahn was the man to find it. But first he must polish off this fellow Lychow, this narrow-minded quarrel-some pedant, this old dug-out from the depths of Brandenburg; the whole clan of them had always been prating and plotting on the wrong side, i.e., against Bismarck. "Let him come," he said softly to himself as he arranged the papers; "he'll find his business settled already." He took down the receiver and said to the sergeant who answered the telephone:

"Matz, wire as follows at once to the Kommandantur at Mervinsk: 'Settle Bjuscheff case according to instructions already received, and report duly carried out within twenty-four hours.' Bring me before half-past four a notification from the telegrapher on duty that the order has gone."

The sergeant answered: "Very good, Sir," repeated the message, and Schieffenzahn hung up the receiver. As he gave the order he felt for an instant an oppression at his heart, but at the same time a sense of grim satisfaction at the thought that Herr von Lychow was coming to waste time over an affair that had long since been settled. For a few seconds he was conscious of this feeling of constriction, and realized that it was due to the strong coffee he had drunk—

coffee of a freshness and purity to which they were unaccustomed in blockaded Central Europe. The room seemed dark for three o'clock in the afternoon, and he went to the window. Courtyard No. IV lay deep and silent beneath its soft covering of white. There were great ridges of snow on the roofs to the right of him, and on the casements, from whose chimneys the yellowish smoke of burning wood swirled merrily upward. The room was pleasantly warm, full of the pleasant fragrance of cigars—a man could sit there comfortably, with plenty of light, and do his work in peace. He switched on the electric light, and its yellow glow beat down from beneath the green shade of the office lamp, and the window turned into an opaque square of blue in the semi-darkness. He leaned his head on his fleshy hand and studied the memorandum of the Austrian authorities, drawn up by the Foreign Minister, and liberally bespattered with notes and comments. If only the Austrians would consent to a German General being appointed member of the new Ukraine Council, with a casting-vote, wherever the new capital might be—in Kieff or Odessa—a great deal could be done to meet their views. There was a certain Hetman Skoropatzki who made himself very prominent; he could be titular head of the new State, just like one of those horses' heads that used to be nailed on the gables of barns. "O Fallada, do you hang there?" suddenly came into his mind from a memory of Grimm's fairy tales: he probably had not thought of it for fifty years. However, he put everything else out of his mind, and concentrated on the text before him and the interplay of political and economic claims involved by it. He paid little attention to questions of nationality, which were set forth at length, such as the claims of the Poles against the Ukrainians, and their demand that the Cholm county should be assigned to the new Polish Kingdom—he was much more interested in the acquisition and transport of the Ukrainian wheat. He suddenly realized that the control of the harvest was the key to the whole position; on this point he must be firm: everything else hung on this. At the end of 1917 it was no easy matter to form a correct estimate of the economic factors of the situation.

Punctually at half-past four the faint clink of Exzellenz von Lychow's spurs was heard at Schieffenzahn's door. At five minutes to five he departed. Their interview was noteworthy in many respects;

both men spoke their minds, and the result was what might have been expected.

Lychow had left his cloak outside, as it was covered with snow. The old gentleman sat, with his gold-laced cap on his knees, a glove on his clenched left hand—he had politely taken off the other to shake hands with the enemy. At first he missed something—of course it was his long straight sword that stood so comfortably between his knees, and was so convenient to hang his cap on; a man cannot express his feelings so pointedly without the support of the long piece of steel which has swung at his side for nearly forty years. Schieffenzahn, in a loose *Litevka,* which he liked to wear unbuttoned, so that he could put his hands in his trouser-pockets, had the advantage of him, thought Lychow.

He began by asking whether the Quartermaster-General was aware of the position: there had been unwarrantable interference with the judicial authority of the Division, and a perfectly regular legal decision had been treated with contempt. His tone had already become rather acid; but Schieffenzahn, with the genial propitiatory smile of a younger man humoring an old man's whim, reassured him.

He had read through the papers himself once again during the last few days and he could not understand what objection His Excellency could have to the decision which the court martial officer at Ober-Ost had recommended to him after mature consideration, and which he thoroughly approved.

Between the two antagonists was a broad expanse of writing-table; on it was an inkpot made of the cast-steel base of a hand-grenade, a flattened brass shell-case for an ash-tray, copper limber-rings for paper-weights, and some unpleasant-looking shell splinters, such as could be picked up everywhere in the lines. On the right was the telephone, on the left the Ukraine papers; in a black papier maché bowl with little golden stars on it lay the fountain-pens, copying-pencils, large colored pencils, red, green, and blue, and ordinary lead pencils with blunt points adapted to Schieffenzahn's well-known marginal scrawls. It seemed to Lychow that the table was getting broader and broader, as if each of them was at the edge of a continent, a flat plain peopled with pigmies, tiny specks called men; and he and Schieffenzahn yonder, swollen to the stature of colossi, crouched or glared in hatred on the confines of this world. He felt he ought never to have come here. His baggy-cheeked junior opposite made him feel that he was certainly the weaker man, perhaps only today because he felt unwell, or perhaps just because he had justice upon his side. A man who recognizes justice, must also recognize that it imposes limitations, he thought, already absorbed in his own reflections before the battle had fairly started. To a man who respects justice, his neighbor's flower-beds are sacred. A man who does not respect it, may perhaps live three stories lower down, but with his thick skin and tough skull, he plunges about in forbidden regions: it is nothing to him if they are forbidden. "I have made a colossal blunder: a man can fight better at a distance. . . ." He began to grow angry with himself at these meandering reflections, took out one of his own cigarettes and tapped it on the case, and asked, with an appearance of unconcern, what was the Major-General's view of the situation as a whole: was he going to abolish completely the independent legal authority of the Divisions, and introduce a new military code, according to which justice might indeed be sought for, but when found, was to be thrown into the waste-paper basket at the caprice of a higher court, or even one of equal jurisdiction, which might happen to think differently?

In reply to which Schieffenzahn growled out that nobody could have more respect for the jurisdiction of so experienced a soldier and one who stood so high in His Majesty's favor, but matters of policy were not everyone's business. Apparently the members of the Divisional court martial had missed the most important aspect of the case, which it was his duty to take into account.

Lychow felt that he must keep calm: this was the core of the dispute between them. But he did not want to plunge rashly into such fundamental issues. So he said quietly: "But, my dear Schieffenzahn, how is my court martial officer, who is a capable man—as I think you will admit—to find out which is the court competent to deal with a given charge? If you thrust your more enlightened views on us in this way, we shan't be inclined to refer our cases to you."

Schieffenzahn was becoming annoyed. Did the old figure-head take him for a child?

In spite of his irritation, he answered in a matter-of-fact tone that if an explanation was due to anyone it was due to him. It was intolerable that a man sentenced to death as a seditious person, a slinking Bolshevik, should have been allowed to survive so long, and he had clearly and unmistakably intimated his wish that the sentence should be carried out. And instead of obeying a plain order, they came to him with quibbles about jurisdiction and legal competence. He, Schieffenzahn, was responsible for seeing that nothing should endanger the German victory, at least on the Eastern Front. He had to keep the army well in hand. When such issues were at stake it was no time to be splitting hairs about justice and injustice. He would be the last man to upset the authority of a General. (That sounds quite Fritz-like, thought Lychow scornfully.) But His Excellency von Lychow was the last man from whom he would have expected to have to endure all this stuff and nonsense about courts and jurisdictions.

Lychow bowed slightly, and he thanked Schieffenzahn for his good opinion. He said that the matter had gone far beyond a mere question of jurisdiction. It was a question of plain justice—whether in Prussia there was to be equal justice for every man, as the Bible says: "One scale, one measure, and one weight shalt thou have for thee and for the stranger within thy gates. I the Lord have spoken it." He was quoting at random and his legs quivered as he spoke.

Schieffenzahn made a polite gesture of agreement. There must assuredly be justice, and therefore no exceptions. As every day a thousand men fell as a sacrifice to the German victory, he supposed that a Russian deserter, who had so disgracefully abandoned his post in the prison-camp, might well fall with them. And he smiled amicably, delighted at the cunning with which he had caught the old gentleman in his own trap.

But Otto Gerhard von Lychow smiled too: he had got Schieffenzahn now; he had managed to lure him on to ground where that laborious intellect was hardly at its best.

"Certainly, Herr Kamerad," he said, "you have put the case very well. Throughout this War, at every moment of the day and night, innocent men have gone to their deaths, all honor to them. But the responsibility for this rests with all the generations that have built up the State, and also with the men themselves. They agreed to take part in the pageant of history, and their children and grandchildren must reap the fruits of their sacrifice. Of course, it was to some extent imposed on them; still, it may be considered voluntary, as long as the country is ready to obey the decisions of its responsible leaders. But now, Herr Kamerad, I am sorry to have to point out a slight flaw in your argument. Let me finish what I have to say," he exclaimed, as Schieffenzahn prepared to answer. "Do I send my men into action with the intention of getting them killed? If I had a voice in the matter they should all come back alive, every one of them, sir! If that is impossible, I submit sorrowfully to the inevitable—as long as war is the ultimate means of making a nation great. But you, on the other hand, are proposing to sacrifice against his will a man well known to be innocent, because in the furtherance of your purposes you think merely to do the State a service. The soldier always goes into battle with a certain degree of willingness, for he thinks there is a shadow of a possibility that he may return; in the last resort, he puts his life in God's hands, for the sake of his home, his country, and his Emperor. But this Russian—the machinery of justice is to be used to put him to death unjustly. Do you dare to compare him with a German soldier?"

"I do," said Schieffenzahn nodding. "Look at the facts. How long does this degree of willingness last? If the German soldier refuses to obey orders, he is shot. And as for that shadow of a possibility of returning—if he's lucky this time, he'll be for it next time. Consider, Exzellenz. Phosgene shells, and gas attacks, are gradually reducing the scope of the Divine Mercy that you mentioned. The art of war, looked at from the technical point of view, seems to be intended to put God in His proper place. I prefer—though I am afraid I shall offend you—to take the plain blunt view of the situation: the State creates justice, the individual is a louse."

Von Lychow leaned back in his chair and said softly: "If I thought that was true, I should feel no better than a dog. The State creates justice, does it? No, Sir, it is justice that preserves the State. I learned that as a boy, and that alone gives a meaning to life, in my view. It is because justice is the foundation of all States, that nations have the right to tear themselves to pieces in their defense. But when a State begins to work injustice, it is rejected and brought low. I know, as I sit here under your lamp fighting for the life of this poor Russian, that I am fighting for something greater than your State—I mean for mine! For the State as the instrument of eternity. States are like vessels: and vessels wear out and break. If these cease to serve the purposes of God, they collapse like houses of cards, when the wind of Providence blows upon them. But I, General Schieffenzahn, know that justice and faith in God have been the pillars of Prussia, and I will not look on while her rulers try to bring them down."

The small dark room, in which the sole illumination was the circle of light from the green-shaded bulbs in the center, seemed to stretch away to infinity round the two men who sat there contending for a man's life. Outside in the vast silence the faint sound of snow could be heard eddying against the window-panes. Von Lychow got up and, absorbed in his reflections, absent-mindedly drew the curtains in this room that was not his. Schieffenzahn looked at him quizzically. To think that an old stick like this should come to him with quotations from the Bible, as if Haeckel's *Riddle of the Universe* had never been written. Did such superannuated old dugouts think that they could guide and preserve the German Empire? At last, as he toyed with a paper-weight in the shape of a Roman sword, made from the limber-ring of a heavy mortar and inlaid with copper, he asked if His Excellency was prepared to take his oath that Prussia had grown up in obedience to God's commandments. Maria Theresa and the Polish nation had expressed quite a different view on several occasions, and the proletariat had the most singular notions on the subject. And, smiling down on von Lychow from the superior height of the nineteenth century, he began cautiously to pull to pieces the old gentleman's political theology: touching upon the franchise, the rights of property, and the distribution of land.

But Schieffenzahn's superior attitude was lost upon von Lychow. Might must not be divorced from Right. If Schieffenzahn's objections were more in accordance with reality, yet he was well aware that all human institutions were imperfect, and the influence of the people still counted for something in the formation of the future. But nothing in the world could justify a State setting in motion the mighty machinery of the law against the innocent, and so destroy a nation's sense of justice. The national sense of justice, he said, quivering with emotion, was the symbol of Divine justice, and if it is thrown on the scrap-heap on political grounds, no one could tell whether, as a result of such an outrage, in the eternal spheres of the Divine justice sentence might not be passed on the State itself: *Mene, tekel, upharsin* might be seen faintly glimmering on the wall of a room in which a General was using his pitiable logic to bring God's commandments into contempt.

"Pitiable logic," indeed! Albert Schieffenzahn started in his chair. He had borne with the pious old dodderer and kept his temper, so long as he had remained polite. But this he could not stand, and in a harsh imperious tone he requested von Lychow to moderate his language. He must remember he was not at Herrenhut or at a mothers' meeting.

Von Lychow slowly drew on his glove. He was familiar with that sort of talk, he said. The Lychows had tried to get rid of it after Saalfeld and Jena, but half Prussia had been swamped by it. "No doubt the Schieffenzahns think it extremely up-to-date," he added. "However, there's no more to be said," and he flicked the cigarette-ash off his trousers.

Albert Schieffenzahn breathed heavily, and thrust out his lower jaw, bulldog fashion, though it was by nature somewhat receding. He thanked von Lychow for his observations: he had enjoyed the lecture on Divine Providence, and now he proposed to make some remarks in return. He flattered himself he knew all about discipline and the best means of enforcing it. He had therefore telegraphed orders to the Kommandantur at Mervinsk to the effect that the sentence should be punctually carried out by the following afternoon. He saw Lychow start, and grip the back of the chair. Yes, he went on, he had done so without the slightest hesitation. His Excellency might, of course, appeal to the Emperor afterward. Then he, Schieffenzahn, who was so unpopular and had already taken so much upon himself, might get into hot water again: but he did not mind. However, he now wanted to make the difference between them perfectly clear. In His Excellency's opinion the execution of the Russian would be prejudicial to discipline, but in his own, it was in the interests of discipline and was, in fact, demanded by political necessity. Their views were diametrically opposed. Very well, then. As His Excellency declined all responsibility—"Of course I do," said Lychow emphatically—he had better give up his leave and let the 5:20 D train go off without him. He could go straight back to Mervinsk by the next train, or by a car which would be at His Excellency's disposal, and personally prevent the Ortskommandant from carrying out the order of the Q.M.G.—in other words, of the Commander-in-Chief. If he, Schieffenzahn, then sent a lieutenant and ten men to take the Russian, dead or alive—and he leaned forward and smiled insolently at his visitor who, with his cap in his gloved fingers, was staring at him, motionless, from behind his chair—His Excellency had better place himself at the head of his Division, and with full understanding of the consequences, resist him by open force, and, with his Bible in his pocket, return blow for blow in defense of what he conceived to be right. "Don't you agree, Your Excellency?" he asked, as Lychow opened his mouth to reply, but merely swallowed and said nothing. "As you decline all responsibility, and are quite sure that you have the interests of the Empire and of justice on your side . . ."

The room was strangely still. The silence that surrounded Lychow was like the silence of an Arctic waste, cut off from all the world.

"God help me," he said at last: "I'm a Prussian General . . ."

"So Your Excellency will proceed on leave, and not declare a private war on me, but yield to my poor logic after all?"

Lychow nodded: he had come into the room pale and determined, but now he turned to go with bowed head and heavy footsteps. Schieffenzahn got up politely, and pushed his chair back sharply and exultantly—the noise he made echoed against the wooden walls like the slamming of a hundred doors. As he stood there, he pushed up the green-shaded electric lamp, the better to illuminate his triumph, so that its yellow glare lit up the battlefield as far as the door.

Lychow walked to the window with his spurs tinkling, just as if he had been alone, pulled the curtain aside, stared out vacantly for a moment, then turned round and looked steadily at his victorious antagonist.

"I am only an old man, Herr Schieffenzahn, nobody can jump over his own shadow, however small it is: and I've cast my shadow for seventy-two years."

Then he laid two fingers on his cap and went.

Major-General Schieffenzahn, standing with his legs apart, watched with a sardonic smile the door close behind a beaten man.

[. . .]

THE BLACK BEAST

In the corner, behind him in the corner, waits the fear of death, the black beast, and watches him. Soon it will leap upon his neck.

Grischa sat at table eating: he was eating a beefsteak and roast potatoes, and on the table was a tin of preserved fruit. He was drinking half a bottle of red wine. Sergeant-Major Spierauge had sent him three cigars, two of which he had given away, one to Corporal Schmielinsky and the other to Corporal Sacht, to smoke as soon as he was allowed tobacco. Grischa had the third in his mouth. He was going to cut the end off and light it, ready at any moment for the black beast, the fear of death, to leap upon him from the corner. He must keep it off. A soldier was going to his death, by God, a Russian Sergeant, Grischa Iljitch Paprotkin, Knight of the Cross of St. George, alone among a horde of enemies, exposed to the eyes of everyone; and he must go like a man. In spite of all he had eaten there still remained between his palate and his tongue a bitter taste he could not get rid of. The cigar was a good one: it drew and tasted well; but he had to smoke it with set jaws, as his heart was pounding so slowly and so heavily. The door of the cell was open. He would be alone long enough; he would get plenty of sleep, too, if sleep it could be called. Now he must see and hear and breathe; his fingers which he kept lying on the table or stuck in his pockets were continually in motion. They felt the lining of his pockets, and the ribbed surface of the deal table, so rough and pleasant to his touch. His eyes could see the golden light of noon pouring through the window, indeed it was past noon. He saw the spiders' webs on the ceiling, and the winter-flies of Russia—several were buzzing and flying sluggishly along the window-pane, and they reminded him of overfed crows. They were safe enough.

Grischa remembered that he was still wearing his woolen waistcoat which he did not want spoilt. He took it off, drawing it over his head, and then put on his tunic again. Grischa's back felt cold, and he quickly buttoned up his tunic. His head felt hot, so he took off his cap. He felt impelled to walk up and down. From the chair under the window to the cell door by the passage was exactly seven paces, and with bent head, as if he were quite alone, he paced them up and down. He still felt cold. He drew on his overcoat, the good warm Russian cloak. Then the desire to empty his bowels came over him, so he went to the corporal who sent a man with him. He liked the sound of his footsteps echoing upward from the stone flags. The snow in the yard crunched deliciously under his hobnailed boots, and the keen blue air felt refreshing against his temples and his nostrils. It is pleasant to sit on a latrine and empty oneself out. All that makes the living man is good, he thought, as he clenched his teeth and wiped away the sweat that burst out on his forehead though it was winter and very cold. It would not last much longer. Then he went back accompanied by the Landwehr man with his rifle. That heavy weight upon his knees had gone. He walked back to his cell much comforted: he felt better now. Next he wanted to wash his face: he was determined to be clean. Hot water takes away the dirt from a man's hands and the skin of his face. The coarse soap, which looks like a soft brown stone, did not lather but it rubbed the dirt off. Anyhow, it would clean him, he thought. Then he asked for the barber—he wanted to be shaved. Erwin Scharski, the company barber, a soldier like the rest, could report in three minutes from the quarters of the first platoon. Grischa was sitting among the South German Landwehr men. They were smoking and reading: two games of nap and a game of chess were going on. It was very silent compared with the usual clatter at that hour. The long tunnel-like room was full of a murmurous hum of talk. With a towel round his neck, pleasantly sprinkled with hot water, lathered with almond soap, Grischa sat with closed eyes— his twilight was upon him. Now that he was being shaved no one could come to fetch him. As long as this business lasted his life was safe. At the moment he had a craving for sleep: but he must be shaved first, and he listened to the barber's gossip while he was stropping the razor.

"I'll put on my St. George's Cross," thought Grischa. "I'll take it out of the pocket of my tunic and hang it on my overcoat: afterward they can send it back to the Tsar. I hope it may be a reproach to him all his days that he did not keep the peace or come to his senses earlier."

The barber was telling him about the huge rats which they had had in their lines in Champagne, how they were as big as squirrels, nearly as big as cats. But when he came to the point of the story, when the rats with the poison in their bellies lay on their backs with their four paws drawn up, forty-one of them in a single trench, he stopped short. He suddenly hated the idea of these rats lying there so stiff and he grew dizzy at the thought. He was telling the story for the seventeenth or perhaps the seventy-seventh time, but this was the first time he told it with a happy ending. This time the rats smelt the poison and generously left it alone. Grischa smiled, and then let himself be shaved. His skin was now smooth, his hair brushed and parted neatly in the way that soldiers like to have it. The cost of the performance would go down to the office account. The barber would not take Grischa's money. And the soldier, the man of the Landwehr into whom, when his work was done, he so obviously changed back again, shook his customer by the hand and disappeared. As he crossed the yard he heard an unknown clear voice outside:

"Section, halt! Order arms! At ease!"

Something struck at his heart, and he ran into his quarters. A clerk brought in an order to Corporal Schmielinsky; the corporal went as white as a sheet, and his lips trembled in his agitation; then he went in to Grischa, who had just lain down for a moment, though a moment before he had got up because he was tired of lying down.

"Comrade," said Schmielinsky, "it has come. Try and keep calm, old boy."

Grischa felt the sensation of a blow that made his heart leap. And he too went pale. The two men stared at each other. Then Grischa made the movements of buckling up his belt: he would not go forth in slovenly and unsoldierly guise, and he mechanically felt for the broad, once black, infantry belt which had been returned to him with the rest of his possessions, and which he had not yet given away, and buckled it round him. Then he adjusted his cloak in the correct folds over his back, smoothed it down in front, put on his cap, his broad peaked Russian summer cap made of thin linen, straightened himself with a jerk, saluted in the Russian manner (not permitted to German soldiers), and said good-bye to the corporal:

"If it's time, then I must go. Thank you, comrade."

The corporal on duty blew his nose, his arms shook, and for an instant his handkerchief covered his eyes.

A breathless stillness fell upon the room. The guards, who had come in from outside, stood at attention. Grischa, standing on the threshold, looked once more around him: the windows above the long table, the stools on which the chess-players sat motionless and stared across at him, the two groups of nap-players, who let their cards fall, men washing, who ceased to wash, and two men sewing, who let their needles and their garments drop, the bunks with their straw mattresses and haversacks.

"All correct," he thought. "Section, march!"

"I wish you good luck, comrades!"

The Germans made no sound, except for a young soldier, pale, and with eyes starting from his head, who answered him hoarsely: "Keep your heart up, comrade, and good-bye," and another, near him, whispered unintelligible words of horror from where he lay upon his bunk.

"Hurry up," came a voice from without.

Grischa felt slightly dizzy: but with chin well out, he marched with the corporal on duty and two Landwehr men past the sentry at the gate. There waited two sergeant-majors on horseback: Spierauge on a fat lethargic mare, and Berglechner, spruce as an officer, on a dark brown gelding. Four files of four men each, all in the same green uniforms, wearing puttees and steel helmets, carbines on their shoulders—there they stood, Jägers of this machine-gun company, ready for the march.

"But the fellow's arms are free," Berglechner called out to his friend from the office.

Spierauge shrugged his shoulders. It was not really necessary to bind Grischa's hands, he said. But Berglechner was punctilious, and without saying a word, Grischa put his hands behind his back and allowed Corporal Schmielinsky, whose hands were still trembling, to tie a narrow strip of leather round his wrists.

"That'll make me stand up," he thought. "I must stick my chest out with my arms behind my back." And with hard, steady eyes he looked at the horseman, whose voice and manner was quite different from that of the Germans whom he had known hitherto— middle-aged men with their experiences behind them. Then he looked the young Jägers up and down: cool, keen-eyed fellows, he thought. Two files in front of him and two behind, and Grischa in the middle,—and the little procession moved off. The two sergeant-majors started their horses. Berglechner took the lead, and Spierauge was to have ridden behind: but Berglechner would not allow it, he wanted company and conversation, so the leisurely old Liese had to move up to the front. Berglechner, who had already reported to Rittmeister von Brettschneider, took command: "Section, march!" and the detachment began to tramp rhythmically through the squelching slush of the main street. They went round the Tverskaia, and through outlying quarters of the city.

Grischa gazed straight ahead. The lower edges of the line of helmets in front of him gave the impression of a long gray shield swaying slightly as it moved forward. The men's leather straps and belts, gleaming with fresh buff polish, their puttees, their worn green trousers, their laced boots, so carefully greased, and on an exact level above the helmets the four muzzles of the rifles, and beyond them another four, now visible and now hidden as the heads of the marching men behind them rose and fell. The place for executions at Mervinsk was well known. It lay outside the town, in an easterly direction, on the way to that fortified outlook known as "Lychow's bunion." Years ago it had been a gravel quarry, scooped out of the hillside, and its steep wall offered an excellent background for shooting, and there was a fairly level stretch of ground on which the men could be drawn up. Veressejeff had a sleigh waiting in front of his house so that if the priest, unhappy man, should still come, he could drive to the place at once. Spierauge, who also had the subject in mind, thought that the clergyman, whoever he might be, would not join them till they were outside the town: but at that moment Sergeant-Major Pont appeared, helmeted and gloved, wearing an artillery cloak with three ribbons; he rode up casually and saluted. He introduced himself briefly and the two others raised their gloved hands to the rims of their helmets. At a slow trot they overtook the little party, which of course had not halted; Pont took up the rear and the two others rode ahead. Some civilians were sauntering up and down the pavements enjoying the afternoon sun, and they were splashed with the flying slush as the men tramped marching with extreme smartness and precision. The two sergeant-majors felt like officers; they stared straight before them over their horses' ears, seeing no one. Murmurs and whispered talk followed them along the Magazinstrasse. Women crossed themselves at the roadside and all the passers-by stared aghast at the solitary Russian with his hands bound behind him, and the St. George's Cross on his chest. As yet nobody knew much about him; but his journey along that humble street of warehouses was to make him known and famous before evening in Mervinsk, and many families—Jews, Catholics, and Orthodox Russians—would learn every detail of his fate. Newspapers were unknown there, but news was passed all the more eagerly from mouth to mouth.

Grischa went forward, took his eyes off the unbearable steel-gray line in front of him and the tiny black mouths of the gun barrels, and let his gaze wander to the houses on the right and left, where lived his friends, who could not help him. He filled his lungs with deep draughts of air. In some marvelous manner, he no longer felt the presence of that fear that had so lately threatened to destroy him. He looked about him and saw all that stood upon the earth.

The shop signs, on which men announced what wares lay stored for sale in the caverns behind them. The openings to these same caverns, four-square windows with wooden frames and crosspieces and little double sashes, moss-grown at the joints. The doorsteps, wooden balks or slabs of stone, smooth and worn with many steps. He saw the smoke rising like pale pennons from the chimneys, melting snow pouring in little torrents from every roof, or falling from the eaves in golden drops; he saw how the wind blew when they had left the last houses behind them. Every step seemed to jerk him violently onward; over that white road, monotonously clanked and tramped a moving body, composed of several members, each of which was itself a man. Embedded in this complex creature, his hands behind his back, his legs mechanically moving, marched in a long buff cloak, the solitary soldier. At last he saw the snowfields, white or pale gold, flecked with bluish shadows. Perhaps the business of this day was a mad business, but if so it was being done with such solemnity and so much as a matter of course, that Grischa alone perceived a little of its madness. His wild eyes wandered to the right and left of him; there was nothing new to see, nothing but crows, snowdrifts, and the dazzling shimmer of the sun's bright golden pathway, before the haze dispersed and gathered into the blue canopy above their heads.

"O God," he thought, "O God." The only thing that comforted him was the feel of his broad leather belt round his middle which kept him stiff and erect. Pride, sad splendid liar, that forced him to preserve his honor in the face of his enemies by a brave death in a far country, was like that belt of his: it too held him together. He kept on swallowing saliva that he noticed had a bitter taste, and while his gaze wandered from left to right, marking all the details of that scene, just below his heart he felt a steady pressure thrusting the overstrained muscle against the vaulting of his ribs. The horses' harness clinked and there was much rattling of chains against leather; the soldiers' heavy laced boots, sixteen pairs of them, crunched in unison into the snow that now began to grow harder, their bayonets beat rhythmically against their thighs and on their shoulders the rifles creaked on the leather straps, sometimes knocking sharply against the steel helmets. This marching body made its own peculiar noises, and had a heart that was full of fear; that heart was Grischa.

The young soldiers strode forward, some with serious, others with different expressions; they were talking in low tones. The little column was the only eminence in that flat, rolling plain; upon it the road stretched away into the distance and cut into its surface like a shallow ravine. Against that glittering scene the soldiers' cloaks looked olive-green, and their faces a deep red, much darker than they really were. They were marching out to execute a spy: that was what they had been told. And this was one of the most solemn duties of a soldier. Not till they were coming back, would they light their pipes or cigarettes, talk and laugh, and wave to the women, carrying five bullets less. At the moment they were the very incarnation of discipline as they marched forward with a steady, swinging step. The two horses in front sent up a faint steam of sweat. Liese tactlessly raised her tail before Spierauge noticed it. The soldiers behind her made indignant grimaces and turned their heads aside. Sergeant-Major Berglechner called his colleague's attention to it, and Spierauge drove his heels into the flanks of the fat old creature, and pulled her in to the side of the road.

The little party moved forward: the form of it was oddly symmetrical—narrow at the head, then broadening and narrowing alternately—four files of four men each, a solitary figure in the center, two horsemen in front and one in the rear. This last horseman, Sergeant-Major Pont, sat meditatively in the saddle. As with all the others the chin-strap of his helmet was drawn tight across his cheeks. But he was the only one of them who realized the martial value of the chin-strap and what many feelings it helped to inspire. All that was distinctive and noteworthy in this game of soldiering he saw before his eyes, and even embodied in himself: war and make-believe, the moving body in front of him, the group soul, if so it can be called, adventure, courage, the solemnity of an official act that was costing a man his life. From his point of vantage he could look over the two files in front of him and their rifles and see

Grischa marching with his shoulders drawn back: (but Grischa alone knew how blue with cold his hands were, and cramped and twisted in their leather strap). An infinite pity for that poor, brave, lonely figure, that ragged Russian, brought back from the depths of his unconscious memory a feeling that a tribune was riding here, and that tribune was himself, Laurentius Pontus, riding behind his cohort, on service somewhere in the mighty Empire, German mercenaries marching to his death some rebel against the Imperial law, symbolized perhaps by Hadrian's or Trajan's bust, some hairy Sarmatian, scowling Scythian, laughing Samogetian, or dark, fanatical Jew. That low, white, rolling plain might just as well be white sand or white snow, or again the white lime dust of Galilee or Gaul: and the unchanging nature of man—at least over such short periods as two thousand years—made his heart heavy.

Suddenly they turned off from the main road. Grischa, like a beast lashed by an invisible whip, tossed his head helplessly from right to left, for this parting of the ways made it too horribly clear that the irrevocable place as near at hand. His breath came heavily as though, within his breast, water was contracting into ice. They had reached the rising ground, and after passing a clump of elder, a black and tangled mass of stems and leaves, they came upon a bend in the road, and followed some wheel-ruts into a sunken track, where a gray cart with two half-starved gray horses, and a lumpish Posener peasant lad in uniform, had drawn to the side; nearby at the entrance to the gravel quarry, a man on a horse in a gray and purple cloak, with a felt hat turned up on the left side, and the brim hanging down on the right like an African rough-rider, a great silver cross hung round his neck, and a puffy, red-cheeked impatient countenance, the man of God sat waiting. Events now moved forward with incredible rapidity, like a torrent rushing down a mountainside. Grischa, confronted by this lofty yellow-gray wall, spattered with snow, and by the young medical officer, Dr. Lubbersch, who was stamping up and down smoking a cigarette; and in the presence of the long narrow box covered with two tarpaulins, this last grim preparation for the end, Grischa realized that until now he had never quite believed that his last moment would really come; he had thought of it all as somehow hardly serious, though in his heart he knew it must be so. Fortunately for him, the last few minutes sped in rushes toward the end. He tried to tear at the straps that bound him, and he opened his mouth to cry out, but an inner power, engrafted in his soul these hundreds of years ago, forced his wrenching fingers to relax and rub themselves together as though for warmth, and stifled his shriek into a gasp for air. Only the despairing glitter of his watery-blue, wandering eyes above his high cheekbones betrayed his agony. Luckily, Sergeant-Major Berglechner thoroughly understood such functions: he had had much experience in Serbia and Ruthenia where he had begun his service in the Archduke Frederick's command.

"Pity to spoil a good cloak," he said to Spierauge, who did not in the least know what were the proper steps, as his office regulations did not cover such performances.

One of the Jägers untied Grischa's hands. Grischa smiled gratefully at him and swung his arms against his chest to warm himself. Meanwhile the man of God had begun to recite the prayers for the dead in Latin, which Grischa did not understand; he said them into Grischa's face, honestly troubled for this poor soul, who was going to damnation, and appealing for the grace of Christ, who died on the Cross for the salvation of even this ignorant Russian, although the apostasy and schisms of His Church seemed likely to put something of a strain on God's goodness. He recited the prayers in a sonorous sing-song. Grischa felt very impatient and would have turned his head away from him, but the silver cross hypnotized him for the seconds it took the soldiers to unhook his belt, unbutton his cloak, and strip it off his shoulders; next they took off his tunic and his arms were free for a moment as he stood there in his patched and threadbare gray flannel shirt. High above him towered the semicircle of the stony crumbling wall of the gravel quarry. The path in front of him was now barred. There stood, drawn up in a line, five men, with their rifles at the ready, terrible to look upon, and waiting for a brief word of command. These were the green cloaks and red faces of his destroyers. Grischa stood helpless and forsaken: a crushing weight lay on his throbbing heart, and he cast a wild, fluttering glance past the elder bushes, and watched the sluggish course of a crow flying upward into the distance, where the town lay hidden below him, that town so full of living men. Sergeant-Major Pont set his teeth, pulled out his handkerchief, and in a quiet matter-of-fact tone that admitted of no question he ordered one of the Jägers to blindfold the prisoner. The priest went on with his muttered ministrations. Now Grischa stood once more with his hands bound and his arms tightly secured. He was terribly helpless now; he could not struggle, he could only groan. He had already almost lost consciousness. The tremendous crushing weight of this thing that was being done to him, and the thought that it was being done without pause or protest, or the least sign of mercy, clouded Grischa's mind. He wanted to beg that he might not be bound or shot, but he could not find the German words to express his anguish, not the Russian words either: all he could think of were the words "Mother, Mother," that came unconsciously to his lips. Then the world was hidden by a soft clean-smelling piece of linen. And within him, ready to spring, crouched that nameless fear, the awful shuddering terror of the black beast, and he stood up tense and stiff with horror, listening for the dreadful sounds that must soon rend his ears. In that instant, as the last order but one suddenly rang out, and he heard the rattle of the rifles brought up to the men's shoulders, the litany came to an end.

The Cross, he thought was turned toward him, that ponderous hewn symbol was being raised to his unseeing eyes. Then, in that moment when Sergeant-Major Berglechner rapped out the sharp command "Fire!" the certainty of death and the extremity of his terror conquered; his soul burst its bonds, and in the same instant his bowels were loosened. The crack of the shots was like a sudden senseless blow shattering a panorama of hurrying pictures in his mind, beginning with the cross in his mother's kitchen at home. He saw Aljoscha with the wire-cutters, the moonlit expanse of the forest camp as he cut through the wires, he smelt the acrid smell of the car in which he had escaped, of the hay in the car next to him when he left the train, the vast white, icy silence of the winter forest, the shuddering loneliness of the deserted artillery position, and there was the black beast creeping toward him, the lynx with her pointed brush-like ears and devilish face, longing to leap upon him and tear him down, yet fleeing in terror at his laughter, his exulting freedom, and the snowball that he threw at her. Once more, now weak and forlorn, he smiled at the beast as she leapt upon him from the five muzzles of the rifle-barrels—this time he knew that she would tear him down. But his sense of life, which had long been broken and effaced from his experience, was suddenly, in the very instant of death, lit by a flame of certainty that burst from the deepest recesses of his soul, a certainty that parts of his being would be rescued from destruction. The ancient germ within him, the mighty source of life, contented with having transmitted itself in women's bodies to new and ever new manifestations, cast into his brain this faint but faithful reflection, and made him believe, as poor besotted men of flesh do believe, in the continuance of the Ego, the immortality of his individual entity which at that very moment had been extinguished.

Three forms of time moved over his fading consciousness. The calculated time of events and hours, the time in which five rifle bullets hiss through space, crash into a body as into a sack full of water, and, rending and flinging aside the contents of that sack, the living, working, breathing human sap and flesh, burrow down into the center-point of life as a mole burrows through the earth. Next, the flashing electric time of hurrying ideas and images, of dreams that go on all night long, those dreams that endure for so brief an instant before they disappear, that they deceive the mind, and the whirling panorama takes on some semblance of reality. And last of all, time that is conditioned by the body, and is contained in the muscles and the nerves that obey the suggestions and the orders of the central soul. In that less-than-second, from the instant when those five bullets pierced the torn and stained shirt like rams' horns, so senselessly tearing that poor, quivering body, until the moment when the blood-filled veins, the hammering heart, all the intricate network of the lungs was wrecked forever, he suffered an agony so deadly, so utterly beyond all human conception—struck, pierced, choked, and broken—that the white heat of that destruction must (one would have thought) have burned away his smile of freedom. But from the moment his body, that was himself, cracked and fell, as though from a new joint in his back, and a gush of crimson blood colored the snow round where it lay, physical time—the time in which his body had lived and functioned—was freed from its vassalage to pain: his body could be no longer altered by it. There lay Grischa Iljitsch Paprotkin, otherwise called Bjuscheff, in the snow, and smiled. His face and muscles had the impress of a cheerfulness that he had not known for this long while. Only his eyes shrieked under their bandage, forced horribly outward by the suffocation of his death, as the blood welled up into his lungs from his veins and arteries, his heart, ripped from its sinews, fell into the hollow of his chest, and five small holes were torn between the ribs of his back.

And so this huddled human heap died. . . . Stones rattled down the sides of the quarry, bringing with them little clouds of powdered snow.

"All correct, I think," said Sergeant-Major Berglechner. "Civilians scream, soldiers behave properly"—and he licked his mustache as if he had drunk something. And he had in fact drunk something—his own blood—for without in the least noticing it, as he gave the order to fire, in the dreadful tension of the last second he had bitten his upper lip.

Dr. Lubbersch, whose expression of polite concern had been very little disturbed by these events—indeed, as a philosopher he felt himself superior and impervious to such everyday events—went up to what had once been Grischa, knelt for a moment by the smiling, side-flung head which, awkwardly for him, was lying on one cheek, undid the bandage, closed the eyes, and said:

"Quite dead; perfectly satisfactory. That's what we call the Hippocrates smile."

At that moment there stirred in that slowly bleeding brain what could be called life, but no one noticed it, for men die more slowly than their fellows like to think.

Laurenz Pont dismounted. The handkerchief with which those poor despairing eyes had been bound lay still knotted in the snow, yellow against the white: not a drop of the blood that was trickling slowly nearer had stained it. He felt it as a symbol of Pontius Pilate or Laurentius Pontus, that he was guiltless of the death of this innocent man.

Meanwhile, the men clicked the safety-catches on their rifles, and showed some anxiety to get out of the cold and back to normal pursuits: they had three bottles of schnapps and a free afternoon to look forward to. The long covered object under the tarpaulin revealed itself as a coffin. But no one could be found who took any official satisfaction in putting that pierced body, while it was still soft and could be handled, into this coffin. The Corporal of Jägers pointed out that Sergeant-Major Spierauge should have detailed some men of the prison guard for this purpose. The driver of his cart stood shivering and silent by his horses.

"It isn't our job," grumbled the Jägers.

The difficulty was solved by Laurenz Pont and Dr. Lubbersch, who was prepared to help Pont to carry out this melancholy but philosophic duty. As the Sergeant-Major got off his horse (at the crack of the rifles Seidlitz had merely twitched an ear, and Pont could not help patting him on the neck for it) and took off his gloves, with the actual intention of lifting the dead spy into his coffin with the help of the elegant Jewish doctor, two of the young Jägers nudged each other, took the dead man by the arms and legs and dragged him over the snow with much care so as not to stain their uniforms (his head was already dangling stiffly and horribly from the collar of his cloak), put him into the coffin and arranged his limbs in an easy attitude and folded his hands.

Suddenly the agitated jingle of a sleigh was heard and out of it jumped a flustered old gentleman with long disordered hair and a straggling beard—the Russian priest. The military police post at Bisasni village had kept him back until they could get confirmation of the fact that he was to be allowed to travel urgently: he flung himself down by the side of the coffin, in his long skirts like those of a woman, and prayed with despairing abandonment for the salvation of a soul that these heretical devils had placed in danger of eternal fire.

Pont, in the saddle once more, saw the group of men sharp and clear before him: he saw the kneeling priest place a brightly colored holy picture framed in tin between Grischa's folded hands, he saw Sergeant-Major Berglechner lighting a cigarette, as the men, without waiting for orders, fell in once more, and the driver waiting to take charge of the coffin and convey it to the cemetery, somewhat troubled as to who would help him get the heavy case into the sleigh after the soldiers had departed, and a deep wearisome feeling of exhaustion made him yawn. He watched the driver standing by, with drooping shoulders and drooping mustache, too tactful to disturb the foreign priest at his prayers; he arranged that the *izvost-chick,* the Jewish sleigh-driver, should give the other a hand with the coffin, and turned Seidlitz toward the town. He would have preferred to ride alone: but Spierauge pulled Liese up beside him, Berglechner sprang on to his gelding, Oberarzt Dr. Lubbersch swung himself easily on to his bay, two sharp orders rifles clattered to the slope, and the little column turned homeward swaying to the rhythm of their march. Pont rode next to the doctor. It was obvious that the soldiers wanted to sing, as is the practice on the way back from funerals when the triumph of continuing life over death is celebrated in the cheerful strains of a military march.

"How smart we must look," thought Pont.

But one thing was noticeable. There were four well-turned-out horsemen and sixteen men—one had been left behind. He was not missed. The men talked away to each other and smoked as they did so. A maniple of the Imperial Army, with minds at ease, was swinging back to their camp barracks, which, whether they are built of wood or canvas, leather or corrugated iron, mean to the soldier what hearth and homes mean to other men. When they turned into the avenue and the ground began to slope downhill, Corporal Leipolt did actually start a song; they sang—those sixteen practiced cheerful throats—about the little birds twittering in the woods and how one day they all would meet at home again; a simple ditty set for three voices (more or less), and the men, tall erect fellows with white teeth and good-humored eyes, made the song ring through the streets of the town. Unfortunately, there was a good deal more slush on the way back and the citizens would have to turn out tomorrow with their great wooden shovels; indeed, the street might well be said to be in a disgusting state, but they must give these Jews and Russians something to listen to. Sergeant-Major Pont thought, as he had done all the afternoon, that men change but little and that it was rather tedious to be a man.

Bertin, who was sitting at a window in the Magazinstrasse with a glass of tea in front of him, grew pale. So they had killed him. . . . Very well, he thought, the time will come when we shall win, and our ideas will rule; then let them look out. The room had three windows, it was a tea-room with a few pale indifferent waiting-maids standing about; hitherto it had merely smelt of stale smoke and was full of the musty odor of a place that is used by too many men every day: but suddenly it reeked of blood. He looked at his watch: he had been sitting here, since the men had passed on their outward journey, less than twenty-five minutes. He stood up, pressed his face against the windowpanes, watched the moving lips of the soldiers as they sang, their steel helmets, their swaying bodies, their cloaks with the corners thrown back and hooked into the eyes sewn on for that purpose—covered his face and fell back in his chair. He wanted to say, "it is fulfilled," but the word was for him too full of painful associations; so he thought to himself, "it's all over and Grischa is done with." The machine has won; this apparatus of command has mighty wheels, and if it once gets going it goes on. How long, O Lord? He felt the need of company, and decided to go and see Posnanski, who was ill in bed with a fever. Probably he had taken cold, but perhaps it was only a fever of the mind; though he could only hope so, for those were days in which the soul of a man meant very little.

Meanwhile, on one of the town sleighs, covered with two reddish-brown tarpaulins, a long wooden chest was being conveyed to the cemetery just outside the town. With it had been another sleigh containing a Russian priest, but where a crossroad led toward the town they parted company, and the priest drove off. Not a single person was present at the burial of this poor Russian. The two Hamburg Landsturmers lowered the coffin into the grave dug that morning with cries of "hold hard!" and "let go!": they were old hands at the work and, though not careless, could hardly take much interest in it. The driver with the drooping shoulders and mustaches stood by and looked dully down into the grave before him.

"They say the fellow was innocent," said one of the Hamburgers with the sing-song intonation of his native harbor.

"I dare say he was," said the other, "but what's the good of that—we're all innocent."

"I didn't want the War," said the driver suddenly.

It was the first outbreak of that smothered blunted soul, slave among the countless slaves on those wide plains. The two Hamburgers looked at him contemptuously. They did not need to assure anybody that they had not wanted the War. They exchanged a mocking glance indicative of the fact that they thought the driver was balmy, and that, anyhow, the only men of intelligence were to be found in Hamburg; then with a practiced gesture they stuck their shovels into the high neat mound of earth that Grischa's body, and not the hands of men, had so raised up.

In that very quarter of an hour Dr. Jakobstadt, the civil doctor, removed the child with forceps from Babka's unconscious body. It was a girl, weighing more than six pounds, well made and with distinctive features whose likeness no one could decide: as a matter of fact, with her short nose, broad cheekbones, and bright blue-gray eyes she bore a ludicrous resemblance to Grischa's old mother whom none of them had ever seen. It did not cry, and while Babka was being attended to, it lay still, groping with its tiny fingers, red all over, in a rush basket on a pillow which later on was to serve as its eiderdown. When Babka came out of the anæsthetic, she refused to see it, but when it was held out to her all the same, she smiled the faintest suggestion of a smile and would not let it out of her hands.

Dr. Jakobstadt and the motherly midwife, Frau Nachtschwarz, exchanged a few remarks in Yiddish.

"I think we may congratulate ourselves," said the woman as she dried her hands.

And the doctor, with his sallow, drawn face and grizzled, pointed beard, shook his head sceptically and answered:

"If you think that being born in such times as these is a matter for congratulation, then I suppose we may.

[. . .]

Translated by Eric Sutton

ALFRED DÖBLIN

The Murder of a Buttercup

The gentleman in black had been counting his steps at first, one, two, three, up to a hundred and back again, as he made his way along the wide road edged with firs up to St. Ottilien, swaying so far to right or left with each movement of his hips that he sometimes staggered; then he forgot it.

His light brown eyes, bulging and friendly, stared at the ground that moved along under his feet, and his arms swung from the shoulders so that his white cuffs fell over his hands. His head jerked whenever the yellow-red evening light between the trees made him squint, his hands made hasty, indignant motions of defense. The slender walking-stick in his right hand swung over grasses and flowers at the wayside and diverted itself with the blossoms.

It became entangled in the sparse undergrowth as the gentleman quietly and absently walked along. The grave gentleman did not pause, but, still sauntering along, tugged lightly at the handle, then, caught by the arm, looked around indignantly, pulled at the stick without effect at first, then, using both hands, successfully wrenched it free and stepped back breathlessly with a swift glance at the stick and at the grass, the gold chain on his black waistcoat flying.

The fat man stood there a moment, beside himself. His top hat was sitting on the back of his head. He stared at the matted flowers, then hurled himself at them with raised stick, lashing out blood-red in the face at the silent plants. Blows whistled right and left. Stalks and leaves flew over the road.

Letting his breath out noisily, the gentleman walked on with flashing eyes. The trees strode past him quickly; the gentleman paid no attention to anything. He had a tilted nose and a flat beardless face, an elderly child's face with a sweet little mouth.

He was forced to watch his step at a sharp rising turn in the road. As he marched on more quietly, wiping the sweat off his nose irritably with his hand, he discovered that his face was completely distorted, that his chest was heaving violently. He grew alarmed at the thought that somebody might see him, one of his business colleagues or a lady, perhaps. He touched his face and convinced himself with a furtive movement of his hand that it was smooth.

He walked quietly. Why was he panting? He gave a shamefaced smile. He had sprung at the flowers and had wrought havoc with his walking stick, had struck indeed with the same violent but well aimed arm movements with which he was accustomed to box his apprentices' ears when they were not sufficiently adept in catching the flies in the office and presenting them to him arranged in order of size.

The grave gentleman shook his head repeatedly over the peculiar occurrence. "One gets nervous in the city. The city is making me nervous," swayed his hips reflectively, took his stiff English hat and fanned the fir-scented air toward his head.

After a short time he began again to count his steps, one, two, three. Foot stepped in front of foot, the arms swung from the shoulders. Suddenly, as his gaze swept vacantly along the edge of the road, Herr Michael Fischer saw a stocky figure, himself, stepping back from the grass, hurling himself at the flowers and cleanly striking the head off a buttercup. What had occurred before by the dark road was taking place tangibly before him. This flower here was exactly the same as the others. This one flower drew his gaze, his hand, his stick. His arm rose, the stick whistled, plop, the head flew off. The head somersaulted in the air, disappeared in the grass. The businessman's heart beat wildly. The separated head of the plant was sinking now, burrowing into the grass. Deeper, deeper and deeper, through the blanket of grass, into the ground. Now it was beginning to rush toward the center of the earth, no hands could hold it any more. And from above, from the stump of a body, there dripped, there welled from the neck white blood after it into the hole, a little at first, like spittle from the corner of a cripple's mouth, then in a thick, viscous stream with yellow bubbles, ran toward Herr Michael, who tried vainly to escape, hopped to the right, hopped to the left, tried to leap over it, surging already against his feet.

Mechanically Herr Michael placed his hat on his head, which was covered in sweat, clasped his hands and the stick to his breast. "What happened?" he asked after a while. "I'm not drunk. The head can't fall, it has to stay lying there, it has to stay lying there in the grass. I am sure that it is lying quietly in the grass. And the blood . . . I don't remember that flower, I know absolutely nothing about it all."

He was amazed, consternated, suspicious of himself. Everything in him was riveted on the furious agitation, was thinking about the flower, the sunken head, the bleeding stalk. He was still leaping over the slimy river. If anybody saw him, one of his business colleagues or a lady.

Herr Michael Fischer drew himself up, grasped the stick in his right hand. He glanced at his coat and drew strength from his attitude. He'd soon subdue these rebellious thoughts: self-control. He, the boss, would put an energetic end to this breach of discipline. One had to face these people very firmly: "Yes? We are not accustomed to that sort of attitude in my company. Janitor, throw the fellow out." And standing, he brandished his stick about in the air. Herr Fischer had assumed a cool, critical expression: now we'd see! In his superiority he even went so far, up on the wide road, as to scoff at his timidity. Wouldn't it be really funny if next morning there was a notice in red on all the advertisement-pillars of Freiburg: "Murder of an adult buttercup on the road from Immental to St. Ottilien, between seven and nine p.m. The suspect" et cetera. Thus scoffed the flabby gentleman in black, enjoying the cool evening air. Down there, the nurses, the courting couples would find what his hand had wrought. There will be screams and horrified running home. The criminal investigators would be thinking about him, the murderer, who would be laughing up his sleeve. Herr Michael shuddered dissolutely at his own mad recklessness, he never would have thought himself so depraved. Down there, however, there lay visible to the whole city the proof of his rash energy.

The stump is jutting rigidly into the air, white blood trickles from its neck.

Herr Michael extended his hands in front of him slightly, defensively.

It is coagulating above, all thick and sticky, so that the ants get stuck.

Herr Michael passed a hand over his temples and exhaled loudly.

And beside it the head is rotting in the grass. It is squashed, broken up by the rain, decomposing. It is becoming a yellow, stinking pulp, shimmering greenish, yellowish, slimy like vomit. It rises, alive, runs toward him, straight toward Herr Michael, tries to drown him, steams slopping against his body, splashes up at his nose. He leaps, hops only on his toes now.

The sensitive gentleman started back. He felt a hideous taste in his mouth. He could not swallow for disgust, could not stop spitting. He stumbled repeatedly, hopping uneasily as he continued on with pale blue lips.

"I refuse, I refuse most emphatically to enter into any contact with your company."

He pressed his handkerchief to his nose. The head had to be got rid of, the stalk had to be covered, stamped down, buried. The wood was reeking of the body of the plant. The smell went along with Herr Michael, grew ever more intense. Another flower would have to be planted in that spot, a fragrant flower, a garden of carnations. The corpse in the middle of the wood had to be got rid of. Had to.

Just as Herr Fischer was going to come to a halt it went through his head that it was ridiculous to turn back, more than ridiculous. What did the buttercup matter to him? Bitter rage flared in him at the thought that he had almost been taken by surprise. He had not pulled himself together, bit his index finger: "Watch out, I'm telling you, watch out, you damned scoundrel." Simultaneously fear cast itself over him from behind.

The scowling fat man looked around nervously, reached into a pocket of his trousers, withdrew a small penknife and opened it.

Meanwhile his feet carried on. His feet began to irritate him. They wanted to become lords and masters too; their rebellious urging forward enraged him. He'd soon quiet those little steeds down. They'd feel it. A sharp stab in the flanks would tame them. They carried him farther and farther away. It almost looked as if he were running away from the scene of the murder. Nobody was to think that. There was a fluttering of birds, a distant whimpering was in the air, and came from below. "Stop, stop!" he shouted at his feet. Then he drove the knife into a tree.

He embraced its trunk with both arms and rubbed his cheeks against the bark. His hands were fingering the air, as if they were kneading something: "We shall not go to Canossa." Brow furrowed with strain, the deathly pale gentleman studied the cracks in the tree, hunched his back as if something were going to jump over him from behind. Over and over he could hear the telegraph connection between himself and the spot ringing, in spite of his trying to tangle and silence the wires with kicks. He tried to conceal from himself that his fury was already paralyzed, that a gentle desire was flickering in him, a desire to capitulate. Deep down there was a greed in him for the flower and the scene of the murder.

Herr Michael flexed his knees tentatively, sniffed at the air, listened in every direction, whispered anxiously: "I just want to bury the head, that's all. Then everything will be all right. Please, please, quickly." He closed his eyes unhappily, turned about on his heels as if by accident. Then he sauntered, as if nothing had happened, straight on down with the nonchalant step of one taking a stroll, whistling softly with a carefree air. Breathing easily, with a sense of relief, he caressed the treetrunks by the wayside. He smiled and his little mouth grew round, like a hole. Loudly he sang a song that he suddenly remembered: "A hare there lay asleep in a dell . . ." He was repeating the mincing, swaying of the hips, swinging of the arms of before. He had pushed the stick guiltily far up his sleeve. Now and again he crept back quickly at a bend in the road, to see if anybody was watching him.

Perhaps she was in fact still alive—how did he know indeed that she was dead already? It flitted through his head that he could restore the invalid if he applied splints, perhaps, and put on a dressing with adhesive tape around the head and stalk. He began to walk faster, to forget his composure, to run. All at once he was trembling with expectation. And fell full length at a bend against a felled treetrunk, catching his chest and chin so that he moaned aloud. When he picked himself up he forgot his hat in the grass; the stick, broken, ripped his sleeve from the inside; he noticed nothing of it. Aha, they were trying to stop him, nothing would stop him; he'd soon find her. He climbed back again. Where was the place? He had to find the place. If only he could call the flower. But what was her name?

He did not even know her name. Ellen? Perhaps she was called Ellen? Certainly, Ellen. He whispered into the grass, bent over to poke the flowers with one hand.

"Is Ellen here? Where is Ellen? Well? She is wounded, her head, a little below the head. Perhaps you don't know that yet. I want to help her—I'm a doctor, a Samaritan. Well, where is she? You can trust me with the information, I tell you."

But how was he going to recognize the one he had broken? Perhaps he had her in his hand at that moment, perhaps she was breathing her last breath close beside him.

That could not be.

He roared: "Hand her over. Don't make me miserable, you dogs. I'm a Samaritan. Don't you understand German?"

He lay right down on the ground, searching, finally burrowing blindly in the grass, squashing and tearing the flowers, his mouth open and his eyes flickering and fixed straight ahead. He gloomed a long time to himself.

"Hand over. Conditions will have to be set. Preliminaries. The doctor has a right to the patient. The law will have to be brought in."

The trees stood black in the gray air by the wayside and all around. Anyway, it was too late, the head had certainly dried up by now. The thought of death, final, horrified him and shook his shoulders.

The black, round shape stood up out of the grass and tottered on down by the side of the road.

She was dead. By his hand.

He sighed and rubbed his brow reflectingly.

They would attack him, from all sides. Well, let them. Nothing worried him anymore. It was all the same to him. They would knock his head off, tear his ears off, put his hands in glowing coals. He could not do any more. He knew they would all be having a marvelous time, but he would not utter a sound to gratify his despicable tormentors. They had no right to punish him, they were depraved themselves. Yes, he had killed the flower, and it was no business of theirs, and he had the right, which he would defend against all of them. He had the right to kill flowers, and he did not feel obliged to justify it in any more detail. He could kill as many flowers as he pleased for a thousand miles around, north, south, east, west, whether they scoffed at it or not. And if they carried on laughing like that he would leap at their throats.

He halted; his glances darted poisonously into the heavy darkness of the firs. His lips were full to bursting with blood. Then he hurried on.

He probably should make his condolences here in the wood to the sisters of the deceased. He pointed out that the accident had occurred through practically no fault of his, drew attention to the sad exhaustion with which he had made the climb. And the heat. Basically, of course, he was indifferent to all buttercups.

Despairingly, he shrugged his shoulders again: "What else will they do to me?" He ran his dirty fingers over his cheeks; he could not see his way out.

What was all this, for God's sake, what was he doing here!

He tried to sneak away from it all by the shortest possible route, down across through the trees, to collect his thoughts once and for all clearly and calmly. Quite slowly, one point after another.

To avoid slipping on the treacherous ground, he feels his way from tree to tree. The flower, he thinks cunningly, can stay by the road where it is. There are enough dead weeds like it in the world.

Horror grips him, however, as he sees a round, pale, bright drop of resin appearing on a trunk he touches; the tree is weeping. Fleeing in the dark onto a path, he soon notices that it is becoming peculiarly narrow, as if the wood were trying to lure him into a trap. The trees are assembling to hold court.

He must get out.

Again he runs hard against a low fir; it strikes down at him with raised hands. He breaks his way through violently, the blood running in streams down his face. He spits, lashes out, kicks the trees, yelling, slides down, sitting and rolling, finally runs headlong down the last slope at the verge of the wood toward the lights of the village, his torn frock coat thrown over his head, while behind him the mountain rustles threateningly, shaking its fists, and everywhere trees can be heard cracking and breaking as they run after him, cursing.

The fat gentleman stood motionless by the gaslight in front of the little village church. He had no hat on his head, there were fir needles and black earth in his tousled hair which he did not remove. He gave a heavy sigh. As warm blood dripped along the bridge of his nose and down onto his boots he slowly took the ends of his coat in both hands and pressed them to his face. Then he held up his hands to the light and was surprised at the thick blue veins on the back of them. He rubbed at the thick lumps and could not rub them away. When a tram sang and howled its way nearer he reeled on home through narrow alleys.

Now he was sitting dully in his bedroom, saying aloud to himself "I'm sitting here, I'm sitting here," and looking despairingly around the room. He walked to and fro, took his clothes off and hid them in a corner of the wardrobe. He put on another black suit and read the newspaper on the couch. He crumpled it up as he read: something had happened, something had happened. And he felt it fully next day as he sat at his desk. He was turned to stone, could not curse, and a strange stillness accompanied him wherever he went.

With feverish eagerness he argued that he must have dreamt it all—but the cuts on his forehead were real. Then there must be things that cannot be believed. The trees had struck out at him, there had been a wailing about the deceased. He sat there sunk in himself and, to the astonishment of the staff, did not even bother about the flies buzzing. Then he began goading the apprentices, abandoned his work and began walking up and down. They saw him several times striking the table with his fist, his cheeks swollen, shouting that he would make a clean sweep once and for all in the business and otherwise. They would see. He would not be made a fool of, by anybody.

Next morning, however, as he made out the books, something made him enter ten marks to the credit of the buttercup. He started, fell into bitter rumination of his powerlessness and ordered the head clerk to take over the accounts. During the afternoon he himself, silently and coldly, put the money in a special box; he even felt it necessary to open a separate account for her; he had grown weary, wanted peace. Soon he was driven to make her offerings from his food and drink. A little dish was set every day for her beside Herr Michael's place. The housekeeper had thrown up her hands when he had ordered this place laid—but the master had forbidden any criticism with an unprecedented explosion of anger.

He was paying, paying for his mysterious guilt. He was performing divine service with the buttercup, and the calm businessman asserted now that each person had his own religion; one had to assume a personal position to an ineffable God. There were things that not everybody could understand. A trace of suffering had appeared in the gravity of his monkey's face; his corpulence had also decreased, his eyes became deep set. The flower, like a conscience, watched over his actions, stringently, from the most important to the smallest everyday deeds.

The sun shone often during this time over the town, the cathedral and the hill with its castle, shone with all the fullness of life. One morning the hardened man broke out crying at the window, for the first time since his childhood. Quite suddenly, cried until his heart was almost breaking. Ellen, the detested flower, was robbing him of all this beauty, accused him now with each one of the world's beauties. Sunshine glows, she does not see it; she cannot breathe the perfume of white jasmine. Nobody will come to see the scene of her shameful death, no prayers will be spoken there: she could throw all this in his face, however ridiculous it was and however he might wring his hands. Everything is denied her: the moonlight, the bridal bliss of summer, the quiet co-existence with the cuckoo, the strollers, the children's prams. He drew his little mouth together; he wanted to hold back the people as they moved up the hill. If the world would only perish with a sigh to shut the flower's mouth! He even thought of suicide as a means of putting an end to this misery.

Between times he treated her in embittered fashion, deprecatingly, pushed her to the wall with a sudden rush. He cheated her in small things, knocked her dish over hurriedly as if by accident, miscalculated to her disadvantage, treated her often as cunningly as a business competitor. On the anniversary of her death he behaved as if he remembered nothing. Only when she seemed to insist more urgently on a silent commemoration did he devote half a day to her memory.

In company one time the question of favorite meals was being discussed. When they asked Herr Michael what he most liked to eat he stated with cold deliberation: "Buttercups. Buttercups are my favorite dish." Whereupon everybody shouted with laughter, but Herr Michael cowered on his chair, listened to their laughing with clenched teeth and savored the rage of the buttercup. He felt himself a monstrous dragon, gulping down living things without qualm, thought of wild Japanese rites and harakiri. Even though secretly he expected a severe punishment from her.

He conducted this sort of guerrilla warfare with her incessantly; hovered incessantly between mortal anguish and ecstasy; he drew anxious comfort from her cries of rage, which he often thought he heard. Daily he thought up new tricks; often, in high excitement, he would withdraw from his office to his room to hatch his plots undisturbed. Thus quietly the war ran its course, and nobody knew anything of it.

The flower belonged to him, was one of the comforts of his life. He thought back with amazement to the time when he had lived without the flower. He often took the walk to St. Ottilien now through the wood, with a defiant expression. And one sunny evening, while he was taking a rest on a fallen treetrunk, the thought flashed on him: here, on the spot where he was now sitting, his buttercup, Ellen, had stood. It must have been here. Melancholy and nervous devotion seized the fat gentleman. The way things had turned out! From that evening to this. He let his eyes, grown slightly clouded, wander in a reverie over the weeds, the sisters, perhaps daughters, of Ellen. After long meditation a roguish expression twitched over his smooth face. Oh, his fine flower would see something now! If he dug up a buttercup, a daughter of the dead one, planted it at home, cultivated it, looked after it, then the old lady would have a young rival. In fact, when he thought it out properly, he would even expiate the death of the old one. For he was saving the life of this flower and compensating for the death of the mother; this daughter was very probably going to rack and ruin here. Oh how he would annoy the old lady, how he would leave her out in the cold! The businessman, well versed in legal matters, called to mind a paragraph on compensation. He dug out a nearby plant with his penknife, carried it home carefully in his bare hand and planted it in a porcelain pot resplendent with gold, which he placed in position on a small inlaid table in his bedroom. On the bottom of the pot he wrote with charcoal: "Paragraph 2403, section 5."

Daily the happy man watered the plant with malicious devotion and made offering to the deceased, Ellen. She was legally, if necessary under pain of police measures, constrained to resignation, got no dish any more, no food, no money. Frequently, lying on the couch, he thought he heard her whimpering, her long-drawn-out moaning. Herr Michael's self-confidence rose in undreamt-of manner. Sometimes he almost had touches of megalomania. Never did life pass so serenely.

One evening, after he had sauntered home in high spirits from his office his housekeeper reported right at the door to him, calmly, that the little table had fallen over when she was cleaning, that the pot had broken. She had had the plant, the common dung-hill weed, thrown into the dustbin along with all the pieces. The sober, slightly contemptuous tone with which the woman recounted the accident showed that she strongly approved of the procedure.

The rotund Herr Michael hurled the door to, clapped his short hands, squealed loudly for joy and swung the surprised female aloft by the hips, as far as his strength and her length permitted. Then he swaggered from the hall into his bedroom with flickering eyes, in extreme agitation; he wheezed noisily and stamped his feet; his lips quivered.

Nobody could point at him; not with the most secret thought had he wished the death of this flower, not offered the tip of a finger of a thought toward it. The old lady, the mother-in-law, could curse now and say what she pleased. He had nothing to do with her. They were finished. Now he was rid of the whole buttercup crew. Right and Fortune were on his side. There was no doubt. He had outsmarted the wood.

Right away he was going to St. Ottilien, up into that stupid, grumbling wood. In his thoughts he was already swinging his black stick. Flowers, tadpoles, and toads too would have to go. He could murder as much as he wanted to. He didn't give a hang for any buttercup.

Convulsed with laughter and malicious joy, the fat, impeccably dressed businessman Herr Michael Fischer rolled on his couch.

Then he sprang up, slapped his hat on his head, and stormed past the startled housekeeper out of the house onto the street.

Boisterously, he laughed and spluttered. And disappeared like this in the darkness of the mountain wood.

Translated by Patrick O'Neill

From Berlin Alexanderplatz

*This book reports the story of Franz Biberkopf, an erstwhile ce-
ment-and-transport worker in Berlin. He has just been discharged
from prison where he has been doing time because of former inci-
dents, and is now back in Berlin, determined to lead a decent life.*

*And, at first, he succeeds. But then, though economically things
go rather well with him, he gets involved in a regular combat with
something that comes from the outside, with something unaccountable, that looks like fate.*

*Three times this thing crashes against our man, disturbing his
scheme of life. It rushes at him with cheating and fraud. The man
is able to scramble up again; he is still firm on his feet.*

*It drives and beats him with foul play. He finds it a bit hard to
get up, they almost count him out.*

Finally, it torpedoes him with huge and monstrous savagery.

*Thus our good man, who has held his own till the end, is laid
low. He gives the game up for lost; he does not know how to go on
and appears to be done for.*

*But, before he puts a definite end to himself, his eyes are forcibly
opened in a way which I do not describe here. He is most distinctly
given to understand how it all came about. To wit, through himself,
that's obvious, through his scheme of life, which looked like nothing on earth, but now suddenly looks entirely different, not simple
and almost self-evident, but prideful and impudent, cowardly
withal, and full of weakness.*

*This awful thing which was his life acquires a meaning. Franz
Biberkopf has been given a radical cure. At last we see our man*

back on Alexanderplatz, greatly changed and battered, but, never-
theless, bent straight again.

To listen to this, and to meditate on it, will be of benefit to many
who, like Franz Biberkopf, live in a human skin, and, like this Franz
Biberkopf, ask more of life than a piece of bread and butter.

[. . .]

On Car 41 into Town

He stood in front of the Tegel Prison gate and was free now. Yesterday in convict's garb he had been raking potatoes with the others in
the fields back of the building, now he was walking in a tan summer
topcoat; they were still raking back there, he was free. He let one
streetcar after another go by, pressed his back against the red wall,
and did not move. The gateman walked past him several times,
showed him his car-line; he did not move. The terrible moment had
come (terrible, Franze, why terrible?), the four years were over. The
black iron gates, which he had been watching with growing disgust
for a year (disgust, why disgust?), were shut behind him. They had
let him out again. Inside, the others sat at their carpentry, varnish-
ing, sorting, gluing, had still two years, five years to do. He was
standing at the carstop.

The punishment begins.

He shook himself and gulped. He stepped on his own foot. Then,
with a run, took a seat in the car. Right among people. Go ahead.
At first it was like being at the dentist's, when he has grabbed a root
with a pair of forceps, and pulls; the pain grows, your head threatens to burst. He turned his head back toward the red wall, but the
car raced on with him along the tracks, and only his head was left
in the direction of the prison. The car took a bend; trees and houses
intervened. Busy streets emerged, Seestrasse, people got on and off.
Something inside him screamed in terror: Look out, look out, it's
going to start now. The tip of his nose turned to ice; something was
whirring over his cheek. *Zwölf Uhr Mittagszeitung, B.Z., Berliner*
Illustrierte, Die Funkstunde. "Anybody else got on?" The coppers
have blue uniforms now. He got off the car, without being noticed,
and was back among people again. What happened? Nothing.
Chest out, you starved sucker, you, pull yourself together, or I'll

give you a crack in the jaw! Crowds, what a swarm of people! How they hustle and bustle! My brain needs oiling, it's probably dried up. What was all this? Shoe stores, hat stores, incandescent lamps, saloons. People got to have shoes to run around so much; didn't we have a cobbler's shop out there, let's bear that in mind! Hundreds of polished windowpanes, let 'em blaze away, are they going to make you afraid or something, why, you can smash 'em up, can't you, what's the matter with 'em, they're polished clean, that's all. The pavement on Rosenthaler Platz was being torn up he walked on the wooden planks along with the others. Just go ahead and mix in with people, then everything's going to clear up, and you won't notice anything, you fool. Wax figures stood in the show-windows, in suits, overcoats, with skirts, with shoes and stockings. Outside everything was moving, but—back of it—there was nothing! It—did not—live! It had happy faces, it laughed, waited in twos and threes on the traffic islands opposite Aschinger's, smoked cigarettes, turned the pages of newspapers, Thus it stood there like the streetlamps—and—became more and more rigid. They belonged with the houses, everything white, everything wooden.

Terror struck him as he walked down Rosenthaler Strasse and saw a man and a woman sitting in a little beer-shop right at the window: they poured beer down their gullets out of mugs, yes, what about it, they were drinking, they had forks and stuck pieces of meat into their mouths, then they pulled the forks out again and were not bleeding. Oh, how cramped his body felt, I can't get rid of it, where shall I go? The answer came: Punishment.

He could not turn back, he had come this far on the car, he had been discharged from prison and had to go into this thing, deeper and deeper into it.

I know, he sighed to himself, that I have to go into this thing and that I was discharged from prison. They had to discharge me, the punishment was over, that's as it should be, the bureaucrat does his duty. I'll go into it, too, but I'd rather not, my God, I can't do it.

He wandered down Rosenthaler Strasse past Wertheim's department store, at the right he turned into the narrow Sophienstrasse. He thought, this street is darker, it's probably better where it's darker. The prisoners are put in isolation cells, solitary confinement and general confinement. In isolation cells the prisoner is kept apart from the others night and day. In solitary confinement the prisoner is placed in a cell, but during his walks in the open air, during instruction or religious service, he is put in company with the others. The cars roared and jangled on, house-fronts were rolling along one after the other without stopping. And there were roofs on the houses, they soared atop the houses, his eyes wandered straight upward: if only the roofs don't slide off, but the houses stood upright. Where shall I go, poor devil that I am, he shuffled alongside the walls of the houses, there was no end to it. I'm really a big duffer, a fellow ought to be able to traipse his way through hereabouts, five minutes, ten minutes, then drink a cognac and sit down. When the given signal rings, work must begin immediately. It can only be interrupted at the time set aside for eating, walking, and instruction. During the walk the prisoners must hold their arms stiff and swing them back and forth.

A house appeared, he took his glance away from the pavement, he pushed open the door of a house, and a sad growling oh, oh, came from his chest. He thrashed his arms about, well, old boy, you won't freeze here. The door of the courtyard opened, someone shuffled past him, stood behind him. Now he groaned, it did him good to groan. In the first days of his solitary confinement he had always groaned like this, and had been happy to hear his own voice, there you have at least something, everything is not lost yet. Many did that in the cells, some in the beginning, others later on, when they felt lonely. Then they started it, it was something human, it consoled them. Thus our man stood in the hallway, did not hear the terrible noise from the street, those mad houses were not there. With pursed lips he grunted to give himself courage, his hands clenched in his pockets. His shoulders in the tan summer topcoat were hunched for defense.

A stranger had stopped beside the discharged prisoner and was watching him. He asked: "What's the matter, anything wrong, are you in pain?" until the man noticed him and stopped his grunting at once. "Are you sick, do you live here in this house?" It was a Jew with a full red beard, a little man in an overcoat, with a black plush felt hat, a cane in his hand. "No, I don't live here." He had to get out of the hallway, the hallway had been all right. And now the street started once more, the housefronts, the show-windows, the hurrying figures with trousers or light socks, all so quick, so smart, each moment another. And making up his mind, he stepped again into an entrance-way, but just here the gates opened to let a wagon pass. Then quickly into the next-door house, into a narrow hallway next to the staircase. No wagon could get in here. He clung to the banister post. And while he held on to it, he knew he wanted to escape punishment (oh, Franz, what do you want to do? You'll not be able to do it), he would certainly do it, he knew now where there was an escape. And softly he started his music again, the grunting and grumbling, and I won't go back to the street either. The red Jew stepped back into the house, did not at first notice the man by the banister. He heard him humming. "Say, tell me, what are you doing here? Are you sick?" He moved away from the post, walked toward the courtyard. As he grasped the gate, he saw it was the Jew from the other house. "Leave me alone, what do you want anyway?" "Well, well, nothing. You moan and groan so, can't a body ask how you are?" And through the crack in the door across the way he saw the blamed old houses again, the swarming people, the sliding roofs. The discharged prisoner opened the courtyard gate, the Jew behind him: "What could happen? Now, now, it's not going to be as bad as all that. You're not going to go under. Berlin is big. Where a thousand live, one more can also live."

He was in a deep dark courtyard. He stood beside the dustbin. And suddenly he started singing in a resonant voice, singing toward the walls. He took his hat off, like an organ grinder. The echo resounded from the walls. That was fine. His voice filled his ears. He sang in such a very loud voice, he would never have been allowed to sing like that in prison. And what did he sing, that it should echo from the walls? "There comes a call like thunder's peal." Martially hard and pithy. And then: "Tra-la-la-la-la-la-la," a bit from a song. Nobody paid any attention to him. The Jew received him at the gate: "You sang beautifully. You really sang beautifully. You could earn gold with a voice like you've got." The Jew followed him to the street, took him by the arm, pushed him farther along, talking endlessly all the way, until they turned into Gormannstrasse, the Jew and the raw-boned, big fellow in the summer topcoat with his lips pressed tight together, as if he wanted to spit gall.

[. . .]

Market Dull, Later Bears Very Active, Hamburg
Depressed, London Weaker

It was raining. To the left in Münzstrasse signs sparkled in front of
the movies. At the corner he was unable to pass, the people were
standing in front of a fence, then it got very steep, the streetcar
tracks ran on planks laid across the space, a car was just riding
slowly over them. Look here, they are building a subway station,
must be work to be had in Berlin. Another movie. Children under
seventeen not allowed. On the huge poster a beet-red gentleman
was standing on a staircase, while a peach of a young girl embraced
his legs, she lay on the stairs, and he stood up above with a leering
expression on his face. Underneath was written: No Parents, Fate
of an Orphaned Child, in Six Reels. Yes, sir, I'll take a look at that.
The orchestrion was banging away. Price sixty pfennigs.

A man to the woman cashier: "Say, Fräulein, is it any cheaper
for an old territorial without a belly?" "Nope, only for children
under five months with a sucking nipple." "Sure. That's our age.
New-born babies on the instutterment plan." "All right, make it
fifty then, get along in." Behind him there meandered a young chap,
slim of build, with a muffler on: "Hey, lady, I'd like to git in free."
"How do you get that way? Tell your Mommer to put you on the
pottie." "Well, kin I get in?" "In where?" "The movie." "There
ain't no movie here." "You really mean it, there ain't no movie
here?" She called through the window of the ticket-office to the
watchman at the door: "Say, Max, come here a minute. Here's a
fellow wants to know if there's a movie here. He's got no money.
Go ahead show him what we got here." "What we got here, young
fellow? You ain't noticed it yet? This is the poor-box, Münzstrasse
division." He pushed the slim fellow out of the ticket-office,
showed him his fits: "If ye want me to, I'll give ye what's comin' to
you right off the bat."

Franz pushed on in. It just happened to be an intermission. The
long room was packed full, 90 percent men with work-caps on,
they don't take them off. The three lamps on the ceiling are covered
with red. In front, a yellow piano with packages on top of it. The
orchestrion makes a continuous racket. Then it gets dark and the
film starts. A goose-girl is to be given culture, just why, is not made
so clear, at least not right in the middle. She wiped her nose with

her hand, she scratched her behind on the staircase, everybody in the movie laughed. Franz thought it was quite wonderful, when the tittering started up around him. Just folks, free folks, amusing themselves, nobody has a right to say anything to them, simply lovely, and I right here among 'em! It went on. The high-toned Baron had a sweetheart who lay in a hammock and stretched her legs vertically in the air. The girl had drawers on. That's something. Wonder why people get so excited about that dirty goose-girl and her licking the platters clean? Again the girl with the slim legs flashed by. The Baron had left her alone, now she toppled out of the hammock, and flopped onto the grass, lay there a long time. Franz stared at the screen, there was already another picture, he still saw her toppling out and lying there for a long while. He gnawed his tongue, hell's bells, what was that? But when finally the one who had been the goose-girl's lover embraced this fine lady, the skin of his chest felt hot as if he had been embracing her himself. It went all over him and made him weak.

A jane. (There's something else besides anger and fear. What about all this bunk? Air, m'boy, and a jane!) Queer he shouldn't have thought of that. You stand at the window of the cell and look into the courtyard through the bars. Sometimes women pass by, visitors or children or house-cleaning up at the old man's. How they all stand at the windows, the convicts, and look, every window occupied, devouring every woman. A guard once had a two weeks' visit from his wife from Eberswalde, formerly he used to drive over to see her once every two weeks, now she made good use of the time, every moment of it, at work his head hangs with fatigue, he can hardly walk any longer.

Franz was now outside on the street in the rain. What'll we do? I'm a free man. I've got to have a woman! A woman I've got to have! Gee, how great, life is nice outside. But I must hold on to myself so I can walk. He was walking on springs, not on solid earth. Then, at the corner of Kaiser-Wilhelm Strasse, behind the market-wagons, he came upon a woman; he posted himself beside her, any old gal will do. The devil, how did I suddenly git such cold feet. He went off with her, but his under-lip, he was so excited, if you live far, I won't come along. It was just across the Bülowplatz, past the fences, through a hallway, to the courtyard, down six steps. She turned back, laughed: "Don't be do dithery, sweetie, why, you'll knock me down." She had hardly shut the door behind him, when he grabbed her. "Boy, just give me time to put my umbrella down first." He pressed her, hugged her, pinched her, rubbed his hands across her coat, he still had his hat on, angrily she let the umbrella drop. "Let me go, won't you." He groaned, and smiled an awkward, dizzy smile: "Whazze matter?" "You're going to ruin all my get-up. Are you going to shell out for it afterwards?" All right then, we never get anything for nothing either." He did not let her go. "Say, you fool, I can't breathe. You must be loony." She was stout and slow, small, he first had to give her the three marks, which she put carefully into the chest of drawers. They key she put in her pocket. He couldn't keep his eyes off her. "It's because I've been behind the bars a coupla years, fat gal. Out there in Tegel, you can imagine it." "Where?" "Tegel, you know."

The flabby wench guffawed. She unbuttoned her blouse at the top. There were once two royal children, who held each other so dear. And the cow jumped over the moon. She grabbed him, pressed him to her. Putt, putt, putt, my little chick, putt, putt, putt, my rooster.

He soon had beads of sweat on his face, he groaned. "Well, whatcha groaning for?" "Who's that bird running around next door?" "It's not a bird, it's my landlady." "What's she doing there?" "What do you think she's doing? She's got her kitchen there." "Well, she ought to stop running around like that. What does she want to run around for now? I can't stand it." "Oh Lordy-lordy, I'll go and tell her." What a sweaty fellow he is, I'll be glad to get rid of him, the old bum! I'll soon put him out. She knocked next door: "Frau Priese, won't you be quiet for just a few minutes? I've got to talk to a gentleman here, something important." Well, that's done, dear fatherland, be comfort thine, come to my heart, but you're going to be ditched soon.

She thought to herself, her head on the pillow: those tan oxfords need soling, Kitty's new boyfriend does that for two marks, if she don't mind, I ain't goin' to swipe him away from her, he can also dye 'em brown to go with my brown blouse, it's an old rag anyway, just good enough to be made into a coffee-cozy: them ribbons'll have to be pressed, I'll ask Frau Priese right away, she's probably still got a fire going, what's she cooking today anyway? She sniffed. Green herring.

Incomprehensible verses keep running through his head in a circle. When you cook soup, Fräulein Stein, I'll get a spoon, Fräulein Stein. If you cook noodles, Fräulein Stein, give me some noodles, Fräulein Stein. Tumbling down, tumbling up. He groaned aloud: "Maybe you don't like me?" "Why not, come on, I'm a lovin' gal, I am." He fell back into bed, grunted and moaned. She rubbed her neck. "I have to laugh myself sick. Just keep quiet there. You don't bother me." She laughed, raised her fat arms, stuck her stockinged feet out from under the cover. "I can't help it."

Let's get out of this. Air. Still raining. What's the matter? I'll have to get myself another gal. First let's get some sleep, Franz, what'se matter wtih you, anyway?

Sexual potency depends upon the concentered action of (1) the internal secretory system, (2) the nervous system, and (3) the sexual apparatus. The glands participating in this potency are: the pituitary gland, the thyroid gland, the suprarenal gland, the prostate gland, the seminal vesicle, and the epididymis. In this system the spermatic gland perponderates. Through the matter prepared by it, the entire sexual apparatus is charged from the cerebral cortex to the genitals. The erotic impression releases the erotic tension of the cerebral cortex, the current flows as an erotic stimulus from the cerebral cortex to the switch center in the interbrain. The stimulus then rolls down the spine. Not unimpeded, however, for, before leaving the brain, it has to pass the brakes of the inhibitions, those predominantly psychic inhibitions which play a large rôle in the form of moral scruples, lack of self-confidence, fear of humiliation, fear of infection and impregnation, and things of this order.

In the evening there he is, shambling down Elsasser Strasse. Don't be afraid, m'boy, don't pretend you're tired. "How much for the pleasure, kid?" The black gal is fine, got hips, a toothsome piece. When a gal's got a man, that she loves, ain't it gran'? "My you're a gay one, sweetie. Did you just come into a fortune?" "And how! You'll get some change out of it." "Why not." But, nevertheless, he is afraid.

And afterward in the room, flowers behind the curtain, a clean little room, a nice little room, why, the girl even has a phonograph, she sings for him, artificial silk stockings, rayon, no blouse, pitch-black eyes: "I'm a cabaret singer, I am. You know where? Any-where I like. Just now I got not engagement, you know. I go into nice-looking joints and I ask. Then I do my stunt. It's a wow. Hey, quit tickling." "Aw, come on." "Nope, hands off, that knocks hell out of my business. My act—be nice now, sweetie—you see, I hold an auction in the place, no plate collection either; whoever gives me something, can kiss me. Crazy, ain't it! In a public place, too. No-body under fifty pfennigs. Say, I get everything. Here on my shoul-der. There, go ahead, it's all right." She puts on a man's top hat, croaks into his face, shakes her hips, her arms akimbo: "Theodore, what did you mean last night, when you smiled at me so gay and bright? Theodore, what was it you hoped to gain, when you stood me to pig's knuckles and fine champagne?"

While sitting on his lap, she pulls a cigarette out of his waistcoat and sticks it into her mouth; she looks yearningly into his eyes, ten-derly rubs her ear on his and chirps: "Do you know what homesick-ness is? When your heart is torn by homesickness? Everything seems so cold and dreary." She hums a tune, stretches herself on the sofa. She puffs, strokes his hair, trills, laughs.

Sweat on his brow. Again that fear. And suddenly his head slith-ers off. Boom, the bell rings, get up, five-thirty, six o'clock, cells opened, boom, boom, brush your coat quickly, suppose the old man makes inspection, no, not today. I'll get discharged soon. Psst, say, one of the boys got out last night, pard, the rope's still dangling out there over the wall, they got the police after him. He groans, he lifts his head, he sees the girl, her chin, her neck. If I only knew how to get out of prison. They ain't going to discharge me. I'm not out yet. She puffs blue rings from the side at him, sniggers: "You're sweet, come on, I'll pour you a glass of Mampe brandy, thirty pfen-nigs." He lies there, stretched out at full length. "What do I care for Mampe? They knocked hell out of me. I did time at Tegel, I did, what for, I'd really like to know. First with the Prussians in the trenches, and then in Tegel. I ain't a human being any more." "Well, but you're not going to cry here. Come on, open your li'l beakie, big mans gotta drink. We're a jolly lot, we are, we're as happy as can be, we laugh and sing with delight from morning until night." And the dump heap for that. Why, they might have chopped off the fellow's head at once, and be done with it, the lousy dogs. Could have dumped me on the garbage heap, why not. "Come on, big man, take another glass. I'd walk a mile for Mampe's brandy, it makes you feel so hale and dandy."

"To think the girls ran after me like a bunch of sheep and I didn't even spit at 'em, and there I was, flat on my nose." She picks up another one of his cigarettes which have fallen to the floor. "Yes, you ought to go to the policeman sometime and tell him." "I'm going." He is looking for his suspenders. And says nothing more and doesn't look at the girl with her slobbery mouth, she smokes and smiles and looks at him, shoves a few cigarettes quickly under the sofa with her foot.

[. . .]

The Rosenthaler Platz is busily active.

Weather changing, more agreeable, a degree below freezing. For Germany, a low-pressure region is extending, which in its entire range has ended the weather prevailing up to now. The few pressure changes now going on indicate a slow extension of the low-pressure area toward the south, so that the weather will remain under its influence. During the day the temperature will probably be lower. Weather forecast for Berlin and surrounding country.

Car No. 68 runs across Rosenthaler Platz, Wittenau, Nordbahnhof, Heilanstalt, Weddingplatz, Stettiner Station, Rosenthaler Platz, Alexanderplatz, Straussberger Platz, Frankfurter Allee Station, Lichtenberg, Herzberge Insane Asylum. The three Berlin transport companies—street car, elevated and underground, omnibus—form a tariff-union. Fares for adults are 20 pfennigs, for schoolchildren 10 pfennigs, reduced fares allowed for children up the age of 14, apprentices and pupils, poor students, war cripples, persons physically unfit for walking as certified by the district charity offices. Get to know about the lines. During the winter months the front entrance shall not be opened for passengers entering or leaving, 39 seating capacity, 5918, to alight from the car, warn the motorman in time, the motorman is forbidden to converse with passengers, getting off or on while the car is in motion may lead to fatal accidents.

In the middle of the Rosenthaler Platz a man with two yellow packages jumps off from the 41, an empty taxi glides just past him, the copper looks at him, a street-car inspector appears, cop and inspector shake hands: damned lucky, that fellow with his packages.

Various fruit brandies at wholesale prices, Dr. Bergell, notary and attorney-at-law, Lukutate, the Indian rejuvenation treatment for elephants, Fromms Akt, the best rubber sponge, what's the use of so many rubber sponges, anyway?

The wide Brunnenstrasse runs north from this square, the A.E.G. runs along its left side in front of the Humboldthain. The A.E.G. is an immense enterprise, which embraces, according to the 1928 telephone directory: Electric Light and Power Works, Central Administration, NW 40, Friedrich-Karl-Ufer 2–4, Local Call and Long Distance Call Office, North 4488, General Management, Janitor, Electric Securities Bank Inc., Division for Lighting Fixtures, Division for Russia, Oberspree Metal Division, Treptow Apparatus Plant, Brunnenstrasse Plant, Henningsdorf Plant, Plant for Insulators, Rheinstrasse Plant, Oberspree Cable Works, Wilhelminenhofstrasse Plant, Rummelsburger Chaussee, Turbine Plant NW 87, Huttenstrasse 12–16.

The Invalidenstrasse trails off to the left. It goes toward the Stettin Station where the trains from the Baltic Sea arrive: Why, you're all covered with soot—yes, there is a lot of dust here.—How do you do? So long.—Has the gentleman anything to carry, 50 pfennigs.—Your vacation certainly did you a lot of good.—Oh, that tan will come off soon.—Wonder where people get all the money from to travel around like that.—In a little hotel over there in that dark street two lovers shot themselves early yesterday morning, a waiter from Dresden and a married woman, both of whom, however, had registered under false names.

From the south the Rosenthaler Strasse runs into the square. Across the way Aschinger provides food as well as beer to drink, music, and wholesale bakery. Fish are nutritious, some are happy when they have fish, and others are unable to eat it, eat more fish, the healthy slenderizing dish. Ladies stockings, a genuine artificial silk, here you have a fountain pen with a 14-carat gold point.

On the Elsasser Strasse they have fenced in the whole street leaving only a narrow gangway. A power engine puffs behind the billboards. Becker-Fiebig, Building Contractor Inc., Berlin W 38. There is a constant din, dump carts are lined up as far as the corner, on which stands the Commercial and Savings Bank, Deposit Branch L, Custody of Securities, Payment of Savings Bank Deposits. Five men, workmen, kneel in front of the bank driving small stones into the ground.

Four persons have just gotten on No. 4 at Lothringer Strasse, two elderly women, a plain man with a worried look, and a boy with a cap and earmuffs. The two women are together, they are Frau Plück and Frau Hoppe. They want to get an abdominal bandage for Frau Hoppe, the older woman, because she has a tendency to navel hernia. They have been to the truss-maker's in the Brunnenstrasse, and now they both want to call by to fetch their husbands for lunch. The man is a coachman named Hasebrück, who is having a lot of trouble with an electric iron which he bought for his boss secondhand and cheap. They had given him a defective one, the boss tried it for a few days, then it failed to work properly, so he is supposed to exchange it, the people refuse to do so, this is the third time he has gone there, today he has been told he has to pay something on it. They boy, Max Rüst, will later on become a tinker, father of seven more Rüsts, he will go to work for the firm of Hallis & Co., Plumbing and Roofing, in Grünau. At the age of 52 he will win a quarter of a prize in the Prussian Class Lottery, then he will retire from business and die during an adjustment suit which he has started against the firm of Hallis & Co., at the age of 55. His obituary will read as follows: On September 2, suddenly, from heart disease, my beloved husband, our dear father, son, brother, brother-in-law, and uncle, Paul Rüst, in his 55th year. This announcement is made with deep grief on behalf of his sorrowing family by Marie Rüst. The notice of thanks after the funeral will read as follows: Acknowledgment. Being unable to acknowledge individually all tokens of sympathy in our bereavement, we hereby express our profound gratitude to all relatives, friends, as well as to the tenants of No. 4 Kleiststrasse and to all our acquaintances. Especially do we thank Herr Deinen for his kind words of sympathy. At present this Max Rüst is 14 years old, has just finished public school, is supposed to call by on his way there at the clinic for the defective in speech, the hard of hearing, the weak-visioned, the weak-minded, the incorrigible, he has been there at frequent intervals, because he stutters, but he is getting better now.

[. . .]

Lina Gives It to the Pansies

But that isn't enough for Franz Biberkopf. He rolls his eyeballs. In the company of sloppy Lina he observes the street life between the

Alex and Rosenthaler Platz and decides to sell newspapers. Why? They had told him all about it. Lina could lend a hand, and it's just the thing for him. Moving to, moving fro, roundabout and away we go.

"Lina, I can't make speeches, I'm not a popular orator. When I'm selling something, they understand me, but it's not just right, either. Do you know what 'mind' is?" "Nope." Lina ogles him expectantly. "Look at the boys on the Alex and here, too, none of them has any mind. The fellows with the stalls and wagons, too, that ain't nothin' either. They're smart, clever boys, a lot of sap in 'em, needn't tell me anything about that. But just imagine a speaker in the Reichstag, Bismarck or Bebel, why, the ones we got now ain't nothing, take it from me, they got mind all right, mind, that means head, not just any old noodle. None of them can get anything out of me with their soft soap. A speaker that is a speaker." "Ain't you a speaker, Franz?" "You make me laugh—me a speaker! Know who's a speaker, well, you'll never believe it, your landlady." "That Schwenk woman?" "Nope, the other one, where I got the things, in the Karlstrasse." "The one near the circus? Don't talk to me about her."

Franz bends mysteriously forward: "She sure was a speaker, Lina, a real one, I tell you." "Not on your life. Comes into my room, and me lying in bed and wants to get my valise on account of one month." "All right Lina, now listen, it wasn't nice of her. But when I went upstairs and asked about the valise, she started off." "I know that bunk of hers. I didn't listen to her. Franz, you mustn't let a woman like that put the skids under you." "I tell you, Lina, she started off about criminal law, the civil code, and how she squeezed out a pension for her dead old man, when the old fool had an apoplectic fit, which didn't have anything to do with the war. Since when has apoplexy got anything to do with the war? She said so herself, but she didn't give in, and she won her case. She's got mind, Fatty, no two ways about it. Whatever she wants she gets, that's more than earning a coupla pfennigs. That's where you show what you are. That's how you get air, baby. I'm still knocked flat." "You go up to see her once in a while?" Franz protests with both hands: "Suppose you go up there, Lina, you want to get a valise; you're there at eleven sharp, you got something to do at twelve, and about a quarter to one you're still standing there. She talks and talks to you, and you haven't got your valise yet, and maybe you trot off without it. She can talk, that one, take it from me."

He meditates across the table-top, and draws a design in a beer puddle with his finger: "I'm going to get a license somewhere and sell newspapers. That's a good thing."

She remains speechless, slightly insulted. Franz does what he pleases. One noon, he's on Rosenthaler Platz, she brings him sandwiches, then he lights out at twelve, plunks the box with the tripod and all the cardboard-boxes under her arms and goes out looking for information about newspapers.

To start with, an elderly man on the Hackesche Market in front of Oranienburger Strasse advises him to take an interest in sexual education. It's now being practiced on a big scale and doing quite well. "What's sexual education?" Franz asks, and hesitates. The white-haired man points to his exhibit. "Better first take a look at this, then you won't ask questions about it." "Those are naked girls painted there." "That's the only kind I got." They puff silently side by side. Franz stands and gapes at the pictures from top to bottom, puffing into the air, the man looks past him. Franz looks him in the eye: "Listen here, comrade, do you get any fun out of this, these here girls and pictures like that? The *Gay Life*. Here they go and paint a nude girl with a little kitten. Wonder what she's after, on the stairs, with a li'l kitty. Suspicious bird. Am I disturbing you, pardner?" The latter, seated on his camp-chair, takes a deep breath and sinks into himself: there are jackasses in this world as big as mountains, the real thing in blockheads, who run around the Hackesche Market in broad daylight and stop in front of a fellow, if he's in bad luck, to talk a lot of tommyrot. As the white-haired man becomes silent, Franz takes a few magazines from the hook: "You mind, pardner? What's this? *Figaro*. And this one, *Marriage*. And this, *Ideal Marriage*. Now I s'pose that's different from marriage. *Woman's Love*. Everything to be had separately. Why a fellow can get all kinds of information here, if he's got any money, but it's mighty expensive. Beside there's a catch in it somewhere." "Well, I'd like to know what kind of a catch is in it. Everything goes. Nothing's forbidden. What I sell, I got authorization for, and there ain't no catch in it. Things like that I leave alone." "I can tell you one thing, I just want to tell you, looking at pictures is no good. I could tell you a thing or two about that. It does a man harm, yes, sir, that botches you up. You start by looking at pictures and afterward, when you want to, there you are, and it won't go naturally any more." "Don't know what you're talking about. And don't spit on my papers, they cost a lot o' money, and don't paw the covers like that. Here read this: *The Unmarried*. There's everything, even a special magazine for people like that." "Unmarried, well, well, why shouldn't there be people like that, why, I'm not married with Polish Lina either." "Well, here; look what's here, if that isn't true, it's only an example: To attempt to regulate the sexual life of the two parties by contract, or to decree conjugal duties in this respect, is the most loathsome and humiliating slavery we can possibly imagine. Well?" "How so?" "Is it true or not?" "That don't happen to me. A woman who would ask a thing like that from a man, is that really possible? Can it happen?" "Well, there you read it." "Well, that's going a bit strong. Just let 'em come and try anything like that on me."

Franz reads the sentence again in amazement, then he gives a start, and shows something to the old man: "Well, and look what it says *here*: I would like to give an example from the work of d'Annunzio, *Lust*, now watch out, d'Annunzio's the name of that superswine, he's a Spaniard or Italian or from America, maybe. Here the thoughts of the man are so full of his distant sweetheart that, during a night of love with a woman who serves as substitute, the name of his true love escapes him against his will. That beats everything. No, sirree, I won't have anything to do with things like that." "Hold on, where's that, lemme see it." "Here. Serves as substitute. Artificial rubber in place of rubber. Turnips instead of a real meal. Did you ever hear anything like it, a woman, a girl, for a substitute? He takes another one, just because he hasn't got his own, and the new one notices something, and that's the end, and I suppose she's not to peep? He gets that printed, the Spaniard! If I was a printer, I wouldn't print it." "Well, cut out that rot! Y' mustn't think you can understand everything with your little brain, what a fellow like that means, a real writer, and a Spaniard or Italian at that, right here in the crowd on the Hackesche Market."

Franz continues reading: "A great emptiness and silence then filler her soul. That's enough to make you climb trees. Nobody'll make me believe that. I don't care who he is. Since when, emptiness and silence? I can talk about that, too, just like that fellow, and the girls probably ain't any different there than anywhere else. Once I had one of 'em, and she noticed something, an address in my note-book, well, boy: she notices something, and then silence? Maybe you think so, heh, but then you don't know anything about women, old feller. You shoulda heard 'er. The whole house shook and roared. That's how loud she bawled. I couldn't tell 'er what it was all about. She kept on going, as if she was on a hot griddle. People came running. I was glad when I got outside." "Say, there's two things you don't seem to notice?" "Which are?" "When anybody takes a paper from me, he buys it and he keeps it. If there's any tripe in it, it don't matter either, he's only interested in the pictures, anyway." Franz Biberkopf's left eye disapproved of that. "And then here we got: *Woman's Love* and *Friendship*, and they don't talk any bunk, I'm tellin' you, they fight. Yes, sir, they fight for human rights." "Why, what's the matter with 'em?" "Penal Code, Section 175, if you don't know it." There just happens to be a lecture in Landsberger Strasse, Alexanderpalais, tonight, Franz might hear something about the wrong done to a million people in Germany every day. It's enough to make your hair stand on end. The man pushed a bunch of old papers under Franz's arm, Franz sighed, looked at the package under his arm: all right, he'll probably be there. What'll I do there, anyway, shall I really go, wonder if it's worth while handling magazines like that? The pansies; he just gives me this stuff and expects me to carry it home and read it. A fellow might feel sorry for those boys, but they're none o' my business.

He left in a great pother, the whole thing seemed to him so far from kosher that he didn't way a word to Lina and got rid of her in the evening. The old news-vender pushed him into a little hall, where there were almost nothing but men, mostly very young, and a few women, who sat apart in couples. Franz didn't say a word for an hour, but grinned a lot behind his hat. After ten o'clock, he couldn't stand it any longer, he had to beat it, the whole thing, and those funny people, it was too ridiculous for words, so many fairies in a bunch, and he right among 'em, he got out quickly, and laughed until he came to Alexanderplatz. As he was leaving, he heard the lecturer talking about Chemnitz and the police ordinance of November 27. This forbids all inverts to go on the streets or use the comfort stations, and, if they are caught, it costs them 30 marks. Franz looked for Lina, but she had gone out with her landlady. He went to sleep. In his dream he laughed and swore a lot, he had a fight with a silly old driver who kept driving him around and around the Roland fountain in the Siegesallee. The traffic cop, too, was running after the car. At last Franz jumped out, and the auto drove like mad around the fountain and around him in a circle, and this went on and on without stopping, and Franz was always standing around with the copper while they consulted together: what are we going to do with him, he's crazy?

Next morning he waits for Lina in the café as usual, he has the mazagines with him. He wants to tell her what boys like that really have to suffer, Chemnitz and the article of the law with the 30 marks, at the same time it's not his business, and they can bother about their articles themselves. And then Meck might come too, trying to get him to do something for the cattle drivers. Nope, all he wants is peace, they can go soak their heads.

Lina sees right away that he has slept badly. Hesitantly he pushes the magazines toward her, the pictures on top. Frightened, Lina claps her hand over her mouth. Then he starts talking again about mind. Looks for yesterday's beer puddle on the table, but there isn't any. She moves away from him: Suppose there's something wrong with him like the kind here in the papers. She doesn't understand, up to now he certainly wasn't like that. He fiddles around, draws lines on the bare wood with his dry finger, then she takes the whole package of papers from the table and throws it down on the bench. At first she stands there like a mænad, and they stare at each other, he looking up at her like a little boy, then she waltzes off. And there he sits with his papers, now he can think about the fairies.

A baldpate goes walking one evening in the Tiergarten, he meets a pretty boy, who hooks onto him at once; they have a lovely stroll together for an hour, then the baldpate has the notion—the instinct, oh the desire, immense at that moment—to be very nice to the youngster. He is a married man, he has often noticed these things before, but now it has to be, ah, it's really marvelous. "You're my sunshine, you're my darling."

And the lad is so gentle. To think that such things exist: "Come on, let's go to a little hotel. You can give me five marks, or ten. I'm quite broke." "Anything you want, my sunshine." He gave him his whole pocketbook. To think that such things exist. That's the nicest part of it all.

But in the room the door has peepholes. The hotel-keeper sees something and calls his wife; she, too, sees something. And afterward they say they won't allow such things in their hotel, they saw it all right and he can't deny it. And they would never permit such things, and he ought to be ashamed to seduce young boys like that, they are going to report him to the police. The porter and the chambermaid also come and grin. Next day the baldpate buys himself two bottles of champagne: Asbach Uralt, and leaves on a business trip. He wants to go to Heligoland, to end it all by drowning while plastered. He gets drunk all right, and takes a boat, but comes back two days later to the old girl; at home nothing has happened.

Nothing at all happens throughout the month, the whole year. Just one thing: he inherits $3,000 from an American uncle and is able to treat himself a bit. Then one day, while he's off at the seashore, a court summons arrives which the old lady has to sign for him. She opens it, and everything's there about those peepholes and that pocketbook and the dear little boy. And when baldpate gets back from his holiday, they're all weeping around him, the old lady and his two grown daughters. He reads the summons, why, that's all dead and buried, that's bureaucracy and a lot of red tape dating back to Charlemagne, and now it has got to him, but it's true, all right. "What have I done, Judge? Why, I didn't offend anybody's feelings. I went to a room, locked myself in. Is it my fault if they have those peepholes? Nothing illegal really happened." The boy confirms his story. "Now what is it I've done?" Baldpate weeps into his fur coat: "Did I steal anything? Did I commit a burglary? I only broke into a dear boy's heart. I said to him: my sunshine. And so he was."

He is acquitted. At home the family all keep on crying. "Magic Flute," dancehall, with an American Dancehall on the ground floor. The Oriental Casino available for private entertainments. What Christmas gift shall I give my best girl? Inverts: after many years of experiment I have at last found a radical antidote against the growth of the beard. Every part of the body can be depilated. Furthermore I have discovered the means of developing a truly feminine breast within an astonishingly short time. No medicines, absolutely safe and harmless. As proof: myself. Liberty for Love all along the front.

A star-clear sky looked down upon the dark realms of mankind. The castle of Kerkauen lay in deep nocturnal quiet. But a fair-haired woman buried her head in the pillows and found no sleep. Tomorrow, tomorrow, her love, the dear love of her heart, would leave her. A whisper went (ran) through the sable, impenetrable (dark) night: Gisa, stay with me, stay with me (don't go away, don't go off on a voyage, don't fall down, take a seat please). Forsake me not. But the cheerless silence had neither ear nor heart (nor foot nor nose). And yonder, separated only by a few walls, there lay a pale slender woman with wide open eyes. Her dark, heavy hair lay in confusion on the silk of the bed (Castle Kerkauen is famous for its silk beds). A shiver of cold shook her. Her teeth chattered, as though she were deeply chilled, full stop. But she did not move, comma, she did not pull the coverlet closer over herself, full stop. Motionless her slender, ice-cold hands lay (as if deeply chilled, cold-shuddering, a slender woman with wide open eyes, famous silk bed) on it, full stop. Her luminous eyes roamed blazing through the darkness, and her lips trembled, colon, quotation marks, Eleanore, dash, Eleanore, dash, quotation marks, quotation francs, quotation dollars—going, going, gone!

[. . .]

Supply at the cattle-market: 1,399 steers; 2,700 calves; 4,654 sheep; 18,864 hogs. Market conditions: prime steers firm, otherwise quiet. Calves firm, sheep quiet, hogs opening firm, closing weak, over-weights lagging.

The wind blows through the driveway, it is raining. The cattle bleat as several men drive a big, roaring, horned herd into the place. The animals close in on each other, they stop in their tracks, then run in the wrong direction while the drivers chase them with sticks. A bull jumps up on a cow in the middle of the bunch, the cow runs right and left, the bull is after her, hugely he rises up on her again and again.

A big, white steer is driven into the slaughter-hall. Here there is no vapor, no pen like they have for the swarming pigs. The big strong animal, the steer, steps in alone, between its drivers through the gate. The blood-bespattered hall lies open before it with the chopped-up bones, and the halves and quarters hanging about. The big steer has a broad forehead. With sticks and thrusts it is driven up to the butcher. In order to make it stand still, he gives it a slight blow on the hind leg with the flat part of the hatchet. One of the drivers seizes it from below around the neck. The animal stands for a moment, then yields, with a curious ease, as if it agreed and was willing, after having seen everything and understood that this is its fate, and that it cannot do anything against it. Perhaps it thinks the gesture of the driver is a caress, it looks so friendly. The animal follows the tug of the driver's arms, turns its head obliquely to one side, mouth upward.

But then the butcher stands behind it with his hammer uplifted. Don't look around! The hammer lifted by the strong man with both his fists is behind you, above you, and then: zoom, down it comes! The muscular force of a strong man like an iron wedge in its neck! And a second later—the hammer has not yet been lifted—the animal's four legs give a spring, the whole heavy body seems to fly up with a jerk. And then as though it had no legs, the beast, the heavy body, falls down on the floor with a thud, onto its rigidly cramped legs, lies like this for a moment, drops on its side. The executioner walks around the animal from left to right, cracks it over the head, and on the temples, with another mercifully stunning blow: you will not wake up again. Then the other man beside him removes the cigar from his mouth, blows his nose, sharpens his knife, it is half as long as a sword, and kneels behind the animal's head; its legs have already stopped their convulsive movements. With short twitching jerks it tosses the hind part of its body back and forth. The butcher searches for something on the floor and before using the knife, he calls for the basin to catch the blood. The blood is still circulating quietly inside, little disturbed, under the impulses of a mighty heart. To be sure, the spine is crushed, but the blood still flows quietly through the veins. The lungs breathe, the intestines move. Now he applies the knife, the blood will gush out, I can see it now, in a stream as thick as your arm, black, beautiful, jubilating blood. Then the whole merry party will leave the house, the guests will dance out into the open, a tumult, and gone are the happy pastures, the warm stable, the fragrant fodder, everything gone, blown away, an empty hole, darkness, a new cosmos emerges! Haha! Suddenly we see a gentleman who has bought the house, new streets being laid out, better business conditions, going to tear down everything. They bring the big basin, shove it up to him, the huge animal throws its hind legs in the air. The knife is thrust into its neck near the gullet, look carefully for the veins, they are covered with a tough skin, well safeguarded. And now it's open, another one too, it spurts forth, hot steaming blackness, black red, the blood bubbles out over the knife, over the butcher's arm, jubilant blood, hot blood, the guests are coming, the transformation act proceeds, from the sun came your blood, the sun hid in your body, now it surges forth again. The animal breathes with huge efforts, it amounts to suffocation, a huge irritation, it snorts and rattles. Yes, the beams are cracking. The flanks heave so fearfully that one of the men helps the beast. If you want a stone to fall, give it a push. A man jumps on top of the animal, on its body, with both legs, he stands up there, bouncing, steps on the entrails, bobs up and down, the blood should come out more quickly, all of it. And the snorting grows louder, it is a long drawn-out panting, panting away, with light defensive blows on the hind legs. The legs quiver gently. Life is going out with a snort, the breathing begins to die down. The hind quarters turn over heavily. That's the earth, that's gravity. The man bobs upward. The other man underneath is already preparing to turn back the hide of the neck.

Happy pastures, damp warm stable.

The well-lighted butcher shop. The lighting of the store and that of the show-window should be made to harmonize. Predominantly direct or semi-indirect lighting should be used. In general, fixtures for predominantly direct lighting are practical, because store, desk, and chopping-block, above all, should be well lighted. Artificial daylight obtained by the use of blue-filter lamps, cannot be considered for butcher shops, because meat always demands lighting under which the natural meat color does not suffer.

Stuffed pig's feet. After the feet have been well cleaned, they are split lengthways, so that the rind remains whole; then they are laid together and tied with a thread.

[. . .]

Rencounter on the Alex, Cold as the Devil. Next Year, 1929, It'll Be Colder Still

Boom, boom, the steam pile-driver thumps in front of Aschinger's on the Alex. It's one story high, and knocks the rails into the ground as if they were nothing at all.

Icy air, February. People walk in overcoats. Whoever has a fur piece wears it, whoever hasn't, doesn't wear it. The women have on thin stockings and are freezing, of course, but they look nice. The bums have disappeared with the cold. When it gets warmer, they'll stick their noses out again. In the meantime they nip a double ration of brandy, but don't ask me what it's like, nobody would want to swim in it, not even a corpse.

Boom, boom, the steam pile driver batters away on the Alex.

A lot of people have time to spare and watch the pile driver whacking away. Up on top there is a man who is always pulling on the chain, then there is a puff on top, and bang! the rod gets it in the neck. There they stand, men and women, especially youngsters, they love the way it works, as if it were greased, bang! The rod gets it in the neck. After that it grows small as the tip of your finger, but it gets another blow and it's welcome now to do whatever it pleases. Finally it's gone, Hell's bells, they've given it a nice drubbing, the people walk off satisfied.

Everything is covered with planks. The Berolina statue once stood in front of Tietz's, one hand outstretched, a regular giantess, now they have dragged her away. Maybe they'll melt her and make medals out of her.

People hurry over the ground like bees. They hustle and bustle around here day and night, by the hundreds.

The streetcars roll past with a screech and a scrunch, yellow ones with trailers, away they go across the planked-over Alexanderplatz, it's dangerous to jump off. The station is laid out on a broad plan, Einbahnstrasse to Königstrasse past Wertheim's. If you want to go east, you have to pass police headquarters and turn down through Klosterstrasse. The trains rumble from the railroad station toward Jannowitz Brücke, the locomotive puffs out a plume of steam, just now it is standing above the Prälat, Schlossbräu entrance a block further down.

Across the street they are tearing down everything, all the houses along the city railroad, wonder where they get the money from, the city of Berlin is rich, and we pay the taxes.

They have torn down Loeser and Wolff with their mosaic sign, 20 yards further on they built it up again, and there's another branch over there in front of the station. Loeser and Wolff, Berlin-Elbing, A-I quality for every taste, Brazil, Havana, Mexico, Little

Comforter, Lilliput, Cigar no. 8, 25 pfennigs each, Winter Ballad, package containing 25 at 20 pfennigs, Cigarillos no. 10, unselected, Sumatra wrapper, a wonderful value at this price, in boxes of a hundred, 10 pfennigs. I beat everything, you beat everything, he beats everything with boxes of 50 and cardboard packages of 10, can be mailed to every country on earth, Boyero 25 pfennigs, this novelty has won us many friends, I beat everything, but I never beat a retreat.

Alongside the Prälat there is lots of room, there are wagons standing there loaded with bananas. Give your children bananas. The banana is the cleanest of fruits, because it is protected from insects, worms as well as bacilli, by its skin. We except such insects, worms, and bacilli as are able to penetrate the skin. Privy Councillor Czerny emphatically pointed out that even children in their first years. I beat everything to pieces, you beat everything to pieces, he beats everything to pieces.

There is a lot of wind on the Alex, at the Tietz corner there is a lousy draft. A wind that blows between the houses and through the building excavations. It makes you feel you would like to hide in the saloons, but who can do that, it blows through your trousers pockets, then you notice something's happening, no monkey business, a man has go to be gay with this weather. Early in the morning the workers come tramping along from Reinickendorf, Neukölln, Weissensee. Cold or no cold, wind or no wind, we've gotta get the coffee pot, pack up the sandwiches, we've gotta work and slave, the drones sit on top, they sleep in their feather-beds and exploit us.

Aschinger has a big café and restaurant. People who have no belly, can get one there, people who have one already, can make it as big as they please. You cannot cheat Nature! Whoever thinks he can improve bread and pastry made from denatured white flour by the addition of artificial ingredients, deceives himself and the consumer. Nature has her laws of life and avenges every abuse. The decadent state of health of almost all civilized peoples today is caused by the use of denatured and artificially refined food. Fine sausages delivered to your house, liverwurst and blood-pudding cheap.

The highly interesting *Magazine*, instead of 1 mark, now only 20 pfennigs; *Marriage*, highly interesting and spicy, only 20 pfennigs.

The newsboy puffs his cigarettes, he has a sailor's cap on, I beat everything.

From the east, Weissensee, Litchtenberg, Friedrichschain, Frankfurter Alle, the yellow streetcars plunge into the square through Landsberger Strasse. Line no. 65 comes from the Central Slaughter-House, the Grosse Ring, Weddingplatz, Luisenplatz; no. 76 from Hundekehle via Hubertusallee. At the corner of Landsberger Strasse they have sold out Friedrich Hahn, formerly a department store, they have emptied it and are gathering it to its forbears. The streetcars and Bus 19 stop on the Turmstrasse. Where Jürgens stationery store was, they have torn down the house and put up a building fence instead. An old man sits there with a medical scale: Try your weight, 5 pfennigs. Dear sisters and brethren, you who swarm across the Alex, give yourselves this treat, look through the loophole next to the medical scale at this dump-heap where Jürgens once flourished and where Hahn's department store still stands, emptied, evacuated, and eviscerated, with nothing but red tatters hanging over the show-windows. A dump-heap lies before us. Dust thou art, to dust returnest. We have built a splendid house, nobody comes in or goes out any longer. Thus Rome, Babylon, Nineveh, Hannibal, Caesar, all went to smash, oh, think of it! In the first place, I must remark they are digging those cities up again, as the illustrations in last Sunday's edition show, and, in the second place, those cities have fulfilled their purpose, and we can now build new cities. Do you cry about your old trousers when they are moldy and seedy? No, you simply buy new ones, thus lives the world.

The police tower over the square. Several specimens of them are standing about. Each specimen sends a connoisseur's glance to both sides, and knows the traffic rules by heart. It has putties around its legs, a rubber mace hangs from its right side, it swings its arms horizontally from west to east, and thus north and south, cannot advance any farther, east flows west, and west flows east. Then the specimen switches about automatically: north flows south, south flows north. The copper has a well-defined waistline. As soon as he jerks around, there is a rush across the square in the direction of Königstrasse of about 30 private individuals, some of them stop on the traffic island, one part reaches the other side and continues walking on the planks. The same number have started east, they swim toward the others, the same thing has befallen them, but there was no mishap.

There are men, women, and children, the latter mostly holding women's hands. To enumerate them all and to describe their destinies is hardly possible, and only in a few cases would this succeed. The wind scatters chaff over all of them alike. The faces of the eastward wanderers are in no way different from those of the wanderers to the west, south, and north; moreover they exchange their roles, those who are now crossing the square toward Aschinger's may be seen an hour later in front of the empty Hahn Department Store. Just as those who come from Brunnenstrasse on their way to Jannowitz Brücke mingle with those coming from the reverse direction. Yes, and many of them turn off to the side, from south to east, from south to west, from north to west, from north to east. They have the same equanimity as passengers in an omnibus or in streetcars. The latter all sit in different postures, making the weight of the car, as indicated outside, heavier still. Who could find out what is happening inside them, a tremendous chapter. And if anyone did write it, to whose advantage would it be? New books? Even the old ones don't sell, and in the year '27 book sales as compared with '26 have declined so and so much percent. Taken simply as private individuals, the people who paid 20 pfennigs, leaving out those possessing monthly tickets and pupils' cards—the latter only pay 10 pfennigs—are riding with their weight from a hundred to two hundred pounds, in their clothes, with pockets, parcels, keys, hats, sets of artificial teeth, trusses, riding across Alexanderplatz, holding those mysterious long tickets on which is written: Line 12 Siemensstrasse D A, Gotzkowskistrasse C, B, Oranienburger Tor C, C, Kottbuser Tor A, mysterious tokens, who can solve them, who can guess and who confess them, three words I tell you heavy with thought, and the scraps of paper are punched four times at certain places, and on them there is written in that same German in which the Bible and the Criminal Code are written: Valid till the end of the line, by the shortest route, connection with other lines not guaranteed. They read newspapers of various tendencies, conserve their balance by means of the semicircular canals of their internal ear, inhale oxygen, stare stupidly at each other, have pains, or no pains, think, don't think, are happy, unhappy, are neither happy nor unhappy.

Rrrr, rrr, the pile drive thumps down, I beat everything, another rail. Something is buzzing across the square coming from police headquarters, they are riveting, a cement crane dumps its load. Herr Adolf Kraun, house-servant, looks on, the tipping over of the wagon fairly fascinates him, you beat everything, he beats everything. He watches excitedly how the sand truck is always tilting up on one side, there it is up in the air, boom, and now it tips over. A fellow wouldn't like to be kicked out of bed like that, legs up, down with the head, there you lie, something might happen to him, but they do their job well, all the same.

[. . .]

Now Franz Biberkopf's earthly journey is ended. It is now time for him to be crushed outright. He falls into the hands of the dark power called death, and that, it seems to him, is a fitting place to stay. But he learns what this power thinks of him, in a way he did not expect, which surpasses everything he has met with up till now.

They settle accounts. He is enlightened concerning his ignorance, his pride, his every blunder. And then our old Franz Biberkopf breaks down, his whole life goes asunder.

The man's broken up. But a new Biberkopf will now be shown, superior to the man we've known, and of whom we may expect that he'll make a better job of things.

[. . .]

Now Franz Hears Death's Slow Song

Lightning, lightning, lightning, the lightning lightning stops. Hacking falling hacking, the hacking falling hacking stops. It is the second night that Franz has screamed. The falling hacking stops. He no longer screams. The lightning stops, His eyes blink. He lies rigid. This is a room, a hall, people are moving about. You mustn't pinch your mouth like that. They pour warm stuff down his throat. No lightning. No hacking. Walls. A little while, just a little while, and then what? He shuts his eyes.

When Franz has shut his eyes, he starts doing something. You can't see what he's doing; you just think he's lying there, perhaps he'll soon be a goner, the man doesn't move a muscle. He calls and moves and roams about. He is calling together all that is his. He walks through the windows, across the fields, he shakes the grass and creeps into the mouse-holes. Get out, get out, what's in here, is there anything of me here? He fumbles in the grass: Outside, you bums, what's all this yapping about, it don't mean anything. I need you, I can't give any of you a furlough, there's lots of things to be done here, let's be gay, I need every one of you.

They pour broth down his throat, he swallows it and does not vomit. He doesn't want to vomit, he doesn't like to vomit.

Franz has Death's word in his mouth and nobody is going to tear it away from him, he turns it around in his mouth, it is a stone made of stone, and no nourishment comes out of it. At this stage many people have died. There was no Farther in life for them. They did not know that they had to suffer only one more pain to advance beyond that, only a little step was needed to get farther, but they could not take this step. They did not know it, it did not come quickly, or not quickly enough, there was a faintness, a spasm that lasted for minutes, for seconds, and already they had passed over there where their names were no longer Karl, Wilhelm, Minna, or Franziska—satiated, darkly satiated, red-flaming in rage and the palsy of despair, they had slept their way across. They did not know they had but to flame up whitely and then they would have become soft and all things would have been new.

So let it come—the night, however black and nothing like it be! So let them come, the black night, those frost-covered acres, the hard frozen roads. So let them come: the lonely, tile-roofed houses whence gleams a reddish light; so let them come: the shivering wanderers, the drivers on the farm wagons traveling to town with vegetables and the little horses in front. The great, flat, silent plains crossed by suburban trains and expresses which throw white light into the darkness on either side of them. So let them come—the men in the station, the little girl's farewell to her parents, she's traveling with two older acquaintances, going across the big water, we've got our tickets, but good Lord, what a little girl, eh, but she'll get used to it over there, if she's a good little girl it'll be all right. So let them come and be absorbed: the cities which lie along the same line, Breslau, Liegnitz, Sommerfeld, Guben, Frankfort on the Oder, Berlin, the train passes through them from station to station, from the stations emerge the cities, the cities with their big and little streets. Berlin with Schweidnitzer Strasse, with the Grosse Ring of the Kaiser-Wilhelm Strasse, Kurfürstendamm, and everywhere are homes in which people are warming themselves, looking at each other with loving eyes, or sitting coldly next to each other; dirty dumps and dives where a man is playing the piano. Say, kiddo, that's old stuff, you'd think there was nothing new in 1928, how about "I kiss your hand, Madame," or "Ramona."

So let them come: the autos, the taxis, you know how many you have sat in, how they rattled, you were alone, or else somebody sat next to you, or maybe two. License number 20147.

A loaf is put in the oven.

It is an open-air oven near a farmhouse, back of it lies a field, it looks like a little heap of tiles. The women have sawed a lot of wood and gathered dry twigs, which they have heaped beside the oven, and now they are stuffing it in. One of them walks across the courtyard carrying big molds containing the dough. A young man quickly opens the door of the oven, it glows inside, it glows and glows, a tremendous heat, they shove the tins in with poles, the bread will rise there and the water will evaporate; the dough will turn brown.

Franz is sitting half up. He has swallowed and now he is waiting; almost everything that was running around outside is back with him again. He trembles, what was it Death had said? He ought to know what Death had said. The door opens. Now it will come. The curtain's up. I know him. It's Lüders. I have been expecting him.

So they come in, awaited with trembling. What can be the matter with Lüders? Franz has made a sign and they thought he had difficulty in breathing, because he was lying flat, but he just wants to lie a bit higher and straighter. For they are coming now. He is lying high. Go ahead.

One by one they come. Lüders, he's a miserable cuss, such a funny little man. Let's see what's the matter with him. He walks upstairs peddling shoelaces. Yes, that's what we did. A fellow goes to the dogs in his rags, still the same old outfit left over from the war, Makko shoelaces, I just wanted to ask you, Ma'am, can't you let me have a cup o' coffee, what about your husband, probably died in the war; claps his hat on. All right now, hand over the change! That's Lüders, he was with me. The woman's face is flaming red, but one cheek's snow-white, she fumbles on her pocket-book, she squeals and topples over. He digs around among kitchen things. A lotta chicken-feed, let's hustle off, or she'll start screamin'. Through the hallway, slam that door, downstairs. Yes, he did it. Hooks something. Hooks a lot. They give me the letter, it's from her, what's happening to me now, suddenly my legs are hacked off, my legs hacked off, but why, I can't get up. Do you want a cognac, Biberkopf, probably a death in the family, yes, oh why, just why, why are my legs hacked off, I don't know. Gotta ask him, gotta talk to him. Listen, Lüders, good mornin', Lüders, how are you, not well, me neither, come here a minute, sit down on that chair, now don't go away, did I do anything to you, don't go away.

Let them come. Let them come, the black night, the autos, the hard frozen roads, the little girl's farewell from her parents, she's traveling with a man and a woman, she'll get used to it over there, got to stay nice and good, and it'll be all right. Let them come!

Reinhold, here's Reinhold. Ugh! the bastard! So here you are, what d'you want here, d'you wanta play the big gazook with me, no rain will ever wash you clean, you crook, you murderer, you big scoundrel, take that pipe out of your mug when you talk to me. It's a good thing you came, I missed you, come on, you dirty louse, haven't they caught you yet, you with your blue overcoat on? Look out, they'll nab you in that outfit. "Who are you, Franz?" Me, you crook? Not a murderer, you know who you murdered? "And who showed me the girl, and who didn't look out for the girl, and I gotta lie under the bed-cover, you fathead you, who was it?" But you needn't have killed her for that. "What of it, didn't you nearly beat her black and blue yourself? And then how about a certain other woman we've heard about, she lived in Landsberger Allee; she didn't get to the cemetery all by herself, did she? Well, what about it? Now you got nothin' to say, what has Herr Franz Biberkopf, our big-mouth by profession, to say now?" You kicked me under the car, you let 'em run over my arm. "Hah, hah, well, you can get one made of cardboard. If you're jackass enough to take up with me!" A jackass? "Well, don't you realize you're a jackass? Now you're in Buch playing the wild man from Borneo, but I'm doin' well: who's a jackass now?"

There he goes, and hell-fire flashes from his eyes, horns grow out of his head, and he yells: Why don't you fight with me, come on, show what you are, Franzeken, Franzeken Biberkopf, dear little Biberkopf, ha, ha! Franz presses his eyelids together. I shouldn't have started anything with him, I shouldn't have fought him. Why did I fall for that so hard?

"Come on, Franzeken, let's see who you are! Have you got any strength?"

I shouldn't have fought. He's teasin' me, he's still teasin' me, makin' me mad, my God, he's a dog. I shouldn'a done it. I can't do anything against him, I shouldn'a done it.

"You gotta have strength, Franz."

I shoud'na had any strength, not against him. Now I see it, it was all wrong. A fine mess I made of things! Away, away with him!

He doesn't go.

Away, away with—!

Franz screams and twists his hands: I must see somebody else, nobody else is coming, why does he stay on?

"I know it, you don't want none o' me. I don't taste nice. But somebody else is comin' right away."

Then let him come. Let them come, the great, flat, silent plains, the lonely tiled houses whence gleams a reddish light, cities which lie along the same line, Frankfort on the Oder, Guben, Sommerfeld, Liegnitz, Breslau, from the stations the cities emerge, cities with their big and their little streets. Then let them come: the cabs driving along, the rushing, gliding automobiles.

Reinhold leaves. Then he stands there once more flashing a look at Franz. "Well, who is the strong man? Who won, Franzeken?"

Franz trembles: Not me, and I know it.

Then let them come.

Somebody else is coming right away.

Franz draws himself up still higher, he has clenched his fists.

A loaf to be put in the oven, a giant oven. The heat is terrific and the oven crackles.

Ida! Now he's gone. Thank God, Ida, you've come. He was the biggest crook the world has ever seen, Ida, it's a good thing you've come. He made me mad and got me excited, what do you think of that? I've had a lotta trouble and now I'm here, you know where that is, Buch, the Insane Asylum, under observation or maybe I'm already crazy. Come on, Ida, don't turn your back on me. What's she doin'? She's standin' in the kitchen. Yes, the girl's standin' in the kitchen pottering about, probably wiping the plates. But why does she keep on crumplin' up like that, her side is crumplin' up as if she had sciatica, as if somebody was kickin' her in the ribs. Don't kick her, you fool, that's inhuman, stop that, oh my, oh my, who's that beatin' her, she can't stand up any more, stand up straight, girlie, turn around, look at me, who's beatin' you so terribly?

"You, Franz, it was you who struck me dead."

Nope, nope, it wasn't me, look it up in the Court Records, it was only mayhem, it wasn't my fault, Don't say that, Ida.

"Yes, you killed me, look out, Franz."

He screams, no, no, he clenches his hands and puts his arm before his eyes, but he can see it nevertheless.

Then let it come. Let them come: the travelers, the strangers with potato-sacks slung on their backs, a boy is coming with a pushcart behind them, his ears are freezing, it's 18 degrees below freezing. Breslau and its Schweidnitzer Strasse, Kaiser-Wilhelm Strasse, Kurfürstenstrasse.

Franz groans: Then I might as well be dead, it's unbearable, it would be best if somebody came along and killed me, I didn't do all this, I didn't know anything about it, he whimpers, stammers, he can't talk. The guard guesses that he wants something. He asks him. The guard gives Franz a sip of warm red wine; the other two patients in the room insist on his warming up the red wine.

Ida keeps crumpling up, don't crumple up, Ida, wasn't I in Tegel for it, I got mine, didn't I? Now she stops crumpling up and she sits down; she hangs her head, grows smaller and darker. There she lies—in the coffin, and does not—move.

Groaning, Franz is groaning. His eyes. The guard sits beside him and holds his hand. Take that away, somebody move the coffin away, I can't get up, no, I can't!

He moves his hand. But the coffin does not move. He can't reach it, and Franz weeps despairingly, staring dully and despairingly at it. Through his tears and his despair the coffin vanishes. Franz, however, continues weeping.

But, ladies and gentlemen, you who are reading all this, I ask you, why is Franz Biberkopf weeping? He weeps because he suffers, and about his suffering and himself as well. Because he had done all this, because he was like this, that's why Franz Biberkopf is weeping. Now Franz Biberkopf is weeping about himself.

It is high noon, and the meals are being served in the house. The kitchen-wagon is moving about downstairs, then back to the main building, the kitchen attendants and two patients less seriously ill push it from the annex.

And now at noon, Mieze comes to Franz. Her face is very quiet, calm and gentle. She is in her street-dress with a tight-fitting hat that hides her ears and covers her forehead. She looks very quietly and tenderly at Franz, the way she did when he used to meet her in the street or in the saloon. He asks her to come nearer and she comes nearer. He asks her to give him her hands. She puts both her hands into one of his. She is wearing a pair of kid gloves. Take those gloves off. She takes them off and gives him her hands. Come here, Mieze, don't be such a stranger, and give me a kiss. Calmly she comes up close to him, looks tenderly at him, so tenderly, and kisses him. Stay here, he says, I need you, you must help me. "I can't, Franzeken. I'm a dead one, dontcha know that?" Please stay. "I'd like to, but I can't." She kisses him again. "Y'know all about Freienwalde, don'tcha, Franz? And you aren't angry with me, are ye?"

She's gone. Franz writhes and tears his eyes open. But he can't see her now. What have I done? Why haven't I got her any more? Why did I show her to Reinhold, if only I hadn't started going around with that fellow! What have I done! And now . . .

A stammering sound comes from her terribly tortured face. She must, she must come back again. The guard who understands only the word "again" pours some more wine into his parched and gaping mouth. Franz has to drink, what else can he do?

The dough lies in the heat, it rises, the yeast thrusts it up, bubbles form, the bread rises, it browns.

The voice of Death, the voice of Death, the voice of Death:

What is the use of all your strength, what is the use of all this being respectable. Oh, yes, oh, yes, look upon it. Know and repent.

All that Franz possesses now surrenders. He keeps nothing back.

Now We Must Depict What Pain Is

Now we must depict what pain and suffering are. How pain burns and ravages. For it is pain that now surges up. Many have described pain in their poems. And every day the cemeteries witness pain.

Now we must describe what pain does to Franz Biberkopf. Franz does not resist, he surrenders and gives himself up as pain's victim. He lies down in the blazing flame in order that he may be slain, destroyed, and burnt to ashes. Now let us acclaim what suffering makes of Franz Biberkopf. Let us set forth the annihilation achieved by pain. A breaking asunder, a lopping off, an overthrow, a dissolution. That is what pain achieves.

To everything its season. A time to strangle and a time to heal, to cast down and to build, to weep and to laugh, to wail and to dance, to seek and to lose, to rend and to sew. Now is the time to strangle, to wail, to seek and to rend.

Franz wrestles, awaiting Death, merciful Death.

Now, he thinks, Death, the Merciful, the All-Ending One, is coming near. He trembles, as toward evening he lifts himself up again to receive him.

They who case him down at noon come now for the second time. Franz says: So be it, it is I. Away with you goes Franz Biberkopf, take me away with you.

With a deep shudder, he greets the specter of that wretch Lüders. Evil Reinhold sloshes up to him. With a deep shudder he encounters Ida's voice, Mieze's face, it is she, everything is fulfilled. Franz weeps and weeps. I'm guilty, I'm not a human being, I'm just a beast, a monster.

Thus died, in that evening hour, Franz Biberkopf, erstwhile transport-worker, burglar, pimp, murderer. Another man lay in the bed, and that other one has the same papers as Franz, he looks like Franz, but in another world, he bears a new name.

This then has been the fall of Franz Biberkopf which I have tried to describe, beginning with Franz's discharge from Tegel Prison up to his end in the Buch Insane Asylum during the winter of 1928–29.

Now I will append a report about the first hours and days of a new man, having the same identity papers as he.

Exit the Evil Harlot, Triumph of the Great Celebrant, the Drummer and Wielder of the Hatchet

Dirty snow covers the fields of the bleak landscape before the red walls of the institution. There is a beating of drums and again a beating of drums. The whore of Babylon has lost. Death is the victor and he drums her away.

The harlot hisses and fusses, drools and screams: "What about him, what can you get out of this fellow, Franz Biberkopf? Preserve him in alcohol, if you want, this funny man of yours!"

Death beats a tattoo on his drum: "I cannot see what you have in your cup, you hyena. This man Franz Biberkopf is here. I have beaten him to a pulp. But since he is strong and good, he may now start a new life. So get out of my way, our argument is ended."

But she becomes mulish and keeps on drooling. Now Death makes a move, gets in motion, his huge gray cloak flutters; scenes and landscapes become visible, they are swimming around him, winding themselves about his feet and upward toward his breasts. And screams and shots and clamor and triumph and rejoicing resound about him. Triumph and rejoicing. The beast whereon the woman rides shies and kicks.

The river, the Beresina, marching legions.

The legions march along the Beresina, icy cold, an icy wind. They have crossed from France and the great Napoleon leads them. Roaring wind, flurries of snow, bullets whine. They fight on the ice, they charge and fall. And always that cry: long live the emperor! Long live the emperor! The sacrifice, the sacrifice—and that is Death!

Rolling of railroads, thunder of guns, bursting hand-grenades, curtain-fire, Chemin des Dames, Langemarck, Dear Fatherland be comfort thine, be comfort thine! Shattered dug-outs, fallen soldiers. Death folds his cloak singing: Oh yes, oh yes, oh yes.

Marching, marching. We march to war, with iron tread, a hundred minstrels march ahead. Red of morning, red of night, shines on us death's early light. One hundred minstrels beat the drum, drumm, brumm, drumm, if we can't walk straight, we'll walk crooked, by gum, drumm, brumm, drumm.

Death folds his cloak and sings: Oh yes, oh yes, oh yes.

An oven burns, an oven burns, before an oven stands a mother with seven sons and the groaning of a people is behind them. They shall deny the God of their people. Quietly radiant there they stand. Will you deny and submit? The first says No and suffers tortures, the second says No and suffers tortures, the third says No and suffers tortures, the fourth says No and suffers tortures, the fifth says

No and suffers tortures, the sixth says No and suffers tortures, the seventh says No and suffers tortures. The mother stands there cheering her sons. Finally, she, too, says No and suffers tortures. Death folds his cloak and sings: Oh yes, oh yes, oh yes.

The woman with the seven heads tugs at the beast, but the beast cannot rise.

Marching, marching, we ride to war, a hundred minstrels march before, the fife and drum, drumm, brumm, for one the road goes straight, for the other it goes to the side, one stands fast, another's killed, one rushes past, the other's voice is stilled, drumm, brumm, drumm.

Cries and rejoicings. On they march, by sixes, by twos, and by threes, the French Revolution marches on, the Russian Revolution marches on, the Peasants' Wars march on, the Anapabtists, all march behind Death, and they rejoice behind him, onward to freedom, to freedom they go, the old world must fall, awake, O morning breeze, drumm, brumm, drumm, brumm, by sixes, by twos, by threes, brothers toward the sun and freedom, brothers toward the light, from the darkness of past ages gleams our future bright, get in step, to the left, to the right, to the left, to the right, drumm, brumm, drumm.

Death folds his cloak and laughs and beams and sings: Oh yes, oh yes, oh yes.

Now Babylon, the Great, can at last pull her beast up onto its legs, it starts trotting, races across the fields, sinks down in the snow. She turns around, howls at the gleaming figure of Death. At her outcry, the beast falls on its knees and the woman sways over the neck of the beast. Death draws his cloak around him. He sings and beams: Oh yes, oh yes, oh yes. The field murmurs: Oh yes, oh yes, oh yes.

The First Steps Are the Hardest

In Buch the detectives and doctors question at great length the death-pale invalid who once was Franz Biberkopf, as soon as he has begun to talk and look around; the detectives, in order to find out what he's been up to, the doctors for their diagnosis. The detectives inform him that a man named Reinhold who played a part in his life, his former life, is in the nets of the police. They talk about Brandenburg, and ask him if he knows a certain Moroskiewicz, and where he is to be found. He has them repeat this several times and keeps very quiet. Now they have left him in peace for a whole day. There is a mower, Death yclept. When he 'gins his scythe to whet, sharper it grows and sharper yet. Look out, little blue flower!

Next day he made his statement to the Chief of Detectives: he had had noting to do with that old Freienwalde case. If this man Reinhold says the contrary, then—he is mistaken. This pale man, this wreck of a man, is then asked to produce an alibi. It takes days before this is possible. Everything in the man struggles against walking back along that road. It seems a closed thoroughfare. Groaning, he utters a few dates. Groaning, he begs them to let him be. He looks anxiously ahead of him, like a dog. The old Biberkopf is gone, the new Biberkopf is still sleeping. He does not utter a single incriminating word against Reinhold. We all lie under the same ax. We all lie under the same ax.

His statements are confirmed, they agree with the statement made by Mieze's gentleman-friend and the latter's nephew. The doctors get a clearer view of the case. The diagnosis of catatonia moves into the background. It was a psychic trauma, involving a sort of twilight coma, his family history is not untarnished, he's been on good terms with old John Barleycorn, that's obvious. When all's said and done, this fight about his diagnosis is the bunk, the fellow certainly was not a malingerer, he had a bat in his belfry, and it was some bat, and that's all there's to it. All right now, that's that. As for the shooting affray in the Alexander Quelle, he is punishable under Paragraph 51. Wonder if we'll get him back here again.

This wobbly fellow, whom we'll call Biberkopf after the dead man, is unaware, as he moves about this house in the capacity of kitchen help, and no questions asked, that a lot of things are still going on behind his back. The detectives are still nibbling at him, what happened to his arm, where did he lose it, where did he receive medical treatment? They make inquiries at the Magdeburg Hospital, but that's old stuff, still, the bulls are interested in old stuff, even what happened as far back as twenty years ago. As it is, they don't get anything out of him, aren't we near the happy end, Herbert's a pimp, too, the boys've all got fine girls, they saddle them with everything and pretend they get their money from them. None of the bulls, of course, believes that, it's quite possible they get money from the girls here and there, but in the meantime they work independently as well. About this subject, however, the boys keep mum.

This thunderstorm also passes over our man, albeit this time he might be let off. This time, sonnie, you got a return ticket.

Then comes the day when he is discharged. The police leave him no doubt about it, they'll keep an eye on him outside as well. They fetch all of old Franz's belongings from the store-room, and he gets everything back; he puts his things on again, there's still some blood on his coat, that's where a cop hit him over the head with the club, I don't want that false arm, you can keep the wig too, if you want, might need it, when you're giving theatricals, we always give theatricals in this place, but we don't wear any wigs, well, here's your discharge paper, good-bye, Chief, look us up one of these days, when the weather's nice out here in Buch, we'll do that all right, you bet, and thanks a lot, I'll open the gate for you.

Well, well, that's behind us, too.

Dear Fatherland, Be Comfort Thine, I'll Watch and Use These Eyes o' Mine

For the second time Biberkopf now leaves a house in which he had been held prisoner, we are at the end of our long road and have just one more little step to take with Franz.

The first house he left was Tegel Prison. Frightened, he had stood beside the red wall, and, as he went away and no. 41 came along and took him to Berlin, the houses did not stand still and the roofs were about to fall upon Franz; he had to walk a long time and sit down until everything was quiet around him, and he grew strong enough to remain there and start all over again.

Now he has no strength. He can no longer see the detention ward. But, lo and behold, as he gets out at Stettin Station, at the suburban section, and the great Baltikum Hotel greets his eyes, nothing moves—nothing at all. The houses keep still, the roofs lie quiet, he can move securely below them, he need not creep into any

dark courtyards. Yes, this man—let's call him Franz Karl Biberkopf, to make a difference between him and the former one, Franz
got that second name, at his christening, after his grandfather, his
mother's father—this man now walks slowly up Invalidenstrasse
past Ackerstrasse, toward Brunnenstrassse, past the yellow Market
Hall, and looks quietly at the stores and houses, what a lot of people there are dashing around, I haven't seen it for a long time and
now here I am back again. Biberkopf had been away a long time.
Now Biberkopf is back again: your Biberkopf is back again.

Then let them come, let them come, the wide plains, the red-tiled
houses, in which light is gleaming. Then let them come: the shivering travelers with bags slung on their backs. It is a reencounter,
more than a reencounter.

He sits in a café on Brunnenstrasse and picks up a paper. Wonder
if my name's in here, or Mieze's, or Herbert's, or Reinhold's. Nothing. Nothing. Where shall I go? Where'll I go? Eva, I must see Eva.

She is not living with Herbert any more. The landlady opens the
door: Herbert's got nabbed, the bulls went through all his things,
he did not come back, his stuff is still up there on the floor, how
about selling it, I'll find out. Franz Karl meets Eva in the West End,
in her gentleman-friend's apartment. She takes him in. She is glad
to welcome Franz Karl Biberkopf.

"Yes, Herbert got nabbed, they sent him up for two years, I do
what I can for him, they asked a lot of questions about you, first in
Tegel, and what are you doin', Franz?" "I'm all right, I'm out of
Buch, they gave me my hunting-permit." "I saw it in the paper the
other day." "Funny, how they always have to write up things. But
I'm weak, Eva. You know what the food is like in a place like that."

Eva notices the expression in his eyes, a dark, silent, searching
expression, she's never seen that in Franz before. She doesn't talk
about herself; as a matter of fact, something's happened to her, too,
something that concerns him, but he is very lame, she gets him a
room, she helps him, he mustn't do anything. He himself says it
as he sits in the room and she is about to go: "Nope, I can't do
nothin' now."

And then what does he do? He starts little by little to go about the
streets, he walks around Berlin.

Berlin: 52° 31' North Latitude, 13° 25' East Longitude, 20 main-line stations, 121 suburban lines, 27 belt lines, 14 city lines, 7 shunting stations, streetcar, elevated railroad, autobus service. There's only one Kaiser Town, there's only one Vienna. A Woman's Desire in three words, three words comprise all a woman's desire. Imagine it, a New York firm advertises a new cosmetic which gives a yellowish retina that fresh bluish tint only possessed by youth. The most beautiful pupil, from deep blue to velvet-brown, can be got from our tubes. Why spend so much on having your furs cleaned?

He walks around the town. There are many things to make a man well, if only his heart keeps well.

First the Alex. It's still there. There is nothing to be seen there. It was terribly cold all winter, so they did not work and left everything lying around, just as it was, the big steam-shovel is now standing on the Georgenkirchplatz, they are dredging sand and dirt from Hahn's Department Store, they've put in a whole lot of rails there, maybe they are going to build a railway station. A lot of other things are happening on the Alex, but the main thing is: it's still there. The people keep crossing the square, the slush is something awful, the Berlin municipality is so noble and humane that it lets all the snow dissolve quietly, *peu à peu*, of its own accord, into mud, nobody's supposed to touch it. When automobiles go by, you'd better jump into the nearest house, or else you'll get a load of garbage, free of charge, all over your top-hat, and you'll risk a suit for appropriating public property. Our old "Mokka Fix" is closed. At the corner there is a new joint called "Mexico," a world sensation: the chef stands beside his grill in the window, Indian Blockhouse. They are putting a fence around the Alexander Barracks, wonder what's doing there, they are tearing down some stores. And the streetcars are chock-full of people, all of them have something to do, the tickets still cost 20 pfennigs, a fifth of a mark in cash: or if you prefer, you can pay 30 pfennigs, or buy yourself a Ford. The elevated also goes by, no firsts or seconds, third-class only, everybody's sitting on comfortable plush-seats, unless they happen to be standing up, which is also possible. Getting off while the train is in motion is prohibited and liable to fines up to 150 marks, but who would dare do that, we'd simply risk an electric shock. Everybody admires the shoe that's brightly polished with "Egu." Passengers are requested to get on and off quickly, during the rush house kindly move toward the center aisle.

All these are nice things that can help a man get on his feet, even if he is a bit weak, provided his heart is in good condition. Don't stand near the door. Well, Franz Karl Biberkopf is healthy all right, wish everybody was as solid as he is! It wouldn't be worthwhile telling such a long story about a man if he were not solid on his legs, now would it? And one day, when an itinerant bookseller was standing in the street, during a terribly rainy spell, cussing about his poor receipts, Cäsar Flaischlen stepped up to the book-cart. He quietly listened to the man's cussing, and then, tapping him on his wet shoulder, said ""Stop that cussing, keep sunshine in your heart!" Thus he consoled him and disappeared. This was the starting-point for the famous sun-poem. It was just such a sun, but different, of course, that Biberkopf had in his heart; and he also poured a little flask of booze and a lot of malt-extract into his soups. Thus slowly he gets in shape again. May I, therefore, take the liberty of offering you a share in my excellent barrel of Trabener Würzgarten, 1925, at the special price of 90 marks for 50 bottles, packing included, F.O.B., or 1.60 marks per bottle, not counting the bottles and boxing which I take back at the agreed price? Dijodyl for arteriosclerosis. Biberkopf has not got arteriosclerosis, he only feels weak, he certainly had a tremendous fast in Buch, nearly starved to death, a man needs time to fill himself out again. That's why he doesn't need to see the magneto-pathologist, where Eva wants to send him, because he helped her once.

A week later, when Eva goes with him to Mieze's grave, she finds cause for surprise right away and she notices how much better he is. No tears are shed, he just puts a handful of tulips on the grave, strokes the cross, and immediately after takes Eva's arm and off they go.

He sits with her in the pastry shop across the way, eating a honey-cake in honor of Mieze, you see she never could get enough of it, it really tastes good, but nothing to write home about, at that. So now we have been to see our little Mieze, a man shouldn't go to cemeteries too much, might catch a cold, maybe next year again, on her birthday. You see, Eva, I don't have to run out here to see Mieze, you can take my word for it, she's always there for me, cemetery or no cemetery, and then Reinhold, well, I won't forget him so easy, either. And even if my arm should grow again, I wouldn't forget him. There are so many things in this world, a fellow would have to be a big boob, and not a human being, to forget 'em. And so Biberkopf talks with Eva, while eating honey cake.

Eva once wanted to be his mistress, but now she's quite given up the idea. This business with Mieze, and then the Insane Asylum, that was too much for her, however much she still likes him. The baby she had expected by him didn't come either, she had a miscarriage. It would have been so lovely, but it was not to be, but it's the best thing in the long run, especially since Herbert isn't there, and her gentleman-friend prefers, by a long shot, that she shouldn't have a kid, as in the end, the good man had found out that the baby might very likely be by somebody else, you can't blame him for that.

They sit quietly together, thinking backward and forward, eating honey cake and devil cake with whipped cream.

Forward March and Get in Step and Right and Left and Right and Left

We see our man once more at the trial of Reinhold and Matter the tinner, alias Oskar Fischer, charged with murder and complicity, respectively, in the affair of Emilie Parsunke, of Bernau, on the date of September 1, 1928, in Freienwalde near Berlin. Biberkopf is not a defendant. This one-armed man excites general interest, quite a sensation, in fact, the murder of his sweetheart, love-life in the underworld, he was mentally unbalanced after her death and suspected of being an accomplice, a tragic destiny.

During the trial, the one-armed man who, as the experts state, has now recovered and can be questioned, gives the following testimony: Deceased (he calls her Mieze), did not have an affair with Reinhold. Reinhold and he were good pals, but Reinhold had a terrible, abnormal craving for women, that's how it came about. Whether Reinhold has predispositions to sadism, he doesn't know. He suspects that Mieze resisted Reinhold in Freienwalde, so he did it in a fit of rage. Do you know anything about his youth? No, I didn't know him then. Has he not told you anything? Did he drink? Yes, I'll tell you how it was: In the old days he did not drink, but finally he did start drinking, how much I can't say, but formerly he could only stand a sip of beer, always drank mineral water and coffee.

That's all they can get out of Biberkopf about Reinhold. Nothing about his arm, nothing about their quarrel, their fight, I shouldn't have done it, I shouldn't have taken up with him. Eva and some members of the Pums gang are sitting in the courtroom. Reinhold and Biberkopf stare fixedly at each other. The one-armed man has no pity for the man in the prisoner's box between the two police-men, who is getting his neck in a sling, he has only a curious devo-tion for him. I once had a faithful comrade, never a better one could there be. I must look at him, keep on looking at him, nothing seems more important than to look at you. The world is made of sugar and dirt. I can look at you quietly, without batting an eye. I know who you are. I now find you here, m'boy, in the prisoner's box, out-side I'll meet you a thousand times more, but my heart will not turn to stone on account of that.

Reinhold has planned, if anything should go wrong at the trial, to expose the whole Pums gang, he'll get them all into trouble if they make him mad, he is keeping that up his sleeve, especially in case Biberkopf starts shooting off his mouth before the judge, that dirty son of a bitch, it's on his account I'm in this hole. But then the Pums crowd are all sitting in the courtroom, that's Eva over there, that's a coupla detectives, we know those bulls. Then he gets calmer, hesitates, thinks things over. A man is dependent on his friends, I'll get out some time, and I may need 'em inside, too, I won't make things so easy for the bulls, and then, strange to say, Biberkopf is acting white. They tell me he's been doin' time in Buch. Funny, how that boob has changed, queer look he's got, as if he couldn't turn his eyes around, they musta gone rusty on him out in Buch, and how slow he talks. He probably still has a screw loose somewhere. But Biberkopf knows that, although Reinhold does not testify, he owes him no gratitude for it.

Ten years' prison for Reinhold, murder while temporarily insane, alcoholism, impulsive disposition, unprotected youth. Reinhold ac-cepts the sentence.

Somebody in the courtroom screams, when the sentence is pro-nounced, and sobs aloud. It is Eva, the thought of Mieze has overpowered her. Biberkopf, hearing her, turns around in the witness box and then he, too, sinks heavily into himself, and holds his hand in front of his forehead. There is a mower, Death yclept, I'm yourn, she came to you so lovable, protected you, and you, oh Shame, cry Shame!

Immediately after the trial Biberkopf is offered a job as assistant doorman in a medium-sized factory. He accepts. I have nothing further to report about his life.

We have come to the end of our story. It has proven a long one, but it had to unfold itself, on and on, till it reached its climax, that culminating point which at last illuminates the whole thing.

We have walked along a dark road, at first there was no streetlamp burning, we only knew it was the right road, but gradually it grew bright and brighter, till at last we reached the light and under its rays were able to make out the name of the street. It was a process of revelation of a special kind. Franz Biberkopf did not walk along the streets the way we do. He rushed blindly through this dark street, knocking against trees, and, the more he ran, the more he knocked against trees. Now it was dark, and, as he knocked against the trees, he shut his eyes in terror. And the more he knocked against them, the greater became his terror, when he shut his eyes tightly. His head all bunged up, almost at his wits' end, at last reached his goal. As he fell down, he opened his eyes. Then the streetlamp shone bright above him, and he was able to read the sign.

Now at last he is assistant doorman in a medium-sized factory. He is no longer alone on Alexanderplatz. There are people to the right, and people to the left of him, some walk in front of him, others behind him.

Much unhappiness comes from walking alone. When there are several, it's somewhat different. I must get the habit of listening to others, for what the others say concerns me, too. Then I learn who I am, and what I can undertake. Everywhere about me my battle is being fought, and I must beware, before I know I'm in the thick of it.

He is assistant doorman in a factory. What is fate anyway? One is stronger than I. If there are two of us, it grows harder to be stronger than I. If there are ten of us, it's harder still. And if there are a thousand of us and a million, then it's very hard, indeed.

But it is also nicer and better to be with others. Then I feel and I know everything twice as well. A ship cannot lie in safety without a big anchor, and a man cannot exist without many other men. The true and the false I will know better now. Once I got myself into trouble for a single word and had to pay bitterly for it, this shan't happen to Biberkopf again. The words come rolling up to us, we must be careful not to get run over; if we don't watch out for the autobus, it'll make applesauce out of us. I'll never again stake my word on anything in the world. Dear Fatherland, be comfort thine, I'll watch, and use these eyes o' mine.

Often they march past his window with flags and music and singing. Biberkopf watches coolly from his door, he'll not join the parade any more. Shut your trap, in step, old cuss, march along with the rest of us. But if I march along, I shall have to pay for it later on with my head, pay for the schemes of others. That's why I first figure out everything, and only if everything's quite OK and suits me, I'll take action. Reason is the gift of man, jackasses replace it with a clan.

Biberkopf is working as assistant doorman, takes numbers, checks cars, sees who comes in and goes out.

Keep awake, keep awake, for there is something happening in the world. The world is not made of sugar. If they drop gas-bombs, I'll have to choke to death; nobody knows why they are dropped, but that's neither here nor there, we had the time to prepare for it.

If war comes along and they conscript me, and I don't know why, and the war's started without me, well, then it's my fault, it serves me right. Keep awake 'mid the strife, we're not alone in life. Let it hail and storm, there's no way of guarding against it, but we can defend ourselves against many other things. So I will not go on shouting as once I did: Fate, Fate! It's no use revering it merely as Fate, we must look at it, grasp it, down it, and not hesitate.

Keep awake, eyes front, attention, a thousand belong together, and he who won't watch out, is fit to flay and flout.

The drums roll behind him. Marching, marching. We tramp to war with iron tread, a hundred minstrels march ahead, red of night and red of day, deathward leads the way.

Biberkopf is a humble workman. We know what we know, the price we paid was not low.

The way leads to freedom, to freedom it goes. The old world must crumble. Awake, wind of dawn!

And get in step, and right and left and right and left, marching: marching on, we tramp to war, a hundred minstrels march before, with fife and drum, drrum, brrum, for one the road goes straight, for another it goes to the side, one stands fast, another's killed, one rushes past, another's voice is stilled, drrum, brrumm, drrumm!

Translated by Eugene Jolas

Lion Feuchtwanger

From Jew Süss

[. . .]

Isaac Simon Landauer, Court Treasurer to the Duchy of Württemberg, had been in Rotterdam arranging credits with the Dutch East India Company in settlement of accounts with the Palatinate. From Rotterdam he was urgently summoned by an express messenger to come to the Countess Würben at Wildbad. On the way thither he had encountered a business colleague, Josef Süss Oppenheimer, Chief Minister of Finance and War for the Palatinate, and also Treasury Agent for the spiritual princes of Cologne. Josef Süss had just completed a succession of interesting and exhausting business deals, and was anxious to recuperate in some spa or other, so he was easily persuaded to accompany Isaac Landauer to Wildbad.

They traveled together in Süss's elegant private carriage. "Costs you at least two hundred rix-dollars a year, this carriage." announced Isaac Landauer, with good-humored and slightly mocking disapproval. In the dicky sat Süss's valet and secretary, Nicklas Pfäffle, once a notary's assistant, a pale, stout, phlegmatic fellow whom he had encountered in Mannheim when he was working in Advocate Lanz's office, a man who could turn his hand to anything and who had accompanied him since on all his journeys as his personal attendant.

Isaac Landauer wore Jewish dress, with a curl on each temple, a caftan and a straggling goatee of reddish yellow turning to gray. He even wore the Jewish badge, in obedience to a custom introduced a hundred years ago into the duchy, a hunting-horn with the letter S on it, although no magistrate would ever have dreamed of exacting compliance from such a distinguished and powerful man, who was high in favor both with the Duke and the Countess. Isaac Landauer was the cleverest financier in the West of Germany. He had connections extending from the Viennese Oppenheimers, the Emperor's bankers, to the capitalists of Provence, from the rich traders of the Levant to the Jewish financiers in Holland and the Hanseatic cities which financed deep-sea voyages. He leaned back awkwardly and stiffly on the cushions, a dirty insignificant-looking man, and buried his cold and bloodless hands in his caftan. Somewhat sleepy with traveling, his small eyes half closed, he studied his companion with a slight smile, good-natured but a little mocking. Josef Süss, handsome, clean shaven, and fashionable, almost dandified, in his dress, sat upright, and took in with his quick keen restless glance every detail of the landscape which was still veiled by a fine rain.

Isaac Landauer looked his colleague up and down with amicable amusement. The elegantly-cut brown coat, bordered with silver, made of the finest cloth, the powdered peruke with its fastidious formal curls and the delicately-pleated lace ruffles, these alone must have cost forty gulden. He had always had a weakness for this Süss Oppenheimer, whose eager and adventurous spirit flamed so fiercely in his great, restless, round eyes. So this was the younger generation. He, Isaac Landauer, had seen enough and to spare of life, the kennels of the Jews' quarter and the pleasure-houses of the great. Confinement, dirt, persecution, arson, death, oppression, utter helplessness—and pomp, spaciousness, despotism, lordliness and beauty. He knew the machinery of diplomacy as only three or four others at most within the Empire knew it, and his eye could examine down to the smallest detail the whole apparatus of war and peace, of the government of men, His countless business interests had given him a keen eye for the connections between things, and he was aware, with a good-humored and mocking awareness, of the absurd and subtle limitations of the great. He knew that there was only one reality in this world—money. War and peace, life and death, the virtue of women, the Pope's power to bind or to loose, the Estates' enthusiasm for liberty, the purity of the Augsburg Confession, the ships on the sea, the coercive power of princes, the Christianizing of the New World, love, piety, cowardice, wantonness, blasphemy and virtue, they were all derived from money and they would all turn into money, and they could all be expressed in plain figures. He, Isaac Landauer, knew that; he was among those who sat at the source and could divert the stream to bring barrenness or plenty. But he was not so simple as to cry his power aloud; he kept it secret, and an infrequent amused little smile was all that witnessed to his knowledge and his power. And one thing more. Perhaps the rabbis and scholars of the Ghetto were right when they expounded in detail, as if they were realities, God, and the Talmud, and the Garden of Eden, and the Valley of Destruction; for his part he had little time for such theories, and was more inclined to believe certain Frenchmen who dismissed things of that kind with elegant scorn. Nor did he bother much about them in practice; he ate what he liked and worked on the Sabbath as on a weekday. But in his dress and appearance he clung obstinately to the traditions of his race. He wore his caftan as he wore his skin. In it he entered the closets of princes and of the Emperor. That was the other secret and more profound symbol of his power. He disdained gloves and perukes. He was indispensable, and this was his triumph, even in his caftan and his ritual curls.

But now there was this Josef Süss Oppenheimer, the younger generation. There he sat, in proud magnificence, with his buckled shoes and his lace ruffles, and puffed himself up. It was not subtle, this younger generation. It did not understand the refined pleasure of keeping power secret, of possessing it without betraying it, and the still more refined pleasure of relishing its flavor quietly and exclusively by oneself. Knickknacks and silk stockings, and an elegant traveling carriage with attendants up behind, and the trumpery external signs of possession, these were of more account to it than a jealously guarded chest containing a bond on the City of Frankfurt or on the Margrave of Baden's Treasury. A generation without fineness, without taste.

And yet he liked Süss. How he sat there, tense in every fiber, eager to cut himself an enormous slice of that cake, the world. He, Isaac Landauer, had given the young man's ship a push out into the open when in spite of all its efforts and its wild tacking it was unable to get away from the shore. Well, now the little ship was sailing bravely in the middle of the stream, and Isaac Landauer observed with quiet curiosity its course and direction.

A post-chaise approached them. A large portly man with a strong, resolute face was inside, and beside him a fat, round, stupid woman. They were perhaps a married couple on the way to a family festivity. While the two carriages were trying to pass each other with much fuss and a noisy crossfire of greetings, jests, and curses from the coachmen, the man set himself to exchange a few friendly words with Süss. But when he saw Isaac Landauer in his Jewish dress, he drew back ostentatiously and spat forcibly and far. The woman, too, tried to impose a severe and contemptuous expression on her stupid good-humored face. "Councillor Etterlin from Ravensburg," said Isaac Landauer, who knew everybody, with a little chuckling laugh. "They can't stand Jews, the Ravensburgers. Since they had that infanticide case, and murdered, burned and pillaged their Jews, they have hated us more than all the rest of Swabia. That was three hundred years ago. Today there are humaner and more complicated ways of stealing money from the Jews. But when such injustice has once been done, of course the victims continue to be hated, even three hundred years later. Well, we'll survive it."

Süss hated the old man at that moment. He hated the filthy side-curls, the greasy caftan, the chuckling laugh. One was compromised by his idiotic, old-fashioned Jewish rig-out. He couldn't understand the man, with his senile follies. He had stacks of money, endless credit, dealings with all the courts and the confidence of all the princes—he, Süss, sat in front of him like a lizard before a crocodile; and the man went about in a dirty gaberdine, inviting people to hoot and spit at him, and was satisfied with amassing wealth which got no further than his bank account. What was money unless it was transformed into prestige, magnificence, houses, horses, gorgeous clothes and women? Did the old man have no desire to spit upon others, as he was spat upon, to go on still further? Why did one seize power, if not to display it? The Ravensburg ritual murder case! That was the kind of trash he brooded on! Long forgotten, out of date, buried. The modern world, thank God, was better, more polished, more civilized. A Jew today, if he only set about it in a politic manner, could sit down to table with great noblemen. Was not his grand-uncle, the Viennese Oppenheimer, in a position to boast in the Emperor's presence that the victory of the Imperial arms against the Turks was in great part due to this Jew's assistance? And the Imperial War Office and Field-Marshal Prince

Eugene had acknowledged the truth of this statement with the best grace, and had formally delivered their thanks under seal. One only needed not to stick obstinately to idiotic notions such as running around in a gaberdine and side-curls. Then even Councillor Etterlin of Ravensburg would exchange compliments and be at one's service.

[. . .]

At Hirsau, in the still, spacious chamber in Weissensee's house, the chamber with the great curtains, sat the Duke with his host, the insinuating Privy Councillor Schütz with the harelip, and the surly Major von Röder with the clumsy paws, almost always gloved. The image of Magdalen Sibylle with her childishly ardent face still hung about the room, and the father could see the girl sitting over her book, in the still circle cast by the lamp, childlike importance on her face, absorbed. He saw her as she had been earlier: the brown, glowing, masculinely keen cheeks, the blue, unwavering eyes on their strange contrast to the dark hair. How much light, how much hope, he had drunk from that face! How sad, how cold, now that it was extinguished!

In the room which had once been filled with his expectations, with his work on the Bible Commentary and the dreams of the girl, the Duke tippled and swore, pleased with his company. Karl Alexander felt young, fresh, in gross health. His green coat was wide open, his doublet unbuttoned, his fair, graying hair untied. It had been a rare thought, to come and hunt here. In Stuttgart and Ludwigsburg things were going excellently, the Catholic plot was in good train. Then the new singer in the opera, Ilonka, pleased him marvelously; really he might have taken her with him. But no, it was better as it was. By day only the wind in your face, in the evening wine and good, strong masculine talk. No women! No politics! No Parliamentary rabble! How young he was! *Mille tonnerre!* he did not feel his fifty years at all! He could still laugh and find pleasure in nothing but a bit of forest and a good shooting.

Neuffer went to and fro and poured out wine. In the shadow, beyond the circle of light cast by the lamp, crouched the Turkish servant. Karl Alexander drank deeply, stretched his limbs, laughed hoarsely over the course obscenities of Röder and the subtle ones of Weissensee, and the very filthy anecdotes which Herr von Schütz snuffled with great aplomb and a copious intermixture of French. He related, then, stories out of the camp, adventures out of his Venetian period.

Weissensee listened with fierce pleasure. When one thought of it, the Jew was responsible that his quiet chamber was being defiled with this vulgar and disgusting talk. Well, when one desired to know something, then one must pay for one's curiosity. But it would repay him, it would repay him!

As the gentlemen, heavy with wine, were going to bed, Weisensee remarked to the Duke that he had prepared a surprise for the next afternoon. He advised with submission that tomorrow they should sleep all the morning, then dine well, and then he would conduct His Excellence to the forest and show him his grand surprise.

"Weissensee!" laughed the Duke. "Old fox! Excellence! President! I am pleased with you. You know something new for every day. You are a very useful prelate." And he clapped him on the shoulder and staggered into his bedroom.

Next day, replete with food and the old wine which Weissensee had cunningly provided, they set out. First they took the main road, then turned into a cart track. There they left the carriage, followed a footpath, and stood at last before a lofty and strong wooden fence. Trees barred their further view.

There they stood before the fence. The south wind was blowing. The wine had not yet evaporated from their brains. They puffed and sweated and joked. The surprise was hidden behind there, then; would it be worthwhile? would not Weissensee give them a hint? He begged them not to shy at the trouble, and clambered over the fence. They followed with difficulty, chuckling, pressed on farther, curious, intrigued, amused.

They reached the flower terraces and the white square house, and were astonished. Confused pictures rose before Karl Alexander; of Venice and Belgrade. But none of them knew what to make of this white, strange house in the middle of the Swabian forest.

"The house belongs to the Magus," said Weissensee, "the uncle of the Finance Director."

They gaped dumbfounded. A nasty aftertaste of the wine arose in Karl Alexander, he felt suddenly heavier in spirit, was conscious of his lame foot, of the wretched, rough path he had come. In an inexplicable embarrassment he gazed at the house, with a vague feeling that stony, troubled gray eyes looked at him out of it. "The Magus! Well! Well!" he said in a hoarse muffled voice. "This is truly a surprise."

"That is not all," Weissensee smiled, his fine, fastidious mouth a little wry. "Does your Excellency permit us to go on?"

Karl Alexander pulled himself together, cleared his throat. "The old sorcerer is due me a talk anyway," he shouted. "Let us give the owl a fright in his own nest."

The gentlemen went nearer, knocked, and nobody stirred, went into the house. The aged, broken-down serving-man intercepted them: What did they want? His master. He was not there. Moreover he received nobody, he added with irritation. Then they would like to look round the house for a little, said Weissensee. What an idea, growled the servant surlily. They should clear out. Nobody had any business there.

"Hold your jaw!" shouted Major Röder angrily.

But the old man repeated with a growl: "Nobody has any business here. Nobody commands here, but my master."

"And the Duke of Württemberg," said Karl Alexander. And the gentlemen passed the gaping servant and entered the Rabbi's chambers. They regarded timidly and jeeringly the folios, the symbols of the Cabbalistic Tree, the Divine Man, he strange inscriptions, and exchanged ironical comments. But the uncanny room subdued their customary exuberance, and made them abashed and quiet.

"Damn it all!' cried Karl Alexander suddenly, "it is as if we were in a church. Wine, Neuffer! Seeing the old sorcerer is not at home, we will find out if his spirits will perform magic at our table for a good glass of wine."

"Should we not have a look at the other rooms first?" suggested Weissensee. "Perhaps we will be able to smell something more out still!" And his fine, long nose seemed to sniff, and his keen restless eyes to search every nook.

While Neuffer set out the wine they looked through the few remaining rooms of the little house. Before a door stood Jantje, the stout, garrulous maid; she sought to keep the gentlemen back. But they thrust her aside and pressed into the room. There in the farthest corner sat the girl, anxious, large-eyed, at bay, dressed in her Eastern costume. Before the loveliness of her clear, pale face and black hair, her eloquent, brimming eyes, they recoiled. "What the devil!" the Duke swore half aloud to himself. "So my Jew has kept this to himself! He has concealed all this from me, the scoundrel! He wanted to keep this peach for his private delectation."

There was still a little space between the girl and the Duke's party. A silence fell. Naemi had sprung up, stood behind the chair, crouching into the corner of the room. The men, struck mute by the strangeness of the apparition, remained near the door and stared.

Into the silence the insinuating voice of the Consistorial President broke smoothly: "The demoiselle is the daughter of the Finance Director." And smiling amiably upon the dumbfounded gentlemen; "Yes, that was my surprise."

"Well, I'm damned! Well, I'm damned!" muttered Major Röder over and over; but nothing else escaped him. But the Duke, recovered from his surprise, became enthusiastic, and devouring the girl with his large blue eyes, grew voluble in extravagantly conventional comparison. "A masterpiece of a girl! A head as if made of ebony and ivory! Like a fable of the orient!" Privy Councillor Schütz chimed in adroitly: the Finance Director was a genius, but the production of his loins were still better than those of his brain.

Weissensee was silent. To please the Duke he could have praised the girl better even that he, or than the dry Schütz or the coarse Röder, who could find no better compliment that his raucous: "Well, I'm damned! Well, I'm damned!" But Weissensee was mute. He only gazed at the girl, looked her up and down, a deep smile round his fastidious mouth. Eh, my lord Privy Finance Director, certainly this is a jewel and well worth to be preserved inviolate. The eighth wonder of the world. A Hebrew Venus! She had eyes that came out of the Old Testament, and she did not look as if she were only lovely to behold. The Apostles came to Magdalen Sibylle and spoke to her. To this girl the prophets might well come. You were slyer than I, my Lord Finance Director, but not sly enough. You should have hidden her farther away and in greater secrecy. *Voila!* Now we will see what curious faces you will make.

Meanwhile the others had been exclaiming over the great beauty of the girl. Even Herr von Röder found something to say, and growled: "Who would have credited the old fox with such a cub?" But Naemi stood in the corner, her whole body tense with fear and repugnance, and looked at them. "What do they call you, then,

Demoiselle?" the Duke asked at last. And, as she did not reply: "Shulamite? Salome? Shall we lay someone's head at your feet?"

But Naemi remained silent, her repulsion and fear wringing her with almost physical pain. "It is not from her father that she has this shyness," opined Herr von Schütz. But Major von Röder, rough and impatient, broke out: "Answer, Jewish brat, when your prince asks a question!"

"Hold your tongue, Röder!" said Karl Alexander. And to the terrified girl, pressing into the corner, he said kindly, as to a child: "I won't harm you; I won't eat you. Shy little dear! Mimosa! Do not be so coy!"

Meantime Jantje, the maid, had pushed her away to the girl, and stout and courageous remained near her, but in obvious anxiety and perplexity. "I am really your sovereign," continued Karl Alexander a little impatiently, "your and your father's well-affected Duke and lord. And now tell me what your name is."

"The demoiselle is called Naemi," replied the maid.

"Now we know it!" grunted Röder, relieved. "Naemi, a comical name!" and spluttered with laughter.

But the Duke commanded: "Come here, Naemi! Kiss the hand of your Sovereign!"

The maid whispered to the child and pushed her gently forward. Slowly, as if drawn against her will, her eyes on the ground, she advanced, and with greedy eyes, pleasantly excited, Weissensee looked.

They went into the study and drank; compelled the child to pledge them. On the walls the Cabbalistic Tree bloomed, blocky characters and confused symbols interwoven; the Divine Man gazed immovable. The child took a sip, but further she would not go. She fled and locked herself in her room, terrified, trembling in every limb, and icy cold.

But in the study, among the drinkers, Herr von Schütz remarked, apropos the magical symbols: "First this place savored of the Jewish College and the churchyard. Now it is redolent of Paris and perfume and the *Mercure galant,* and the whole ghostly atmosphere has fled. It is extraordinary how a little piece of fresh femininity can destroy the prestige of the most learned Magus."

The party broke up. Röder and Schütz went first, then the Duke with Weissensee, last of all Neuffer. The massive Duke supported himself graciously on the arm of the frail and slender Weissensee. "You arranged that cunningly," he congratulated him. "We will have some fun out of that for a long time. Such a secretive slyboots, my Jew. We will baste him, until he turns all colors." But that was not Weissensee's intention, to go away now and have a little fun in future at the expense of the Jew, that was not enough for him. He had not taken all his trouble for that. The Jew was sly, the Jew knew what he possessed in his child. He would send her out of the country, far away; in any case he would not bring his daughter to court, as Weissensee had done. The Jew had his wits about him; and even when they were flattered, there was always the magus to restrain him. And if the Duke went now, he would not be brought a second time to Hirsau. Then Weissensee's great, consuming curiosity would have to remain forever unsatisfied.

The President of the Church Council saw the child before him, crouching into the corner, her great eyes in her pale face with a horrified disgust in them, and a soft, gentle feeling overcame him. But this feeling perished in the wild, tormenting curiosity which filled him completely, which lay like a sickly oppression on his heart and caught his breath.

He walked more slowly, begged the Duke not to over-exert himself, advised him to rest for a little. Neuffer had wine still; Weissensee attended upon the Duke. Karl Alexander drank. Weissensee turned the conversation perpetually on the girl; in his courteous, insinuating voice, in half hints, the compete connoisseur, he praised her charm, how young and yet how ripe she was. In their bloom these Jewesses were beautiful, were unique, the best of all, with a cool fire like the wines of the South. But their bloom was very brief, afterward they withered and were loathsome.

They must be taken when they were as shy and ardent as this one; whoever drank the cream of this had tasted a unique joy which would remain with him all his days.

So he dropped his poison into the Duke's ears. Karl Alexander drank and felt his blood careering through his veins, mounting, falling. Evening came, the wind blew in warm gusts, among the trees the image of the girl floated before him, her shy, tender form; he sighed softly. "So might the women have looked," Weissnesee spoke his thoughts aloud and they were the Duke's as well, "the women whom King Solomon took to himself. He had a thousand wives. Thus lived the Kings in the Old Testament. The Testament of the Finance Director." And he laughed his tiny, quiet laugh.

Suddenly Karl Alexander stood up, brushed from his coat a few dried leaves and twigs, and said to Weissensee in a smothered voice that he wished to walk for a little in the forest alone. Weissensee would make his excuses to the other gentlemen; they should not wait for him; they were to go home and send the carriage back; Neuffer he kept with him. The Consistorial President bowed and went. As soon as he was alone he breathed freely, lifted his arms in triumph, his mobile face contorted, strange, smothered, babbling sounds coming from his lips.

Meanwhile Karl Alexander, followed by his Chamberlain, went, as fast as his lame foot allowed him, back through the forest; night was falling. When he came to the house with the terraces it was already dusk; dark, ragged clouds hurried across the sky; there was no moon; he struggled for breath against the strong, warm gusts of wind. A great adventure! He was young, young! He clambered over the fence, and stole like a thief through the trees. Oh, this was good, better than wrangling over clauses with the lousy rabble in Parliament. If one had only a mask on, one might feel as young as in Venice.

Was there a dog about the house? Perhaps the Magus had drawn a magic circle, closed the threshold with sorcery, so that whoever crossed it would not be able to stir.

He told Neuffer to remain behind, and surreptitiously surveyed the house. He had noted the simple ground plan of the building. There lay the girl's room; it was dark. Where the light burned, that was the room with the magical drawings. Would she be there? It would be easy to climb the espalier. He would look.

Softly groaning he climbed up to the window. "Yes, there she sat, her arms rigid, quite still, with her great, anxious, helpless eyes. "Hst!" he whispered to her, smirking, blinking, sly.

She leapt up in terror, saw the red massive face, the blue, greedy, insistent eyes, and recoiled, her body convulsed, her eyes fixed on the panting Duke. He laughed. "Have I scared you? Stupid child! Have no fear!" He swung himself completely into the room and came toward her, panting and sweating: "Look, that shows you how good your sovereign is at climbing." She, feeling her last moment had arrived, fluttered in to the farthest corner of the room, babbling senseless, inaudible prayers, cowering into herself. Coming nearer he spoke with pacifying words as to a child, but his horrible kindness only added to her terror. Her eyes like frozen pools, her lips white, she stared at him, until at last, impatient, brutal, he wrested her to him, showered kisses upon, her, fumbled for her breasts. Then she slipped from between his hands, cried with little, toneless, childish cries for her uncle, tore herself free, reached the door, fluttered up a ladder. The ladder led to the roof.

Once up there, she inhaled deep, quick breaths of the warm night wind. The moist, sultry wind took her in its arms, carried her forward. She listened for a sound behind her; all was still. She extended her arms, she felt free; her uncle had helped; now the good, moist wind carried the fumes and exhalations of that beast away. She walked forward, almost dancing, to the edge of the flat roof. Were not those voices coming out of the forest? The deep, silkily caressing voice of her father, and the surly ill-tempered, but oh! so comforting voice of her uncle. And she smiled into the night.

Then up the ladder stumbled the beast, panting, softly cursing. But now she had no fear. Hither it floated from the forest, a coach drawn by aerial horses, and stopped at the roof. Smiling, with a noiseless movement, she stepped in.

When he reached the top Karl Alexander saw nothing. She had gone up the ladder, and there was no other exit. Hell and damnation! had she, practiced in the magical arts of the old man, changed herself into a night bird? Was she floating up there like the black ragged clouds and laughing at him? Cursed little creature! He stood grim and disabused; a strong wind blew, and tore at his coat and his hair, matted with sweat. Old ass that he was! If he had only taken the Jewish brat below there, the little prude, and thrown her over the table, not heeding her pretences and affectations! Of what use, devil take it, was his sovereignty? Now he had been done out of his night, and the people at Hirsau would be justified if they laughed at him.

In deep vexation he groped his way down the ladder again. His foot pained him and he was dog-tired. Painfully and with difficulty he got through the window and out of the house. Then he heard the Chamberlain's voice sunk to a hoarse whisper, frightened and agitated: "She is lying among the flowers!" He thought she had hidden herself there, laughed: "The rogue," and stumbled hastily through the uncertain darkness in the direction which Neuffer indicated.

Yes, there she lay among the flowers. The flowers were tossed wildly to and fro by the wind; they shook a thousand arms; but she lay quite motionless. He cried playfully to her: "You rogue! How did you manage to get here?" As she did not reply he gripped her cautiously by the arm, bent her head back, felt it hastily, recoiled in horror; recognized that she was dead, but did not understand.

Rags of clouds flew above. Hard colored, the curve of the new moon appeared, giving a little light. The Chamberlain stood apart timidly. But the Duke of Württemberg knelt by the corpse of the young Jewess, in the wind, among the flowers, in stupid, perplexed discomfort, a poor insignificant human being amid the wind and the night.

Had this really happened? Had she stepped into space? Had it been intentional? In some way he was connected with this dead girl, was the cause of her death.

Bah! He had jested a little. Who could have guessed that the girl was so prudish? With others of the same age he had had very different luck, and what had they been? Daughters of the highest Swabian blood! So the Jewess had no need to treasure herself so highly. It often happened that children, only if one gave them a bad word, would throw themselves into a pool or do something to themselves. That often happened. They were insane, they did not know what life was. And those who were, perhaps, the cause of such things could surely not be blamed for them.

Nevertheless he could not rid himself of his oppressive, overpowering discomfort. The Jew had hidden her, hidden her so deep and so securely, and yet there she lay now, rigid and stiff, and all his cunning had not been able to keep her safe. A gust came from somewhere, who knew whence? and the light was quenched. Singular, that, and very perplexing. There she had sat in the light a little while ago, her eyes glowing with life, and now she lay in the night and no warm wind could keep her from growing cold.

The forest lay dark, hostile and full of mystery. Voices came out of it, confused, mocking. The man kneeling in the wind was afraid. The fairy-tales of his childhood wavered before him, thronged round him—figures in a magical forest, filled with the spirits of the damned; they tore him by the neck, by the hair; long, ghostly arms stretched toward him. And suddenly he entered again into that dumb, shadowy dance; before him the Magus held his right hand, behind, Süss held his left. And there, curtsying, almost bowing to the ground, was that not the girl too, in the ring? And he heard the surly, ill-tempered voice of the Magus. He heard every sound distinctly, and strained his mind to understand; but he could not. And all was so melancholy, mistlike, colorless!

With a snarling curse he tore himself out of his trance. He was dog-tired, now he would sleep. There lay a corpse in the wind. Well, he had seen many a corpse. When he ordered an attack, and the dead fell around him, he was ultimately responsible there too. It was madness, it was over-fastidious, to think so long about it. Why should he think so much more of the dead Jewess than of thousands of gallant Christian officers and soldiers who had died beside him and through his agency? For this he was Duke. God had so disposed it that where he went life bloomed or death fell.

He would go now and sleep. And the girl? Should he let her lie like that? Truly wind or rain could not hurt her anymore. If he went now, the affair would be done with, concluded, *finito*. Tomorrow the domestics would discover the girl, send word to Süss. Süss would rack his brains to discover how and by what agency she had died. But probably he would not go any further. He would hold his tongue. He would bury his girl in all secrecy and hold his tongue. And those who were with him, the Duke, Weissensee and the others, would do the same. The affair would be done with, dead and dumb and buried; an end of it.

So he would—no, he would not! Should he turn tail? Hoho! that might look as if he feared the Jew. He would awaken the domestics, send a messenger on horseback to Süss, await him here, and say to him: "Fine tales you tell, you rascal! Your daughter has been found here, dead, in the wind. If you had not concealed her, you Jew, you secretive, crafty fellow, if you had brought her safe to Stuttgart, this would never have happened."

Yes, this must be a great blow, a deep affliction, for the Jew. The cursed, uncanny, incomprehensible pack! First he brings one into ridicule and contempt with the Esslinger affair. And then he has this strange child, and before one can touch her, she is dead. There would never be an end to the story even if he were simply to go away now and return to Stuttgart and never speak a word of it to anyone. This child's face was harder to forget than the faces of a thousand dead, distorted, disfigured soldiers. He recalled the Jew's face, very pale, with the red, small, voluptuous mouth, the quick, arched eyebrows. It was smooth and white like the face of the child. Even from the first the fellow had made up to him, insinuated himself into his confidence, with his cursed, slavish, oriental dog's eyes. Truly, when one thought of it, there was nothing much to be got out of him at that time. A petty prince whom the Parliament would not even grant a trifling advance; no great capital or profit was to be wrung out of him. And if eventually things turned out differently and Süss's trust had been paid back with usury, the business had not turned out well for him in the end. If he was so concerned for the Jew Jecheskel, he must be far more concerned for his child, so tenderly cherished. And there she lay now on the ground, a little morsel for the worms, lay in the wind and was dead.

To be rid of him! To be rid of the Jew! He would dismiss him. He might keep his savings and gold and precious stones and bonds and what he had embezzled at the expense of the country, might take them with him, unhindered. He, the Duke, would add a monster *douceur* to it. But he must go! He must go!

But no, he should not go. That would seem as if he, the Duke, had a guilty, oppressive feeling in his presence. No, he would not dismiss him.

But an end now! He would think it over later! Meanwhile, devil take it, he would sleep. He went to the door, knocked loudly, brutally pointed out the corpse to the old, sleepy, surly servant who opened; without further explanation went past the mute, staring man. The old servant broke out in animal howls, the maid babbled and moaned and whined her grief. Karl Alexander paid no attention to their cries, went into the house, and had only a scornful grimace for the fearful imaginations of Neuffer, who was terrified of the bewitched house with the corpse. The Duke threw himself on an ottoman in his clothes, and slept, snoring, rattling in his throat, in deathly profound slumber.

[. . .]

Back in Stuttgart, Süss flung himself with wild fury into his work. He burst recklessly now into the Catholic plot, seized upon everything that happened to fall within the utmost reach of his competence. He cast away his crutches of servility and amiability. With immeasurable, mocking arrogance he ruled his whole entourage, made ministers skip like lackeys. There flared out of him a gloomy, sardonic contempt for all that is usually called human worth, freedom and responsibility. In a kind of dreadful play he imposed upon his subordinates ever new, superfluous humiliations, and when they stood exposed, their little scrap of manhood ruined and in tatters, he sneered at them with his quiet, open scorn, and feasted his abysmal contempt for mankind on their ignoble patience.

Quite openly, now, and with both hands, he plundered the Ducal money chest. He abstracted monstrous percentages for himself, sold the Duke worthless baubles at colossal prices. He laid new burdens on the groaning, fainting land, and what he extorted in this way he put openly into his own revenues, not Karl Alexander's. If hitherto he had oppressed the Duchy with business-like efficiency to extort money, now he throttled and strangled it out of a perverse joy in extortion. He did all this with the most audacious effrontery, did it so openly that Karl Alexander must notice it, and sought in every way to exasperate the Duke by his conduct of affairs. But the Duke was silent.

The Jew's appearance was altered. His graceful, elastic step was harder, with an officerlike brutality. Harder, more decisive, too, his jaw; and the rich, chestnut-brown hair, which earlier he had worn free wherever he went, he concealed now always under a severe peruke. The whole man was older, more hard. His gloomy voice had lost all its insinuating sweetness; often now it barked imperiously, roughly—with a Jewish intonation, said his enemies. His eyes remained keen and attentive, even full of untiring devotion usually; but when he was off his guard, they had something biting and venomous, and subdued only with pains their hostile, yellow, gloomy fire.

More heavily stepped under her rider the mare Assjadah. No more did she carry her radiant, hated and yet admired, nobly free lord; she carried a load, a sullen task-master, sunk into himself, the enemy of all and hated by all.

He gave splendid parties as before. But their atmosphere was poisoned, and brought no enjoyment to the guests. On such occasions he loved to pursue this one or that with well-aimed, humiliating jests, either in fun or otherwise, and expose their domestic or political misery; and he knew very well how to hit the place that hurt most.

To women he gave a mocking, supercilious gallantry. One there had been; her skin was white, in her eyes were the dreams of thousands of years; if she spoke the song of the nightingale was like a croaking compared to her tiny voice. Now she lay in Frankfurt, earth over her, earth beneath her. What did the others want here? They existed, tattled, laughed and gave themselves in return for a little flattery. That was their existence, but the other one had lived.

Weissensee had emerged out of his profound confusion and perplexity of mind, and now always hung about Süss. Something fermented and worked in that monstrous, exorbitant man, who was unlike everybody else; something was growing in him, a grandiose, thousand-hued catastrophe. He was not like him; he was not the man to cringe and submit. In voluptuous expectation the Consistorial President smelt already the sulphurous fumes of the approaching eruption, and only the lust to see it, to be in it, kept the broken man going.

And Süss's challenging arrogance grew. He behaved openly as if he were lord of the country, and recognized no limitations.

At this time happened the affair of young Michael Koppenhöfer. It was like this:

After two years' travel for the purpose of study through Flanders, France, and England, the young man, nephew of Professor Johann Daniel Harpprecht, related, too, to Philip Heinrich von Weissensee, returned to his native Swabia, to enter as actuary into the service of the Ducal authority. With a strong, brown, keen face, clear blue eyes under dark hair, the young man—he was twenty-three—looked like a brother of Magdalen Sibylle. From his travels he had brought back mad ideas about human freedom and human responsibility, with an intense hatred of all despotism; all the young, springlike, pure thoughts of a new and better state, a more just and humane order, filled him with exuberant ardor, almost burst the bosom of the young enthusiastic man.

He stayed with Harpprecht. The aging man, whose wife had died very young after a few months of marriage, had brought up the nephew; he had missed him bitterly during his two years abroad; he showered now all his inarticulate love upon the youth.

During his tour Michael Koppenhöfer had become doubly proud of the constitution of his native land, freer than that of any other German state. True, he had always known of the military autocracy of the Duke, the Jesuitical autocracy of the Würzburgers, the economical of the Jew. But it was one thing to read of it in letters and brochures, and another to be in the midst of it, to see with one's eyes, to feel with one's mind the insolent oppression, the naked, derisive presence of tyranny. The young man saw the trade in official posts, the sale of justice, the oppression of the people. The rich, lovely fertile land, bled white and eaten up; thousands pressed to the colors; tens of thousands in hunger and misery; hundreds of thousands corrupted in body and mind. An unbridled court vaunting itself in intemperance and lust; power swaggering in gay uniforms, with mocking casuistries maliciously setting aside the clear and noble provisions of the constitution. The administration corrupt, justice a harlot, freedom, his dear, much-prized freedom, a mockery, a rag with which the Duke, the Jesuit and the Jew wiped themselves.

A holy consuming indignation filled the youth, gave his brown, keen face the look of manhood, burned more urgently in his keen, blue eyes. Oh, his slender young eloquence! Oh, his noble rage and exaltation! Consuming grief over the foulness of his native land had shaken badly and crippled old Johann Daniel Harpprecht. Now the simple, straight-forward man put all his hopes in the youth, and his sterile, lonely evenings bloomed and became young in that fresh young presence.

Süss felt unsympathetic to the actuary from the first. The tall statue of the young man, his stiff, angular dignity, in which nevertheless there was nothing of the lout or the yokel; all this exasperated him. Even the transparent honesty of the young man's political convictions put him into a temper. But before the catastrophe at Hirsau he would have feared the youthful impetuosity of the actuary, Michael Koppenhöfer, as little as he had feared the hackneyed pathos of the publicist Moser; would have let the one as he had let the other go free without question: officials of the most revolutionary temper had not been visited with the slightest reprimand.

But now, after the happening at Hirsau, Süss's poisoned nature burned with a more gloomy fire against the unbroken freedom of spirit and generous daring of the youth. He fixed his gloomy gaze upon him, and maliciously, playfully, crouched for a spring. The young man's imprudence provided him very soon with grounds for a sharp and severe warning.

For a long time old Johann Daniel Harpprecht had foreseen a conflict of this kind; but he could not bring himself to throw water on Michael's fine ardors. It was the right of youth to be imprudent, to straighten out what was crooked, even if it should break its arm in the attempt. But he felt a load on his breast, a bitter taste in his mouth, when he thought that his weary evenings would again be solitary, without the warming glow of the youth's presence. Always he hoped that his own great prestige would prevent Süss from proceeding more strongly against Michael.

Amid the misery of his fatherland, the waste of corruption around him, the actuary Micheal Koppenhöfer saw a great and gentle light. This was Demoiselle Elisabeth Salomea Götz, the daughter. Her blond, pastel-like loveliness impressed deeply the enthusiastic, easily fired young man. As soon as he heard that she gently but persistently rejected Karl Alexander's advances, she became to him the symbol of human freedom. Their images swam into each other, and he spoke of his beloved freedom and the dear Demoiselle Elisabeth Salomea Götz in the same breath.

By this time Süss thought he need pay no more attention even to Harpprecht. On the grounds that in spite of being warned he had not kept in mind his due respect for the Duke, and had delivered unseemly, godless and blasphemous speeches against him, young Michael Koppenhöfer was deprived of his post. By an act of special clemency and grace, he was not proceeded against as a criminal. But he had to leave the country within fourteen days, and his banishment was to last all his lifetime.

This had always been on the horizon. But now that it had come it was unexpected and broke old Harpprecht to pieces. Oh, to sit alone and dull in the great, empty room, only with books and parchments, his company only the shadows beyond the lamplight! They formed themselves into images of haggard, bent exiles, hungered and ragged; or they stretched thin, covetous Jewish fingers toward him. Whatever they were they oppressed and stifled him. And if the youth were to be there, obstinate and living, and were to lift his thick dark eyebrows, the shadows would fly away; his piercing blue eyes would drive out of every corner the menacing, chilly twilight. But he is not here; the Jew has banished him out of the country; the Jew will not let him come back.

In heaviness of spirit the old man wrestled with himself, came to a decision, stood before the Duke. He had never begged for anything, he had never asked for more than his just due, he was accustomed to have others come to him and beg. It was an acute trial for the upright man to stand there as a suppliant, and his words came awkwardly and with difficulty. The judgment was right, and not at all too severe. Yet the Duke should reflect that many things in the land were not in a good way, and if the young man spoke out his disaffection openly, that was better perhaps than if he had dealt, like others, in hidden poison. Karl Alexander listened gloomily, pressed Harpprecht's hand warmly, promised hesitatingly that he would think it over.

Brusquely he demanded a report of the case. Süss himself came. Yes, it was exactly as the professor had related. Only Süss and the professor had different opinions about what was needed for the protection of a prince's dignity. The Duke was vexed, cast upon Süss the blame for getting him into such a distressing position, from which he must either retreat now or else refuse a faithful and highly-esteemed man his first and only request. Impudent and venomous, Süss retorted that he knew it would vex His Excellency more to have to refuse a request by the German professor than one by his Jewish Finance Director. He had had other and very good grounds, however, for putting the actuary out of the way. If, to come to the point, he added, pert and confidential, the Duke did not advance much with the Götz ladies, the young man was the chief cause that His Excellency, at least with Demoiselle Elisabeth Salomea, was so much at sea. Growling darkly, the Duke relapsed into silence.

Alone, he decided in spite of all to let the actuary remain in the country. The Jew was off his head as well as insolent. Ho! would he, then, Karl Alexander, have any fear that a rascally democrat and rebel should put his nose out of joint with the lady? Or did the Jew imply that now, after Hirsau, the Duke was scared before every little virgin, and trusted no more in his manhood? A ferocious lust came over him. *Mille tonnerre!* He was Karl Alexander, Duke of Württemberg and Teck, and in spite of every rebellious scoundrel, he would make this virgin small and humble. In any case the rivalry did not scare him, and he would annul the sentence now.

But when he was about to dictate the order, it occurred to him to think it over one more time, and leave the decision to the next day. Next day he went to Ludwigsburg. Amusements, presentations, other political activities thronged upon him. They day arrived when the sentence came into force, and no counter order had appeared. Young Michael Koppenhöfer must go out of the country, and the evening of Professor Johann Daniel Harpprecht's life was left barren and lightless.

Now Karl Alexander could take no retrospective measures that would help. When he thought of the Götz ladies he was very relieved on the whole. But this he would not admit. He was seized, rather, with a sullen rage against the Jew. He was responsible for everything; he had set the choice before him; Harpprecht or him, the Jew.

Süss knew that Karl Alexander had never committed a deliberate piece of trickery, and that he would not admit his real motives for this banishment. This made him itch to pester the Duke continually, so that this verdict might become a thorn in his flesh. He would drop casually: "Now your affair with the Götz ladies will go better, seeing we have got rid of young Koppenhöfer." The Duke would be on the point of breaking out, but he would content himself with a growl, and respond without much vigor: "We? We?" But Süss would only smile, and remain silent.

It came to the ears of Süss's enemies that his proceedings against young Koppenhöfer had been too hasty for the Duke's taste, and not desired by him. They could not understand the long-suffering of the Duke, and utilized the opportunity to raise a protest against his incomprehensible patience. They brought up the fact, and garnished it with statistics, that Süss oppressed the land and sucked it dry only for his own purse, without anything accruing to the Duke; that over every transaction the Duke was cheated and plundered. They spoke for almost two hours, and Karl Alexander did not repulse them; he heard them to the end, he even listened while they explained details which he did not quite understand; he listened most attentively of all to Dom Bartelemi Pancorbo, who showed at great length how shamelessly Süss humbugged and swindled him over inferior precious stones. When the gentleman were finished he courteously dismissed them without expressing any opinion.

Next day, without being summoned, Süss appeared at the palace. He heard, he said, they were intriguing anew against him. He wished to be spared the shame of having his papers shuffled through a second time. He reiterated his request therefore, most submissively but resolutely, to be given his demission.

"Listen, Jew," said Karl Alexander. "You bought a stone for me in October for more than five thousand ducats. What is the stone worth?"

"Today hardly five hundred," said the Jew. And his eye meeting the Duke's, he added with an impudent, provocative smile: "Yes, such stones as these have collector's prices, and their value changes."

"Very well," said Karl Alexander. Then both were silent. The Duke rang, and commanded Court Chancellor Scheffer to come, at once. Twenty minutes passed, however, before the Chancellor came, and during these twenty minutes neither of the two men spoke a word. They did not even think of one another. There was a deep, wonderful, complete silence in the spacious and glittering room. Pictures and dreams came and went between the Duke and Süss, Süss and the Duke. The surly voice of the Magus was in these dreams, and the dead child was in them, her fingers arranged to make the symbol of Shin.

At last Herr von Scheffer came. He was counted now among the enemies of Süss; he sweated when he saw the Jew, imagining that the Duke wished to confront him with the Jew, and conjecturing that he would have a hard task against that diabolical man.

But it happened differently. Hardly had the Chancellor entered before the Duke took up a position, and severe, military, cold and imperious, addressed the confused Minister: "The Finance Director, present now, complains of slanders touching his conduct of affairs, and demands his resignation. In recognition of his services, performed to our full and gracious satisfaction, we with that everything should be done to retain him. Will you, then, Your Excellence, prepare immediately a deed, a deed of legitimation or absolution or whatever you like to call it, a Ducal order, that the Finance Director in all his transactions, past and future, is answerable to nobody. By no one, whoever it may be, can he be brought to book for any of his actions. Will you prepare this document immediately and in proper form, and give to us for signature, so that next week it may be published in the official gazette. We are waiting."

Karl Alexander's voice while he said this was so icily precise, that the terrified Chancellor did not venture upon any remonstrance. Neither the Duke nor the Jew spoke a single word while Schefffer drew up the document. Without speaking, too, Karl Alexander signed his name. Then, scarcely able to constrain himself any longer, he ordered the Chancellor: "To the official gazette with the rubbish!" The Minister retired trembling.

Süss gave thanks with the most servile, devout protestations for this enormous, unearned favor, this extraordinary proof of trust. But his eyes were not grateful, they were bold and challenging and sardonic. Dumb and hostile the two men surveyed each other, and Karl Alexander recognized that he had not bought himself off.

"Go, Jew!" he cried at last, raging. And Süss went, but not like the Chancellor. He went slowly with his head lifted high, consciousness of his power in his deep, malignant smile.

But the Duke, alone, foamed and raged; tore, tugged, chafed himself sore against the invisible, inextricable, horrible thing which bound him to that man.

[. . .]

On two grandstands, each accommodating six hundred people, sat the ladies and gentlemen, the senior civil servants and officers, the foreign ambassadors, the members of the Commission and of Parliament. Privy Councillor von Pflug was well to the fore. He had been afraid up to the very last that the Hebrew beast would escape after all through some crafty Jewish trick. But now the hour had come, now the aim of his life had been achieved. Now, now this very minute, his hated enemy would swing aloft and be strangled. The Privy Councillor's hard eyes greedily spied out under the coat collar the Jew's neck, the place for the halter. It is glorious to look on at the death of an enemy, it is as balm to the eyes; pleasant and lovely is the sound of the death-drums. And the clang of the bell. Among the ladies were many who had known Süss intimately and yet escaped the inquisition for some reason or other. They now gazed at the man with whom they had been involved, alienated and shuddering. For he had passed as very young, and he had possessed a young man's strength, as they knew, and he could not be more than forty at the very most; but now he had white hair and looked like an old Rabbi. One should really feel ashamed of having been in bed with him. But it was remarkable that they did not feel ashamed. They gazed at this extraordinary man with eager fascination. In a minute he would be dead, in a minute he would be dumb forever, and all danger would be over and they would be disentangled from him by a forcible and gruesome deed. They sat waiting for that, eager and trembling, yearning for it, and shrinking from it in terror. Most of them would rather have lived all their lives in fear of discovery if he could have been kept alive.

Young Michael Koppenhöfer was also on the grandstand. At last the millstone would be ground to powder which had for so long hung round the country's neck; at last the corrupter of the land would die a disgraceful death. But—this man had not been dismissed by Elisabeth Salomea, casually and hastily among bundles of books and underclothing, this man had taken her, without even having to exert himself particularly. The old and broken Jew, what was it he possessed? What was his secret? With bitter envy he stared at the man in the gallowscart. But the young Privy Councillor Götz, sitting among the Commissioners, looked on with silent and gloomy satisfaction. Now his mother's and sister's disgrace would be wiped out. Let everybody dare to look askance at him after this! How he would blast them! How well he would know what to do!

Weissensee, old and won, sat, elegant and feeble, on the tribune. Thou hast conquered, O Judaen! Thou hast conquered, O Judaen! Ah, the Jew had triumphed over him again. The Jew had tasted of every dish—had relished with his eyes, his sense and his brain all the daintiest pleasures of the world, had emptied to the dregs every cup of triumph and despair, had been filled with the tragic end of his child and then had prepared and accomplished a conspicuous, oversubtle, hellishly diabolical revenge; and now he died this death with the eyes of the whole world upon him, this romantic and apparently voluntary death, much more heroic than death on the field of battle. Surrounded by raucous hate and cherishing love, ambiguous and great. What would be left of himself, Weissnesee? A couple of lamentable verses by his poor bourgeoise daughter. But the other was sure of immortality. What he was, his life, his observations, his thoughts and his death, would be of perpetual interest to later ages;

his ideas, his life, his feelings and his death would be appreciatively reenacted.

Süss was unbound from the gallowscart. He stood blinking, his limbs numb. He saw the people in the boxes, the periwigs, the painted faces of the ladies. He saw the troops, who made a cordon round the gallows place. Aha, they had exerted themselves! There were at least five companies round the gallows alone. Of course Major von Röder was in command, and conspicuously at his post. Yes, it needed a lot of strategy to get him completely out of the world. Süss saw the tens of thousands of faces, curious women, with their mouths ready to bawl, men ready to smack their lips and growl with satisfaction, children's faces, chubby and large-eyed, destined to become as empty and malicious as the ugly visages of their parents. He saw the breath of the mob, rising in a white vapor, very solid in the clear frost, the ravening eyes, the stretched necks, which had formerly bowed before him so devotedly. He saw the bird cage, the complicated and dishonorable devices for his execution. And while he was looking at all this something lowed and bleated in his ear. It was the Town Vicar Hoffmann who had insisted on waiting for him by the gallows and was now speaking to him once more of heaven and earth, forgiveness of sin, of God, faith and atonement. Süss gazed around him while he listened to the other, and then slowly looked the Town Vicar up and down, and turned away and spat. Eyes opened wide, and a low hiss of indignation arose from the crowd and as quickly died away.

Now the assistant hangmen in their gaudy new uniforms seized him and opened his coat. At the touch of their coarse, clumsy hands he recoiled with disgust, his numbness disappeared and he hit out desperately to defend himself. All necks were stretched still further. It was curious to see how the man in the white beard and the fine clothes, with the diamond blazing on his hand, fought and struggled with the assistants. The children laughed with glee and clapped their hands; on one of the stands a rouged lady began to scream shrilly and continuously, and had to be removed. The Jew's cap fell on the damp ground and was trodden into the slush. The hangmen seized him firmly, tore off his coat, pushed him into the cage and put the halter round his neck.

There he stood. He heard a little breeze, the breathing of the mob, the clattering hoofs of horses, the curses of the clergymen.

Were these the last things he was to hear on earth? He thirsted to hear something else, he opened wide his heart and his ears, yearning to hear something else. But he heard nothing else, save his own breathing and the pulse of his own blood. The cage was already rocking and rising. And then, through the empty and cruel hubbub there soared another sound, the sound of loud and guttural voices crying: "One and Eternal is the God of Israel, Jehovah, Adonai, the Everlasting, the Infinite!" It is the Jews, the small Jaakob Joshua Falk, the burly Rabbi of Fürth, the shabby Isaac Landauer. They are standing wrapped in their praying-cloaks, they and seven others, making ten as is prescribed; they pay no heed to the crowd, which turns its eyes away from the gallows toward them; they sway their bodies wildly, and they stand crying, shrilling, wailing the prayer for the dying, clear over the broad square. "Hear, O Israel. One and Eternal is Jehovah Adonai!" The words mount from their lips as white vapor in the strong frost, up to the ears of the man in the cage, and the son of Marshal Heydersdorff opens his mouth and cries in answer: "One and Eternal is Jehovah Adonai."

Nimbly the gaudy hangmen swarm and clamber up the ladders. The cage rises, the halter tightens. Underneath, the Town Vicar execrates the dying man: "Depart into hell, accursed Jew and villain!" But the shrill Adonai of the Jews is in the air and in the ears of everyone. It is returned from the cage, until the voice is strangled by the halter.

[. . .]

Translated by Willa Muir and Edwin Muir

From The Oppermanns

When Dr. Gustav Oppermann awoke on the sixteenth of November, which marked his fiftieth birthday, it was long before sunrise. That was annoying. The day would be a strenuous one and he had intended to sleep late.

From his bed he could distinguish a few bare tree tops and a bit of sky. The sky looked distant and clear, there was no sign of the fog that is so common in November.

He stretched and yawned. Then, resolutely, now that he was well awake, he threw back the clothes from the broad, low bed, swung both his feet lightly to the floor, emerging from the warmth of the sheets and blankets into the cold morning, and went out on the balcony.

Below, his little garden sloped, in three terraces, down to the woods; to right and left wooded knolls rose, and beyond the more distant tree-covered area further hills and woodlands appeared. A pleasantly cool breeze ascended from the little lake, which lay out of sight to the left, and from the pines of Grunewald. In the profound silence that precedes daybreak, he breathed the forest air deeply and with enjoyment. The strokes of an axe came faintly from the distance; he liked the sound; the rhythmic blows emphasized the stillness.

Gustav Oppermann, as he did every morning, rejoiced in his house. No one, if he were suddenly transported here without warning, could suspect that he was less than three miles from the Memorial Church, the center of the West End of Berlin. Really, he had chosen the prettiest spot in Berlin for his house. He had here all the peace of the countryside and in addition, every advantage of the great city. It was only a few years since he had built and furnished this little place in Max Reger Strasse, but he felt as though he had grown together with the house and the woods, as though each one of the pines surrounding him were a piece of himself. He, the little lake, and the sandy street below, which, fortunately, was closed to motor vehicles, belonged together.

He stood for a time on the balcony, drinking in the morning and the familiar landscape, without thinking much about anything. Then he began to shiver. He was glad he still had a short hour before his daily morning ride. He crept back into the warm bed.

But he could not sleep. That damned birthday. After all, it would have been wiser to leave town and escape the whole bother.

As he was here, he might at least have done his brother Martin the favor of going to the office today. The employees would be vexed, considering the sort of people they were, that he would not be there to receive their congratulations personally. Ah, well. It was too much of a bore to mope about and listen to people's clumsy congratulations.

A self-respecting senior partner ought to take that sort of thing for granted. Senior partner. Rot. No doubt about Martin being the better businessman, to say nothing of his brother-in-law Jaques Lavendel and the chief clerks Brieger and Hintze. No, he was quite right to steer as clear of the business as possible.

Gustav Oppermann yawned noisily. A man in his position should damned well be in a better mood on his fiftieth birthday. Hadn't those fifty years been good years? Here he lay, the owner of a fine house that suited him exactly, of a substantial bank account, of a valuable business partnership; he was a collector and acknowledged connoisseur of fine books, and a gold medalist in sports. His two brothers and sister were fond of him, he had a friend whom he could trust, a host of entertaining acquaintances, as many women as he wanted, an adorable mistress. What ailed him! If anyone had reason to be in good humor on a day like this, it was he. Then, damn it, why wasn't he? What was to blame?

Gustav Oppermann snorted peevishly, threw himself on his other side, determinedly closed his heavy eyelids, and kept his strong, virile head motionless on the pillow. He would go to sleep now. But his fretful resolution was of no avail, he could not sleep.

He smiled like a mischievous boy. He would try a remedy that he had not used since childhood. "I am doing well, better, superlatively well," he thinks. Again and again, mechanically: "I am doing well, better, superlatively well." By the time he will have thought this two hundred times, he should be asleep. He thinks it three hundred times and remains awake.

Nevertheless, he really was doing well. Physically, materially, and spiritually. He had, he could honestly say, in spite of his fifty years, the appearance of a man in the early forties. And that was how he felt. He was not too rich and not too poor, not too wise and not too foolish. Achievements? Gutwetter, the author, could never have succeeded without him. He also had put Dr. Frischlin on his feet. As for what he had published himself, those few essays on eighteenth-century life and literature, they were decent enough books, written by a cultivated man. No more, he didn't deceive himself. All the same they were pretty good for the senior partner of a furniture store. He was a mediocre man without any particular talent. To be mediocre was best. He was not ambitious. At any rate, not very.

Ten minutes more, then at last he could get ready for his morning ride. He grounded his teeth together lightly, closed his eyes but he no longer thought of sleep. To be quite honest, there were, of course, a few things he still wanted. Wish number one: Sybil was a mistress and many people justifiably envied him. The beautiful and clever Ellen Rosendorff was fonder of him than he deserved. Nevertheless, if he didn't get a certain letter from a certain person today, it would be a bitter disappointment to him. Wish number two: he really could not expect the Minerva Press to undertake the publication of his biography of Lessing. Nor was it important in these times whether the life and works of an author, who died a hundred and fifty years ago, were described all over again or not. But all the same, if the Minerva Press refused the book, it would be a blow to him. Wish number three:

He opened his eyes. They were brown and deep-set. He did not feel as peaceful or as resigned as, scarcely a moment ago, he had believed himself to be. Deep, vertical furrows above the strongly moulded nose, thick eyebrows angrily drawn together, he scowled gloomily at the ceiling. It was remarkable how his keen face instantly reflected each change in his impetuous, ever-changing moods.

Should the Minerva people accept the Lessing book, there would still be a year's work on it. If they refused it, he would lock the manuscript, just as it was, in some drawer. In that case, what could he do all through the winter? He might go to Egypt, to Palestine. For a long time he had intended going there. One should have seen Egypt and Palestine.

Should one really?

Rot. Why spoil this beautiful day by thinking about such things? Thank goodness, it was time for the ride at last.

He walked through the little front garden toward Max Reger Strasse. His figure was rather thickset, but in good training. He walked with precise, quick steps, his entire sole firmly pressing the ground, but he carried his massive head high. Schlüter, his servant, stood in the gateway and wished him many happy returns. Bertha, Schlüter's wife, the cook, came out too and wished him the same. Gustav, beaming, acknowledged their meetings in a loud, hearty voice. They all laughed. He rode away, knowing that they were standing looking after him. They would have to admit that he kept himself in damned good form for a fifty-year-old. He looked particularly well on horseback, too, taller than he actually was, his legs being a little short, though his body was long. "Just like Goethe," as his friend of the Bibliophile Society, Headmaster François of Queen Louise School, remarked at least once a month.

Gustav met several of his acquaintances along the road, waved cheerfully to them, without stopping. The ride did him good. He came back in high spirits. It was fine to have a rubdown and a bath. He hummed lustily and out of tune a few not altogether easy melodies, and snorted mightily under the cold shower. He ate a hearty breakfast.

He went into his library and paced up and down a few times with his precise quick step. He felt pleasure in the fine apartment and its tasteful furnishings. At last he sat down before the massive desk. The large windows scarcely separated him from the landscape, he sat as though in the open air. Before him, a bulky pile, lay his morning letters, the birthday letters.

Gustav Oppermann always looked at his correspondence with pleasurable curiosity. One had, from one's first youth, put many feelers out into the world. What was the reaction? There were birthday greetings and congratulations. What else? He rather hoped that perhaps among these forty or fifty letters there might be something to bring excitement into his life.

He did not open the letters, but arranged them according to their senders, those he knew and those he was not sure of. Now, at last, he felt a sharp little thrill. Here was the letter from Anna which he had expected. He held it in his hand for a moment. His eyelids twitched nervously. Then a boyish smile spread over his face, he put the letter to one side, quite out of reach. He was going to postpone reading it, like a child who leaves the most coveted morsel to the last. He began to read the other letters. Birthday wishes. It was nice to have them, but they were hardly exciting. He reached for Anna's letter, balanced it in his hand, took up the paper-knife. Then he hesitated. He was really glad that a visitor came in to disturb him.

The visitor was his brother Martin. Martin Oppermann came toward him, a little heavy on his feet, as usual. Gustav loved his brother and wished him well but this did not prevent his quietly noting that Martin, though he was two years younger, looked the elder. The Oppermanns resembled one another; everyone said so, it must be true. Martin had a large head, like his; his eyes also lay rather deeply in their sockets. But Martin's eyes had a slightly dull, oddly sleepy expression. Everything about him was clumsier, fleshier.

Martin stretched out both hands to him. "What shall I say? I can only hope that everything will stay just as it is for you. I wish this most heartily." The Oppermanns had deep voices. With the exception of Gustav, they disliked showing their feelings. Everything about Martin was reserved and dignified. But Gustav was well aware of his sincerity.

Martin Oppermann had brought his birthday gift with him. Schlüter fetched it in. The coverings were stripped off a big parcel, revealing a picture. It was a burst portrait, oval in shape. Above a stiff collar in the fashion of the eighties, a large head rested on a rather short neck. The head was fleshy and the brow, above deeply set rather sleepy eyes—the Oppermann eyes—was heavy and protruding. The expression was shrewd, thoughtful, and kindly. It was the head of Immanuel Oppermann, their grandfather, the founder of the furniture firm of Oppermann. This was his likeness at the age of sixty, shortly after Gustav's birth.

Martin placed the picture on the big desk, and held it there in his fleshy, well-kept hands. Gustav looked out of his own brown, pensive eyes into the brown, shrewd eyes of his grandfather Immanuel.

No, the picture was not very remarkable. It was old-fashioned and had little artistic value. But the four Oppermanns prized it. It had been dear and familiar to them from their early youth, undoubtedly they saw more in it than there actually was. Gustav liked to keep the light walls of his house undecorated. Only one picture hung in the entire house, in the library. But it had always been one of his dearest wishes to have this portrait of Grandfather Immanuel for his study. Martin, on the other hand, believed it should hang in the private office of the business. Gustav, well as he got on with his brother in other respects, had taken it amiss that he had been denied possession of the picture.

Thus the sight of the portrait filled him with joy and satisfaction. He knew it had been a wrench for Martin to part from it. Beaming, he expressed his pleasure and gratitude volubly.

When Martin had gone, Gustav called Schlüter and instructed him how to hang the picture. He had long made up his mind where it should go. Now it was really going to be put there. Gustav waited impatiently for Schlüter to finish. At last it was ready. The study, the library, and the third room of the ground floor, the breakfast-room, led into one another. Slowly and thoughtfully Gustav let his eyes pass from the portrait of Immanuel Oppermann, his grandfather, his past, to the other, the hitherto unique picture in the house, the one in the library, the portrait of Sybil Rauch, his mistress, his present.

No, the picture of Immanuel Oppermann was really not a work of art. The painter, Alexander Joels, who had executed it on commission for the friends of Immanuel Oppermann, had at that time been grotesquely overrated. Today he was forgotten. But what Gustav Oppermann liked about the picture was actually something apart from its artistic merit. He and his brothers and sister could see in this familiar portrait the man himself and his work.

The life-work of Immanuel Oppermann was nothing great in itself. It was merely successful commerce. But it meant more in the history of the Jewish inhabitants of Berlin.

The Oppermann family had been established in Germany from time immemorial. They originally came from Alsace. There they had been bankers on a small scale, merchants, gold- and silver-smiths. The great-grandfather of the present generation of Oppermanns had come to Berlin from Fürth in Bavaria. The grandfather,

Immanuel Oppermann, had filled important contracts as purveyor to the Germany armies operating in France in the years 1870–71. A framed document hung in the private office of the Oppermann firm, in which the taciturn Field Marshal von Moltke attested that Herr Oppermann had rendered the German army good service. A few years later Immanuel had founded the furniture firm of Oppermann. It was an undertaking which manufactured household furniture for the middle classes and, by standardizing its products, was able to give good value. Immanuel Oppermann took a personal interest in his customers, sounded them, tempted their obscure desires into the light of day, created new needs for them, and then proceeded to supply these needs. His jokes were repeated everywhere. They were an excellent combination of lusty Berlin common sense and his individual brand of genial scepticism. He became a well-liked personality in Berlin and soon his popularity began to extend beyond the city. It was by no means due solely to personal vanity that the Oppermann brothers later registered his picture as the trademark of their firm. Through his integrity and manifold connections with all sorts of people, he contributed toward making the emancipation of the German Jew a fact, not a mere printed paragraph: giving them a real home in Germany.

[. . .]

In the Lower Sixth of the Queen Louise School, during the five minutes' recess between the mathematics and the German lesson, the boys stood about and talked excitedly. The authorities had now at last made up their minds who was to succeed Dr. Heinzius, the master who had come to so lamentable an end. Their choice had finally fallen upon Dr. Bernd Vogelsang, hitherto senior master at Tilsit School, the man whom Rector François had referred to at Gustav Oppermann's birthday party as causing him a certain amount of uneasiness. The boys were anxious to see their new form master. Much depended, for each one of them, upon what type of man the new teacher was. As a rule, it was a snap for the Berlin boys to have to deal with provincial schoolmasters. They felt themselves superior to them from the very start. What could a man from Tilsit know about life? Was there a sports pavilion there, or a subway, or a stadium, or an aviation field like the Tempelhof or a Luna Park or a Friedrich Strasse? Besides the boys knew already that Dr. Vogelsang was tainted with Nationalism. In the Queen Louise School, under the mild and liberal Rector François, Nationalism was not popular.

Kurt Baumann, one of the boys, related for the hundredth time a case which had occurred in the Kaiser Friedrich School. The fellows there had found a peach of a way of showing the Nationalist senior master, Schultes, which side his bread was buttered on. As soon as he got going with his nonsense they started humming with their mouths shut. They had practiced for days, so that the combined humming drowned out the voice of the master, without anything being noticeable on the boys' faces. At first the senior master Schultes thought the reason for the noise was an airplane. He had been encouraged in this belief. When, however, the airplane regularly turned up every time he started his sickly rot about the Fatherland, he smelt a rat. But they kept their secret. Immense pains were taken to discover the reason for the noise, a thousand conjectures were made. Was it the central heating, the water supply, or men in the cellar? They kept the fellow guessing. He was a nervous, sensitive man, that Nationalist senior master Schultes. When the humming started for the fourth time, he burst into tears and turned his face to the wall. Later, to be sure, when the board of trustees took up the investigation, the Nationalists in the class gave the game away and the ringleaders were punished. All the same, what the boys at the Kaiser Friedrich School had managed to do had been pretty good. The idea might also come in handy at the Queen Louise School, in case the gentleman from Tilsit tried to abuse them.

Heinrich Lavendel did not consider the idea practicable. He was sitting on his desk opposite his place, fair-haired, sturdy, swinging his legs alternatively as though he were doing gymnastics. Heinrich Lavendel, in spite of the fact that he was rather short, looked healthier and stronger than most of his companions. They were nearly all pale and had an indoors look about them. His delicate skin was fresh and bronzed. He devoted all his spare time to taking exercise in the open air. Gazing with interest at the tips of his swinging legs as they flashed in and out, he said thoughtfully: "No, that's no use at all. It might work the first and second time, but we would be caught the third time." "What can we do, then?" asked Kurt Baumann, slightly hurt. Heinrich Lavendel stopped swinging his legs, looked around, opened his extremely red lips, and said lightly, shrugging his broad shoulders: "Passive resistance, my lad. That's the only sensible line to take."

Berthold looked thoughtfully with his piercing gray eyes at his cousin Heinrich Lavendel. That chap had an easy time of it. To begin with he was an American. Sometimes, even now, an English word often rose to his lips out of memories of his early years. Secondly, he was the indispensable guard of the Lower Sixth's football team. These were two facts which were bound to make an impression on a Nationalist teacher. His, Berthold's, position was more difficult. Not only because the new man was to teach German and history, Berthold's favorite subjects, but, above all, because it depended on this man whether he would be allowed to make his speech on "Humanism."

A group had gathered around another of the boys, Werner Rittersteg. There were six or seven of them and they were the Nationalists of the class. They had not had an easy time of it so far, they were coming into their own now. They held their heads together. They whispered and laughed and put on important airs. The senior master Vogelsang was a member of the executive committee of the "Young Eagles." That was important. The Young Eagles were the secret society of the youth of Germany, the atmosphere around that society was full of adventure and secrecy. They formed blood-brotherhoods, they had a secret court. Whoever betrayed their slightest plan was cruelly punished. The whole thing was enormously exciting. The senior master Vogelsang would certainly let them join.

This senior master Vogelsang, meanwhile, was sitting in Rector François's office. He sat erect, not leaning back, his reddish hands, covered with downy fair hair, resting on his thighs, his pale blue eyes fixed unwaveringly on François, determined to get this interview over with as few gestures as possible. Involuntarily, Rector François looked for the sabre at the side of his new senior master. Bernd Vogelsang was not tall, but he made up for his lack in stature by an excess of vigor. The upper and lower parts of his face were separated by a flaxen mustache. A long scar divided his right cheek into two sections and a straight parting divided his hair.

Already, two days ago, when he reported to Rector François, Bernd Vogelsang had received no favorable impression of the establishment. Everything he had hitherto seen confirmed all his previous gloomy forebodings. Of the entire staff of the place he only approved of a single person, Mellenthin the porter. He had stood at attention to the new senior master. "Were you in the Service?" Bernd Vogelsang had asked. "In the 94th," Mellenthin the porter had answered. "I was wounded three times." "Right," Vogelsang had replied. But so far that had been the only good mark he had been able to give. That milksop, Rector François, had let the school go to the dogs. It was a good job that he, Bernd Vogelsang, had turned up in time to put new life into the thing.

Rector François gave him a friendly smile from under his white, trim moustache. Frau François had told him to be sure and make himself agreeable to the new master. The new master was not making it easy for François. His curt way of speaking, the concise, sharp, and at the same time banal arrangement of his phrases, his hackneyed, editorial style, were all deeply repugnant to him.

The new man had turned, with a sudden jerky movement, to contemplate a fine, old marble bust. It was an ugly, profoundly shrewd head, that of the author and scholar, François Marie Arouet Voltaire. "Do you like that bust, my dear colleague?" asked the Rector politely. "I like the other better," declared the new master bluntly in his broad, squeaking East Prussian accent, pointing to the opposite corner, at the bust of another ugly man, the head of the Prussian author and king, Friedrich von Hohenzollern. "I can understand, Herr Rector," he went on, "why you have placed the great king's antithesis facing him. On the one side the man of spirit in all his grandeur, on the other the creature of intellect in all his paltriness. The dignity of the German is emphasized by the contrast. But allow me to confess frankly, Herr Rector, that I should find it disagreeable to have that grinning French rascal before my eyes all day long." Rector François continued to smile, doing his best to be polite. He found it difficult to make contact with the new teacher. "I believe it is time," he said, "for me to introduce you to your class."

The boys stood up as the two gentlemen entered. Rector François spoke a few sentences. He spoke more of the dead Dr. Heinzius than of Dr. Vogelsang. He gave a sigh of relief when he had closed the door between himself and the new master.

Dr. Vogelsang had stood stiffly erect during the Rector's speech, with his chest thrown out and his pale blue eyes staring straight before him. He now sat down, smiled, and did his best to be genial. "Well, boys," he said, "now we're going to see how we shall get on with one another. Show me what you know." Most of the boys had disliked the new teacher at first sight. The high collar, the affected air of smartness, did not impress them. Provincial, from the darkest corner of the provinces at that, they had said to themselves. But his first words were not clumsy ones, that was not a bad tone to take with the Lower Sixth.

It was a lucky chance for Vogelsang that they happened to be reading just then "Arminius's Fight," by Grabbe, a piece by a semi-classic poet of the first half of the nineteenth century, crude, weak in ideas, but full of genuine passion, at times extremely picturesque. The battle fought by Arminius, the magnificent entry of the Germans into history, this first great victory of the Germans over the Romans was a favorite theme of Bernd Vogelsang's. He compared the poems written about Arminius by Grabbe, Klopstock, and Kleist. He asked few questions himself, he gave his tongue free rein. He was no lover of subtleties, he did not care for shades of meaning as the dead Dr. Heinzius had, his object was to infect the boys with his own enthusiasm. He occasionally allowed them to put in a word. He assumed the tone of a comrade, wanted to find out at the start to what extent they were familiar with patriotic poetry. One of them mentioned Kleist's wild hymn, "Germania to Her Children." "That's a magnificent poem," cried Vogelsang with enthusiasm. He knew the piece by heart and recited some of the powerful lines of insane hatred against the foreigner:

> *Every hiding place and meadow*
> *Color with their bones ash-gray;*
> *Whom the fox and whom the raven*
> *Scorned, let them be fishes' prey;*
> *Choke the Rhine with their foul corpses,*
> *Let it—heaped with their dead bones—*
> *Change its foaming course and circle*
> *The Palatinate's proud stones.*
> *'Tis a frolic when the huntsman*
> *Finds the wild wolf's hidden lair.*
> *Strike him dead! The law of nations*
> *Questions not your reasons fair.*

Vogelsang recited the hate-verses with ecstasy. The scar which divided his right cheek turned red, but the rest of his face remained as rigid as a mask, while the words issued from between his high collar and his small, flaxen moustache. They had a particularly odd effect in his broad East Prussian accent. The entire man was a little ridiculous. But Berlin boys have a delicate ear for what is honest and what is put on. The boys of the Lower Sixth were well aware that the man who stood before them, ludicrous as his appearance was, spoke from the heart. They did not laugh. They looked, instead, with a certain abashed and inquisitive air at this fellow, their teacher.

When the school-bell rang, Bernd Vogelsang had the impression that he had won all along the line. He had got the Lower Sixth of a liberal, hostile Berlin school well in hand. Rector François, that milksop, would be astonished. The class was, of course, already deeply corrupted by the subversive poison of Berlin intellectualism. But Bernd Vogelsang was full of confidence: he would manage to rock his nurseling's cradle.

In the quarter of an hour's recess which followed he sent for the two boys who were scheduled to give the next lectures. Talking is more important than writing. He considered that thesis of the Leader of the Nationalist party sacrosanct, he took the lectures very seriously. He soon came to an understanding with the first boy, who intended to speak on the Nibelung legend, on the subject: "What is the lesson for modern times of the struggle of the Nibelungs with King Etzel?" "*Bon!*" said Vogelsang. "We can do a great deal with that."

But what was the intention of the other boy, that gray-eyed one? "Humanism and the Twentieth Century"? He took a good look at the gray-eyed boy. A tall chap, of striking appearance. The black hair and the gray eyes didn't go together. A boy like that might fit all right in Berlin: in a band of young men, marching in step, he would be incongruous. "I beg your pardon?" asked Dr. Vogelsang. "Humanism and the Twentieth Century? How can one usefully discuss such a gigantic theme in a mere hour?" "Dr. Heinzius gave me a few tips," said Berthold modestly, his fine, deep, manly tones much subdued. "I am surprised that my predecessor approved of subjects of such an abstract character," continued Dr. Vogelsang. His voice sounded sharp, squeaky, and pugnacious. Berthold was silent. What could one answer? Dr. Heinzius, who would certainly have had something to say, lay in the cemetery at Stahnsdorf. Berthold himself had thrown a shovel of earth on the coffin. Dr. Heinzius could not help him now. "Have you been working long at the subject?" the squeaky voice asked again. "I have pretty nearly finished the lecture," Berthold answered. "I was to give it next week," he added almost apologetically.

"I'm sorry for that," said Vogelsang, courteously enough. "I don't like such abstract subjects. I should like to forbid them on principle." Berthold pulled himself together, but he could not prevent his chubby features from twitching just the tiniest bit. Vogelsang noticed it, not without a certain satisfaction. To conceal it, he repeated: "I am sorry you have gone to so much trouble. But, *principiis obsta.* After all, work is its own reward."

Berthold had really grown a little pale. But the other was right. One could hardly explain humanism in an hour. Vogelsang was not a sympathetic figure to Berthold; but he was a devil of a fellow, he had shown that during the lesson. "What subject would you suggest to me, sir?" he asked. His voice sounded hoarse.

"Let's see," meditated Dr. Vogelsang. "What's your name, by the way?" he asked. Berthold Oppermann told him. Ah, thought the teacher, that explains it. That was the reason for choosing that odd subject. He had already noticed the name, particularly, in the class-list. There were Jewish Oppermanns and there were Christian Oppermanns. No need for a long investigation. The Jew, the despoiler, the enemy, betrays himself to the expert at a glance. Humanism and the Twentieth Century. They always hide themselves behind masks of long words.

"How would it be," said he lightly, in the tone of a comrade—in dealing with this dangerous boy it was worthwhile taking double precautions, "how would it be if you took Arminius the German as the subject for your lecture? What do you say, for instance, to the theme: 'What can we learn today from Arminius the German?'"

Senior Master Vogelsang sat motionless at his desk, his eyes fixed inflexibly upon the boy. Is he trying to hypnotize me? thought the latter. Arminius the German, indeed. His name was Arminius the Cheruscan, man. Anyhow, whether it's Arminius the Cheruscan or Arminius the German, that makes no difference to me. It doesn't interest me. He stared hard at the teacher's scarred face, at the precise parting of his hair, at his staring, pale blue eyes, at his high collar. It doesn't interest me. I don't care a hang about it. But if I say no, he'll think me a coward, for certain. Humanism is too abstract for him. Arminius the German. He's only trying to provoke me. I get you, my boy. I shall say I'll think it over. Then he'll answer, yes, do, my boy. And it'll sound as if he said: shirker. Am I a shirker?

"'What can we learn today from Arminius the German?'" came the squeaky voice of Vogelsang once more. "What do you say, Oppermann?"

"All right," said Berthold.

The sound of his answer had not yet died away, when he wanted to take it back. He ought to have said: I'll think it over. He had wanted to say that. But it was too late. "That's fine," Vogelsang approved. He was having a good day of it. He had emerged the victor from this interview too.

Berthold, when the others asked him during the next recess how he was getting on with the new chief, was monosyllabic. "He's just half and half. We'll have to see." He did not say more.

He generally went a good part of the way home with Heinrich Lavendel. The two boys rode their bicycles, their books and notes fastened with leather straps to the handlebars, now close to each other, one's hand on the other's shoulder, now separated by the traffic.

"He's messed up my lecture for me," said Berthold. "That's tough," said Heinrich. "The swine. He just thinks to himself: 'I'm master.' It's simply personal spite." Berthold did not answer. They were separated by passing cars. At the next red light they found themselves side by side again. They kept close together, each with a foot on the roadway, hemmed in by cars. "He suggested to me: 'What can we learn from Arminius the German?'" said Berthold. "Did you agree to it?" asked Heinrich, amid the hooting of motorhorns. "Yes," said Berthold. "I wouldn't have," said Heinrich. "Look out, he's trying to put you in a tough spot." Yellow light, green light, they rode on. "Have you any idea what he may have looked like?" asked Berthold when they found themselves together again. "Who?" asked Heinrich, who was thinking about the afternoon's football practice. "Arminius the Cheruscan, of course," said Berthold. "I expect he looked just as much a wild Indian as the rest of them," was Heinrich's opinion. "Think it over a little, will you?"

begged Berthold. "OK," said Heinrich. Often, when he wanted to speak heartily, the words he had used as a child came to his lips. Then the boys' roads separated.

Berthold wrestled with his subject. The whole thing was one great battle and Dr. Vogelsang was the enemy. Vogelsang had had the luck to choose the ground. He had the sun and the wind in his favor, and knew the lay of the land better than Berthold. Vogelsang was wily. But Berthold was plucky and tenacious.

He sat brooding over the books which dealt with his subject, Tacitus, Mommsen, Dessau. Had Arminius the Cheruscan actually accomplished anything? His victory had been precious little use to him. Only two years later, the Romans were across the Rhine again; they recovered two of the three lost eagles of their legions. The whole thing was only a colonial war, a kind of Boxer rebellion, which the Romans soon settled. Arminius himself, when he had been conquered by the Romans, was slain by his own countrymen. His father-in-law looked on from the Emperor's box while Arminius's wife and son walked in chains in the Roman triumphal procession.

What can we learn from Arminius the German? General considerations were no use to Berthold. He had to have striking pictures: The fight. Three legions. A legion means about six thousand fighting-men. With its baggage-train and other appurtenances, ten to twenty thousand. Swamps, forests. It must have been very much like Tannenberg. A camp of fortified baggage-wagons, the thickening fog. Above all, the Germans hated the Roman law-makers. They temporarily spared heir lives so as to put them to death later on with exquisite tortures. The Germans, Berthold read in the book by the nationalistic historian Seeck, believed that common law was inimical to personal honor. They did not want any law. That was the chief reason for their rebellion.

It was essential to know what Arminius had looked like. That point had struck Berthold at once. Again and again, with concentrated effort, he tried to get an idea of him. The monument in the Teutoburg Forest, a tall pedestal with a conventional statue upon it, didn't help at all. "Look here, man, that Arminius of yours was no fool," Heinrich Lavendel said to him. "Those boys must have had a different kind of intelligence from ours, a sort of American

Indian point of view. He was a cunning devil, that's certain." No doubt he had that Nordic craftiness, Berthold meditated, about which everyone talked nowadays. Dr. Vogelsang had it too.

Berthold lay awake during the night, he often did now. He had only the small lamp on his bed-table switched on. The wallpaper had a delicate design, repeated a hundredfold: an exotic bird sitting on a drooping twig. If one half closed one's eyes, the line which formed the bird's breast, taken with the line of the suspended twig, produced the contour of a face. Ah, now he had it. That was the face of Arminius. A broad forehead, a flat nose, a big mouth, a short but strong chin. Berthold smiled. Now he had got his man. Now he had got the better of Dr. Vogelsang. He went peacefully to sleep.

Up to now, Berthold had not confided his difficulties to anyone except Heinrich Lavendel. From then on his taciturnity left him. Only in the presence of his parents did he keep silent. They noticed that the boy was excited about something, but they knew from experience that if they asked him what it was, he would only get stubborn. So they waited for him to speak of his own free will.

But Berthold talked to a good many others, and collected a good many opinions. There was, for instance, that experienced man of the world, the chauffeur Franzke. For him, the battle in the Teutoburg Forest held no problem. "The whole thing is clear," he decided; "in those days there might have been some justification for National Socialism." Jaques Lavendel, on the contrary, declared that the barbarians had made the same mistake at that time that the Jews made seventy years later, that is to say, they had blindly revolted against a brilliantly organized stronger power. "That sort of thing never succeeds," he concluded, putting his head on one side, and drawing his lids far down over his blue eyes.

Much more sympathetic to Berthold than this sober interpretation, was his uncle Joachim's opinion. Berthold regarded his mother's brother, Joachim Ranzow, with reverence and affection. Government Director Ranzow, tall, slender, and elegant, precise in speech and character, had won the boy's heart by treating him as an adult. What Uncle Joachim had to say on the problem of Arminius the German was romantic. Berthold did not quite understand it, but it made an impression on him. "You know, my boy," said Uncle

Ranzow, carefully pouring him out a strong schnaps with his long hand, "the fact that the affair ended badly doesn't prove anything.

> *One man may ask: "Is this thing safe?"*
> *The second: "Is it right?"*
> *Their queries show us in one phrase*
> *Which free man is, which wight.*

Arminius was right. It was only by means of revolt, even at the risk of defeat, that the Germans came to understand their own natures, crystallized themselves, learned to live. If they had not revolted in those days, they would never have entered history, they would have had no history and would have vanished into obscurity. It was only through Arminius that they won a name and arrived. Name, reputation, is all that counts. What sort of a man the real Caesar was, is without interest: what lives is the legendary Caesar.

If Berthold understood that correctly, it was not alone a true likeness of Arminius that was important. The face of the statue in the Teutoburg Forest might also have a part to play. It was therefore not enough for him to have an idea, now, how Arminius looked. That was confusing. He was still far from his goal.

A chance conversation with his cousin Ruth Oppermann did not help to simplify matters. Ruth patronized him, treated him as a small boy who had grown up with misguided ideas. Well, he was young, it was necessary to free him from his prejudices, to make the truth clear to him. It was such a simple truth, too. She did her very best to rescue him. Whenever Berthold saw that plain girl with her high-strung manner, he got annoyed. But in spite of that, he was always looking for fresh opportunities to quarrel with her. It was true that she was weak in logic; but her aims harmonized with her, she was a personality, she was sound.

To Ruth Oppermann, Arminius's procedure was the only possible one. He did what a few centuries before the Maccabees had done, he rose against the oppressors and drove them out of the country. What else could one do with oppressors?

As she stood there, the great eyes flashing in her olive-tan face, her hair a bit dishevelled, as usual, Berthold was reminded of the Germanic women who went into battle with their husbands, to defend their wagon-camp. They were fair-haired, those German women, of course, their skin was white, their eyes were blue. But their hair, too, must have been dishevelled, their eyes big and wild, their whole expression probably identical.

His cousin Ruth was right, Uncle Joachim was right. He himself, Berthold, admired Arminius. The only confusing thing was that, unfortunately, Uncle Jaques, too, was right, that, in the end, nothing whatever had come of the victory of Arminius.

In any case the enemy, Senior Master Vogelsang, behaved himself, in the weeks that preceded Berthold's lecture, in a perfectly unexceptionable manner. Bernd Vogelsang did not want to be in too much of a hurry about anything. The Queen Louise School was dangerous ground, it was necessary to advance carefully, with Nordic craftiness. Vogelsang suspected adversaries all through the school. He classified them. Out of the entire Lower Sixth, he could find, for the time being, only two boys fit to join the ranks of his Young Eagles, Max Weber and Werner Rittersteg.

Werner Rittersteg had a pale and unhealthy complexion and a high, piping voice. He was the tallest boy in the Lower Sixth. His classmates had nicknamed him "Long Lummox." He had found Dr. Vogelsang an impressive figure from the start. He had fixed his bulging eyes on the new teacher with such doglike submissiveness, that the latter had at once noticed him. Bernd Vogelsang approved of blind subjection to authority, he interpreted it as manly loyalty. He considered the boy Rittersteg worthy of acceptance into the ranks of the Young Eagles.

The only son of wealthy parents who wanted their boy to go far, Werner Rittersteg had never hitherto, in spite of his height, distinguished himself among the rest. Of average intelligence, slow of judgment, he had not got on well under senior master Heinzius. His reception into the Young Eagles was the first great success of his life. His narrow chest swelled. It was he whom Dr. Vogelsang had chosen, and he had, with one single exception, rejected the others.

There was no doubt that the air of secrecy which hung over the Young Eagles, over their blood-brotherhood, their extraordinary, mysterious rites, their secret court was extremely attractive to the other boys, so that they envied Weber and Rittersteg. Even the level-headed Heinrich Lavendel, when he heard of the enrollment of these two, had said, "Lucky dogs!" The Long Lummox wished that Heinrich Lavendel had said more. It was precisely that boy, among all his companions, upon whom he would have liked to make an impression. He envied and admired the strength and skill with which the other was able to whirl, turn, and twist his short, sturdy body about. In a groping, clumsy way he constantly sought to win Heinrich's approval. He had actually learned English in his honor. But even when he had greeted him, one day, with the words: *"How are you, old fellow?"* Heinrich had remained perfectly cool. It was a torment to Rittersteg that even his great success did not alter this indifference.

Apart from the appointment of the two Young Eagles, nothing sensational occurred in the Lower Sixth. The boys quickly came to terms with their first Nationalist teacher. He was not particularly popular and not particularly unpopular. He was a master like any other, nobody got excited about him any longer. Soon the phenomenal performances of Heinrich Lavendel at football again became more interesting than Dr. Vogelsang's occasional Nationalist utterances.

Rector François, too, calmed down. He sat mildly and peacefully in his big study between the busts of Voltaire and Frederick the Great. Nearly three weeks had now passed without the occurrence of any untoward incident. There was only one thing that worried him. Herr Vogelsang's frightful German, that stiff, trite, editorial, Nationalist New German. At night when he retired, he would sit on the bed, carefully unfastening his suspenders, and lament to his wife: "He is ruining everything I've given the boys. Thought and speech are identical. We have struggled for seven years to get the boys to use straightforward, lucid German. Then the Ministry of Education lets this Teuton loose on them. You can train the skull of a newborn babe to any shape you like, make it long or broad. Is the careful speech of our boys sufficiently drilled into them to withstand the influence of this cramped, affected, early-Germanic jargon? It would be a pity if the boys were to go out into the world lacking clear ideas as well as clear speech." His kindly eyes gazed with a worried look through the strong lenses of his rimless glasses. "Those are not the things to worry about now, Alfred," Frau François declared in a resolute tone. "Be thankful that you have gotten along with him all right so far. One can never be careful enough these days."

Frau Mellenthin, the porter's wife, was disappointed. From what her husband had said, she had expected that the new man would at once distinguish himself by some great deed. Mellenthin, the porter, however, did not allow himself to be dissuaded so soon from his first opinion. "Tannenberg was not won in a day either, he'll do something yet," he declared emphatically. Frau Mellenthin took heart and repeated her husband's opinion to others; for he had a good nose for changes in the weather, and could scent every storm two days before it came.

[. . .]

In the five minutes' recess before the German lesson Berthold assumed a manly attitude, behaving as if he had forgotten what lay before him and talking on indifferent subjects to his companions. Senior Master Vogelsang also behaved as if the forthcoming event were not of any consequence to him. He came in, sat down stiffly at his desk, and turned over the pages of his notebook. "What was it we were going to do today? Ah, I have it. Oppermann's lecture. Now then, Oppermann." And as Oppermann came forward, Vogelsang added, obviously in a very good humor today, in a kindly bantering and encouraging tone: "Wolfram von Eschenbach, begin."

Berthold, standing between the teacher's platform and the boys' benches, showed no sign of nervousness. He appeared unconcerned and casual, his right foot advanced, his right arm hanging down, and his left hand resting lightly on his hip. He had not chosen the easiest road, he had not shirked any of the difficulties. He had seen it through. He was quite certain now what we, or at any rate what he, could learn from Arminius the German. From the standpoint of a rationalist, the achievement of Arminius might appear useless. But such an interpretation became meaningless in view of the unbounded admiration which the heroism of this man, in the cause of liberty, had kindled in the heart of every German, especially in a German of today. Berthold wished to pursue this train of thought in accordance with the good old rules he had been taught: general introduction, statement of subject, point of view of the lecturer, the objections, the refutation of the objections, then finally, once more, the lecturer's thesis. Berthold had set down in writing, to the last comma, exactly what he wished to say. But speaking came easily to him, so he had disdained to learn his manuscript by heart in parrot fashion. He wished, while keeping to his fundamental design, to leave the wording of the individual points to the inspiration of the moment.

He stood there, then, and spoke. He saw the faces of the other boys before him: Max Weber's, Kurt Baumann's, Werner Ritters-teg's, and Heinrich Lavendel's. But he was not speaking to them. Only to himself and to that fellow behind him, the enemy.

For Senior Master Vogelsang had taken up a position at Berth-old's back. He sat there stiffly, uncompromisingly, and listened. Berthold could not see him, but he knew that Vogelsang's gaze was fixed hard upon him, exactly on the nape of his neck. He felt the place underneath his collar that Vogelsang's gaze was set upon. It was as though someone were pressing the tip of his finger there.

Berthold took pains to think of nothing but his phrases. He was to speak for fully thirty minutes. He had got through about eight minutes. The introduction was over, the subject had been stated, and his thesis outlined. He had got as far as the "proof." Then he became aware that Vogelsang's gaze was no longer upon him. Yes, Vogelsang had risen, very quietly, in order not to disturb the lecture. He was advancing. Berthold saw him, next, against the wall to the left. He walked along the left-hand row of benches on the tips of his toes with measured but careful steps. Berthold heard the slight creaking of his boots. Vogelsang went to the rear of the room and stood in the left-hand corner. He wished to have Berthold in front of him, watch the words come out of his mouth. There he stood, behind the last bench, very upright (was not one hand resting on the pommel of an invisible sabre?), his pale blue eyes fixed unwa-veringly upon Berthold's mouth. Berthold began to feel uncomfort-able under his scrutiny. He turned his head for a moment in the teacher's direction, but this made him still more uneasy. He looked straight in front of him, made a slight movement, and tossed his head as if he wanted to drive away a fly.

He finished the "proof." He was not talking so well now as he had at first. It was very warm in the room; the rooms in the Queen Louise School were, as a rule, overheated. His upper lip was per-spiring slightly. He came to the "objections." The achievement of Arminius, he said, had perhaps not, from the point of view of sober reason, resulted in any permanent, external consequences. It had to be admitted that the Romans were, a few years later, in exactly the same position as they had been in before the battle. Indeed—

He stopped for a moment, suddenly realized that he could not go on. He tried to concentrate. In his mind's eye he could see the narrow pages of his Latin edition of Tacitus, the large Roman type of his fine German edition of Tacitus. He glanced again at that corner on the left. There stood Vogelsang, still motionless, attentive. Berthold opened his mouth, closed it and opened it again, looked down at the tips of his toes. It must be at least eight seconds since he had stopped speaking. Even ten. What was it he had said last? Oh, yes, that the achievement of Arminius had really had no external consequences. There was no question but that Luther's translation of the Bible and Guttenberg's discoveries had been more important to Germany and to her position in the world than the battle in the Teutoburg Forest. The achievement of Arminius, we must admit, remained, practically, without significance.

Did he want to express himself quite like that? No, he wanted to give the idea much more discreet, less blunt, less harsh expression. Well, anyhow. Get on, Berthold. Get it over. Only, no more pauses, the first had already lasted an eternity. But now he had the threads again. Now nothing more could happen to him. He would get into his stride after the "refutation." A second stop? No, Herr Doctor, impossible.

He smiled triumphantly across the room toward the far corner. "But all the same," he began again. Hallo, what was this? Why was Vogelsang's face suddenly changing in such an extraordinary manner? Why was the scar which cut through his cheek getting so red? Why was he opening his eyes so wide? None of that will do any good, Herr Doctor. I've got hold of the threads again now. You can't faze me now. "But all the same," he began, in a brisk and vigorous tone, "admitting all that——"

At that point he was interrupted. A sharp, squeaking voice issued from the corner: "No, not admitted. I do not admit that. No one here admits that. I am not going to put up with it. I refuse to listen to such a thing any longer. Who do you think you are, young man? What sort of people do you suppose you have sitting here before you? Here, in the presence of Germans, in this time of German need, you dare to characterize the tremendous act which stands at the beginning of German history as useless and devoid of meaning?

You admit that, you say. You have the effrontery to utter arguments of the rankest opportunism and then you say: you admit that. If you, yourself, have lost every spark of German feeling, you might at least spare us, who retain our love for our Fatherland, your foul abuse. I forbid it. Listen to me, Oppermann. I forbid it, not only for my sake, but for the sake of this institution, which still remains, for the present, a German one."

A deathly silence had fallen. The thoughts of most of the boys had been wool-gathering in the warm room. They were sprawling, day-dreaming, but now, at the sharp, squeaking voice of Vogelsang, they looked up at Berthold. Had he really said something so awful? And what was it, actually, that he had said?

It had been something about Luther and Gutenberg. They did not quite understand Vogelsang's rage, but probably Oppermann had really gone a little too far. In these lectures one ought to say just what was in the lesson-books, no more and no less. It looked as though he had got himself into a nice mess.

Berthold himself, when Vogelsang had interrupted him, was at first deeply astonished. What was the matter with the man? Why was he shouting so? He might have had the decency to let him finish. It had not hitherto been the custom to interrupt the lecturer. Dr. Heinzius had never done so. But he was now under the ground, in the cemetery at Stahnsdorf. And that fellow was shouting. The "objections" had to be stated. They ought not to be suppressed, they had to be refuted. That was what we have been taught, such were the rules, Dr. Heinzius taught us that.

I didn't say anything at all against Arminius. The thing was an "objection." I was going to refute it. There's my manuscript. I stated my own attitude quite clearly at the beginning of Part B. He really ought to stop, he ought not to go on shouting so.

I had an uncomfortable feeling as soon as he suggested Arminius to me. I ought to have stuck to "Humanism." Heinrich said straight away that he was a swine, that it was pure personal spite.

He's talking utter nonsense. My manuscript is on the desk, in my satchel. Anyone who read it would realize that the swine is talking utter nonsense.

What was it I really said? I don't remember exactly. It was not in the manuscript. Nevertheless, I could cite it as evidence. Then everyone would see what I meant to say.

I won't cite my manuscript as evidence. Arminius was a wild Indian. I can't bear him. The "objection" was a fair one. I had said so, that ends it.

He had abandoned his unconcerned attitude. He stood very erect, his fleshy head held high, his gray eyes looking straight ahead. He let his enemy's words patter over him.

The fellow at last seemed finished talking rot. Berthold stood there, gnawing his underlip with his big white teeth. Now he should pull out his manuscript and say: "I don't know what you mean, Herr Senior Master. Here is the manuscript." But he did not say it. He remained silent, embittered and impenitent. He kept his gray eyes fixed unwaveringly upon the other's pale blue ones. Finally, after a pause that seemed to last an eternity he said in a clear but quiet voice: "I am a good German, Herr Senior Master. I am as good a German as you are."

This colossal nerve on the part of the young Jew struck Dr. Vogelsang dumb for a moment. Then he felt an impulse to give his fury rein. But he held all the trumps in his own hand. He did not want to throw them away in a burst of temper. He controlled himself. "I see," he contented himself with saying, as quietly as the other. "You are a good German, are you? Well, will you be so good as to leave it to others to decide who is a good German and who is not? A good German, indeed." He gave a scornful snort. And then, at last, he came out of his corner, but not quietly. Every step was loud and firm. He came straight up to Berthold. Then he faced him, eye to eye. Before the tensely silent class, amidst breathless excitement, with simulated calm and moderation, he inquired: "Will you, at least, apologize for what you have said, Oppermann?"

Berthold, for the fraction of a second, had also thought of apologizing. He had said something he had not intended saying. He had said it in an unconcentrated moment and in a crude and unfortunate manner. Why not admit it? Then the whole matter would be settled, he could finish his lecture and everyone would be bound to see that he was a good German and that the fellow opposite was doing him an injustice. But confronted by Vogelsang's stare, by his disgusting, arrogant, slashed face, this impulse vanished before it had become a real thought.

The other boys all stared at Berthold. Vogelsang's attitude had impressed them. It seemed as though Oppermann had bitten off more than he could chew. But, naturally, he must not eat humble pie on that account. They waited, curious to see what he could do.

He and Vogelsang were standing eye to eye with each other. At last Berthold opened his mouth. "No, sir," he said very quietly, even modestly, "I shall not apologize, sir." Everyone was satisfied.

Vogelsang, too, was satisfied. Now he had really won. Now, owing to this attitude of Oppermann's, he would have the opportunity of showing how a German schoolmaster crushed corruptive elements. "Very well," he said. "I'll remember that, Oppermann. Be seated."

Berthold went to his seat. What he had done was certainly not very wise. He could see that by his enemy's attitude, by the light that flashed in his eyes. But if he were to be given a choice again, he would do the same thing. He could not apologize to that man.

The other decided to practice moderation at all costs. But he could not resist calling out to the boy, as he sat down among the others: "Perhaps some day, Oppermann, you will be glad if people are satisfied with such amends." His voice was casual but just this tone emphasized his triumph and his scorn. "We'll go on now with our reading of Kleist," added Bernd Vogelsang and thus concluded the incident in a lofty manner.

The report of what had occurred spread rapidly through the whole school. Even Rector François heard of it before the morning was over. He was not surprised when Senior Master Vogelsang paid him a visit.

Vogelsang scarcely allowed himself a disapproving glance at the burst of Voltaire, so full was he of the recent event. But he kept himself in hand, deliberately avoided all exaggeration, and gave an accurate account of the matter. François listened to him with evident uneasiness. His small, well-kept hands stroked his trim moustache nervously. "Unpleasant," he said several times after Vogelsang had finished. "Exceedingly unpleasant."

"What steps do you intend to take to punish the boy Oppermann?" inquired Vogelsang in a restrained tone.

"He's a conscientious lad," was Rector François's opinion, "particularly interested in German essays and his lectures. No doubt he had carefully prepared his manuscript. Perhaps we ought to have a look at it before we come to a definite decision. It is probably a case of *lapsus linguae*. In that event it would be a mistake, with all due respect to your feelings, my dear colleague, to punish a slip of the tongue too severely."

Vogelsang raised his eyebrows in astonishment. "In my opinion, Herr Rector, it would be impossible to punish such a case too severely. At a time when the shameful peace treaty, the treaty of Versailles, is creating havoc, a young chap has the audacity to decry by means of insipid logic one of the most sublime of German achievements. While we Germans, especially we recognized Nationalists, are having such an immeasurably hard struggle to awaken our people, a schoolboy, a mere child, insults the efforts made by our forefathers to shake off their chains. Such behavior would perhaps have pleased your friend Voltaire, Herr Rector. But how anyone can take the trouble to look for excuses when a boy belonging to a school which, after all is a German one, reaches such a height of presumption, that, I must frankly confess, is more than I can understand."

Rector François stirred uneasily in his chair. The thin, rosy skin of his face twitched. He was almost as much disturbed by the fellow's phraseology as by his topic. The bombastic German, the ranting, mass-meeting oratory made him physically uncomfortable. If only the chap were nothing more than an opportunist. The worst of it was that he sincerely believed the gibberish he was talking. Due to an inferiority complex, he had encased himself in an armor of the cheapest nationalism, through which not a ray of common sense could penetrate. And he, François, had to listen to all this rubbish with attention and courtesy. What terrible days these were. Once more Goethe was right: "There is nothing the rabble fear more than *Intelligence*. If they understood what is truly terrifying, they would fear *Ignorance*." Yet he, François, knowing what was right, had to sit there with his hands tied. He was not allowed to protect the clever lad against that bully of a man, his teacher. For, unfortunately, Little Thundercloud was right. If one got carried away, if one dared openly to espouse the cause of reason, then the whole herd of Nationalist newspapers would begin to bellow. And the Republic is weak, the Republic always eats humble pie. It leaves one to the mercy of the bellowing herd. One loses one's job, one's bread and butter, one's children are pauperized, and one loses the best thing life has to offer: a tranquil old age.

Dr. Vogelsang, meanwhile, was explaining his view of the case point by point. *"Lapsus linguae,"* said he, "slip-of-the-tongue, you claim. But does not the importance of these school lectures lie precisely in the fact that they release, through his contact with an audience, the real sentiments of the lecturer?" He was on his favorite topic now. "Talking is more important than writing. The glorious example of the Leader proves it. And what the Leader says on that subject in his book, *My Battle*—"

At this point, however, Rector François interrupted him.

"No, my dear colleague," he said. "I refuse to follow you into this field." His mild voice sounded unusually resolute, his friendly eyes flashed through the big lenses of his glasses, his cheeks flushed, he drew himself up—one realized he was taller than Senior Master Vogelsang. "You know, my dear colleague, that since the establishment of this school I have been fighting for the purity of German speech. I am not a fighter by nature; life has demanded many a compromise from me. However, I can make one statement: I have been uncompromising in this fight. And I shall remain so. Of course, I have been shown your Leader's book. Some colleagues of mine have placed it in their school libraries. But I have not. I know of no other work so disfigured by sins against the spirit of the language as that one. I cannot permit that book to be even quoted within the walls of my establishment. I most emphatically request you, my dear colleague, not to quote that book in this house, not to me and not to my pupils. I will not have the speech of the boys ruined."

Bernd Vogelsang sat with his thin lips compressed. He was painstaking and thorough. He knew his way about the German language and its grammar. He had made a mistake. He ought not to have quoted the Leader's book to this misguided man. It was unfortunately only too true. Rector François was right in a certain sense. The greatest living German, the Leader of the German movement, was not familiar with the rudiments of the German language. He had that in common, to be sure, *mutatis mutandis,* with Napoleon, with whom he also shared the attribute of not having been born on the soil of the realm that he had come to liberate. Just the same, Vogelsang suffered because of the linguistic failings of his Leader. In his spare time he labored at the task of eliminating the most flagrant errors in the book entitled *My Battle*—that most important document of the German liberation movement—and to transpose it into a German which would be grammatically and stylistically perfect. As usual, he would have to swallow the Rector's insolence without comment. There was no counterargument he could advance. The invisible sabre had fallen from his hands. He sat silent, lips compressed.

Rector François at first thoroughly enjoyed his own indignation. Life often compelled one to sacrifice the intellect. Little Thundercloud had wrested many a concession from him in that direction. But he had not yet fallen so low as to allow anyone to bespatter him with the mud of the book entitled *My Battle* and call it perfume. By degrees, however, the sinister look of anger on the face of his senior master and his ominous silence began to alarm him. Rector François had stoutly defended his beloved German and that was enough. He became again the conciliatory gentleman he was by nature. "Please do not misunderstand me, my dear colleague," he said soothingly. "Far be it from me to say anything against your Leader. You remember how the Emperor Sigismund silenced the bishop who corrected his grammatical mistakes. *'Ego imperator Romanus supra grammaticos sto.'* No one requires your Leader to be an expert on German grammar. But I require it of the pupils of Queen Louise School."

It sounded like an apology. But it remained a piece of impudence on the part of that fellow François to have spoken so disrespectfully of the Leader's failings. What he, Vogelsang, might think, it was not right that this effeminate creature should blurt it out. Bernd Vogelsang would not permit himself, in any case, to be diverted from his object. Not by a long shot!

At that moment vengeance for the crime which the boy Oppermann had committed became Senior Master Bernd Vogelsang's lifework.

"Let us return to the point, Herr Rector," he squeaked. The invisible sabre was back again now. "The case of Oppermann is not only one of a slander against the German race, a slander that borders upon treason in such times as these, it is also an uncommonly impudent breach of school discipline. I must ask you again: What steps do you propose to take to punish the refractory boy Oppermann?"

Rector François sat on, tired, courteous, harmless as ever. "I will consider the matter, my dear colleague," said he.

Rumor traveled swiftly in Queen Louise School. A year ago, the porter, Mellenthin, had saluted young Oppermann, the son of the furniture people, obsequiously. Now he looked the other way when Berthold left the building. However, when saluting Vogelsang, he would remain stiffly at attention even after the senior master had walked past. Who was it who had always said that the new man would, one of these days, show these donkeys what was what? And who was showing them now? Once more it was proved that Mellenthin, the porter, had a good nose.

[. . .]

It was not until after Berthold's burial that Gustav received the news of his death. Mühlheim, who was the only person who knew his address, had delayed notifying him in order that Gustav might not run any risks by returning.

During these days he had been wandering about the beautiful and delightful city of Berne. It was spring, the air was clear, the towering peaks of the Oberland stood out in infinitely delicate and pure contours against the horizon. But Gustav took no pleasure in the view, his mind was stunned by the events which had taken place in Berlin. When he got the news, he felt as though he had received a shock which he had long been expecting.

He could not bear anyone near him now, he went off into the mountains, he had to be alone. He could not understand the things which were happening, he had to think things out for himself. The place where he finally stopped was situated at the base of the Jungfrau. But there was no more snow and he was the only guest at his small hotel. He avoided the crowded mountain railway and carried his skis himself as far as the snow-line. With some difficulty he ascended a slope that lay apart from the main route. He lay down in the snow and the sunlight. The outlines of the mountains rose high and smooth into the marvelously pure air. He was alone.

He began a searching self-examination. He had remembered old Jean, but not Berthold. He was largely to blame for what had happened. He had always done the wrong thing. He had led a useless, indolent, self-absorbed existence. He had gone to Sybil instead of to Anna. If he had only interested himself in politics, in political economy, in some branch of the business, it would have had more purpose than the things he had done. He had proved that Lessing had written a certain letter on the 23rd of December, not on the 21st. What of it? That phrase might be an appropriate caption for his entire life.

Perspiring in the heat of the sun, he squatted in the snow and took stock of himself. The result was not gratifying.

He spent four days in this manner, in the quiet of his mountain retreat. The narrow road up which, day by day, he trailed his snow-shoes, ran the length of the valley, overlooking it from a great height. Tiny villages lay on the slopes opposite. The towering peaks of the Jungfrau spread before him in sunlit whiteness. He would sit for hours on his secluded lofty peak. There was a clean fresh warmth in the air. The roar of the avalanches, deadened by distance, came to his ears. He saw what lay before him and around him but he appeared conscious of neither the air nor the view. His senses were benumbed. The same thoughts continually occupied his mind, revolved and pierced ever deeper and deeper into his consciousness. The wisest thing for him to do was to overtax his body until he would be too exhausted to think. He sometimes managed this on the way home. Then he would sit by the roadside, actually glad of his utter fatigue, his mind a blank, nodding his head mechanically and laughing like a half-wit. Sometimes the road would be empty for hours. Once a young boy with a cart passed. He stared at him in astonishment and turned his head to look back at him for a long time.

This stupor lasted for four days, paralyzing him; his head felt as though it were wrapped in cotton-wool. Suddenly, on the morning of the fifth day, after a long night's sleep, the mists about him lifted. Gustav raised his head, looked about him, emerged completely from the shadows. Five days had actually passed since he had had news from Germany, since he had seen a newspaper. There could be few Germans, just now, who were so devoid of curiosity. He obtained whatever papers he could: German, Swiss, English, French. With the big bundle under his arm, he climbed his usual beautiful road. He felt a sudden mad anxiety which he could scarcely control. Although the ground was still damp, he sat down by the roadside and began to read.

As he read, all the blood seemed to rush to his head. Keep quiet, don't lose control, keep steady, think quietly. In days like these it is impossible to stop all sorts of absurd rumors from getting about.

All his life he had been interested in compiling accurate source materials, he was not going to be taken in now by the ravings of a few overimaginative reporters. What papers were these? They were the *Times,* the *Frankfurter Zeitung,* the *Neue Zürcher Zeitung,* the *Temps.* And the reporters were not just anybody, they were people with reputations. The statements were concise, businesslike. Correspondents of high standing could not afford to publish such monstrous things in such minute detail unless they were sure of their ground. There was no question but that the Nationalists had carried out their program point by point, that program at whose primitive barbarism people had so often smiled; he himself had been among the most incredulous. They had arrested, kidnapped, illtreated, killed all those who were in disfavor with them, destroyed or confiscated their property, simply because these persons were their adversaries and for that reason had to be annihilated. Gustav read names, dates. Many of the names were known to him. Many of these men were his close friends.

His quiet, animal-like despair was over. A violent rage against himself and against the Nationalist party overcame him. He read the insane speeches of the Leader. The aged President had handed the Reich over to them in good order. They had ruthlessly broken their solemn pledges, trampled law underfoot, and substituted caprice, disorder, and brutality for civilization and order. Germany had become a madhouse in which the patients had overpowered their warders. Did the world realize this? What was it doing about all this?

He traveled back to Berne that same day. Had he been mad to hide away in that lonely place without even giving his address? Did he imagine this horror would have less effect upon him if he wrapped his head up in cotton-wool? He was determined to know, he must know, more, everything, every detail.

In Berne he found telegrams, letters, and newspapers. The mercenaries had entered his house, too, and searched it, destroying much and pilfering more. There was a telegram from Frischlin, asking Gustav to ring him up. He did so.

It gave him a peculiar sensation to hear Frischlin's voice. It was the voice he knew so well and yet it was altered, it was tense, anxious, full of energy. Gustav wanted to ask questions but Frischlin interrupted him at once. He stated that he had made a good deal of progress with the Lessing but he considered it would be best if he came to Berne and made his report personally. Moreover, that was also Mühlheim's opinion.

He arrived the very next day. "I should prefer to stay at a different hotel from yours," he said, almost before he had left the train. "It would be a better policy if our names were not reported as being on the same register. I suggest that we then take a walk. I can give you a better report if I am sure we cannot be overheard." He spoke with modesty, yet with assurance. Gustav noticed with amazement how much the man had changed. In Berlin, with his long thin legs and his long thin hands protruding from sleeves which were always too short, with his shy, awkward manner, he had always impressed Gustav as a student whose inner and outer qualifications had been inadequate. Now, for all his simplicity, he had acquired the firmness of manner of a man who knew exactly what he wanted.

They drove out to the Gurten. It was a dazzling day of early spring, the white outline of the mountain ranges gave an effect of extreme delicacy and clarity. It was still too cold to sit for any length of time on the natural platform overlooking the view. They walked up the wooded heights. Gustav slackened his rapid, firm stride and Klaus Frischlin made his report.

The mercenaries had appeared in Max Reger Strasse during one of the first nights after his departure; it had been toward morning, there had been eight of them. Fortunately, the day before, Frischlin had deposited the manuscript, the most important of the Lessing literature, and the card index of notes with persons above suspicion. All the documents that remained had been pilfered or damaged. They had spared many of the books; at any rate their devastations had been a good deal worse in some other houses. They were very erratic in the choice of the books which they tore up or took away with them. They seemed especially enraged by the many editions of Dante's *Divine Comedy,* which they took for propaganda literature in behalf of the "godless movement"; probably they had been misled by the word "Comedy." They had confiscated the car and the typewriter. The portrait of Fräulein Rauch had shared the same fate. The portrait of Immanuel Oppermann, on the other hand, was untouched. Frischlin had now placed it in safekeeping. They had also overlooked a stack of private correspondence. This Frischlin had sent on to Gustav's present address by a circuitous route. It should arrive during the next few days. The servant Schlüter had proved himself very reliable. They had beaten him severely on the first occasion. Nevertheless, immediately after the looting, he had rescued the remaining property with the aid of his brother-in-law's widow. It was a good thing he had done so, for the very next night they had come again and got their talons into what was left. Frischlin had put the things which he believed Gustav especially valued in Fräulein Rauch's house.

"Was Fräulein Rauch able to help you?" Gustav asked. "Not much," returned Frischlin. She had been very willing to help but, somehow, very little had come of it. Fräulein Rauch was very busy with her own affairs, he added with marked reserve. However, he spoke with enthusiasm of Mühlheim, with whom he had apparently come to an excellent understanding. Mühlheim wanted Gustav to telephone him, if possible, between six and seven that evening, at the Hotel Bristol.

It was nearly six o'clock when Gustav returned to his hotel. He must telephone Mühlheim at once but he did not want to hear anything of business or anything of the sly schemes which, to be sure, was the only sensible method to employ against the Nationalists. All the same, his house, of which he was very fond, was at stake. It was horrible to think that Nationalist troops might soon be wallowing in those beautiful rooms. He must really speak to Mühlheim. But when the hotel operator answered, he gave her, at the last moment, not Mühlheim's number but Sybil's.

He soon heard Sybil's voice. She was surprised, and her surprise had an element of fear in it, as he noted with quickly aroused suspicion. Perhaps it was imprudent to telephone anyone from abroad just now. But as far as Sybil was concerned, the risk was exceedingly slight and she need not have been so aloof. He remembered how briefly and coolly Frischlin had spoken of her. Yet he longed to see her, he longed for the fragrance of her childlike body. Very earnestly he begged her to come, told her how much he needed her now. She readily assented. But when he wanted to set a definite date, she hesitated. She would wire tomorrow or, at the latest, the day after. Gustav did not know she was thinking of Friedrich Wilhelm Gutwetter. But he realized that she was hiding something from him and was much distressed.

Frischlin's report, too, clear and detailed as it was, now seemed insufficient to him. The fact of the matter was that public events in Germany were beginning to interest him more intensely than his house and his manuscript. He had always hoped Frischlin might begin to tell about them of his own accord. But Frischlin had not done so and he hesitated to rush the deliberate, level-headed fellow.

At last, that evening, in a very pretty little restaurant which Gustav had discovered, Frischlin gave him some account of conditions in general. It was not easy, he began, to secure authentic details in Germany today, the authorities successfully tried to shroud everything in uncertainty. His account would, therefore, be very incomplete. But Gustav soon found that the names, dates, and places which Frischlin was sure of were alarmingly numerous.

Of all the detachments of mercenaries stationed in Berlin the most notorious were the shock battalions 17 and 33, the so-called Murder Battalions. The places which were spoken of with the greatest horror were the cellars of the Nationalist quarters in Hedemann Strasse, in General Pape Strasse, and several in Köpenik and Spandau. In these spots, Frischlin observed, and this comment sounded disconcerting in the midst of his otherwise extremely sober narrative, there may well be erected—when the power of the Nationalists is finally broken—memorial tablets to the deepest blot on the reputation of the German people. The most dreadful thing about the activities of the secret police and the mercenaries, he continued, was the system, worked out to the smallest detail, the thorough organization, the half-military, half-bureaucratic regulations in accordance with which the ill-usage and the slaughter proceeded. All was duly registered, signed, and recorded. After each case of ill-treatment the victim had to state in writing that he had not been ill-treated. In the case of killings, the doctor certified that the man who had been killed had died of heart failure. The body was delivered to the relatives in a sealed casket, the opening of which was forbidden under the severest penalties. Those who were dismissed after mistreatment were supplied with fresh suits and underclothing, so that their blood-bespattered garments would not be too conspicuous. They had to guarantee in writing to return the fresh clothing within twenty-four hours properly cleaned. Furthermore, payment had to be made for board and the services rendered in the Nationalist barracks. Not much, to be sure: one mark a day for lodging and one mark for board and services. The board and services of those who had been killed, that is to say those who had "died of heart failure" or who had been "shot while trying to escape," had to be paid for by the surviving relatives. Services rendered also comprised spiritual things and were not devoid of a certain grim humor. The prisoners, for instance, had Nationalist songs played to them on a phonograph while they were undergoing treatment. They had to join in the songs, the rhythm was impressed upon them with steel rods and rubber truncheons.

The Nationalists apparently intended to carry out their system on a grand scale. They established enormous concentration camps in which the prisoners were taught "the qualities of mind required by the spirit of the new age." For this educational process, psychological methods were also employed. For example, they drove the prisoners through the streets in long, ridiculous processions and forced them to make grotesque utterances in chorus such as: "We're Marxist swine, we're Jewish swindlers," and so on. Or they forced individuals to mount on boxes and make genuflections and after each genuflection to call out: "I am a Jewish swine, I have betrayed my country, I have seduced Aryan girls, I have stolen public funds," and so on. Occasionally prisoners had to climb trees, poplars for instance, and proclaim similar traits from aloft for hours.

In addition to this, the prisoners in the cellars of the mercenaries' barracks, as well as those in the concentration camps, had the opportunity of thoroughly familiarizing themselves in a very short time with the program of the National-Socialist party and the Leader's book. The method of instruction was rigorous. Harsh penalties awaited those who made mistakes or were careless; the era of liberalism and humanistic drivel was past. Many, as already stated, did not survive the instructions. In Berlin alone he knew of seventeen cases, attested by documentary evidence, which had ended fatally.

Such then was the information imparted by Dr. Klaus Frischlin to Dr. Gustav Oppermann in the little wineshop in Berne, the capital of the Swiss confederation. He spoke in a low monotonous voice, for there were people sitting at the next table. From time to time, to moisten his throat, he took a sip of the light, sparkling wine and when he did this his hands looked remarkably long and thin as they emerged from his sleeves. Gustav ate little that evening, nor did he speak much. There were not many questions he could ask.

Klaus Frischlin told his story accurately and precisely. The only occasions when his German was not precise were when he quoted the words of the Leader which the ill-treated had to learn by heart.

[. . .]

It was a fine, sunny day when the man with the passport made out in the name of Georg Teibschitz crossed the frontier. He was a heavily built, slow-moving, amiable-looking man in a worn gray suit and he carried a shabby suitcase.

He traveled about, in South Germany to begin with, in Baden, in Swabia, in small towns and villages; that merchant Georg Teibschitz, a man who had at one time been independent and made a lot of money, who had later been employed by others but who, for the time being, was without a job. His papers were in perfect order. A man in Bandol had provided him with a number of further proofs of identity. He could substantiate everything he said.

He was in no hurry. He breathed German air, gazed on the German countryside, heard German voices. He drifted along as on a calm sea, in a state of peace and happiness. He walked about the streets, traveled across country in that miraculously lovely season of early summer, breathing deeply and gazing his fill. He was more content with himself and with his destiny during these days than he had ever been before. Life glided on, quietly, evenly, strongly, and he let himself drift.

But just because the peace and order of Germany at once enfolded him, because he adjusted his tempo to that of the others and began to think their thoughts, he doubly realized the danger of this deceptive calm and the urgent necessity of revealing what an impudent swindle this apparent tranquility really was.

He commenced his activities slowly. The fact that he had gossiped so much, during these last weeks, down there beside the southern sea, with fishermen, with bus drivers, and all sorts of people in humble walks of life, now proved useful to him. He entered into long-winded conversations with small tradesmen, peasants, and laborers. These people made no secret to him of their private affairs. But as soon as he began to talk politics, they became speechless. The times were in favor of silence. Nevertheless, he managed to make a few of them talk.

He was disappointed. The pictures which the stories of Frischlin, Bilfinger, and Teibschitz had conjured up had been wild and colorful, whereas reality had a gray and prosaic look. People shrugged their shoulders over the atrocities committed by the mercenaries. It was an old story that the Nationalists were dirty dogs. There was no need for anyone to come and tell them that. The facts that prisoners were beaten, that their miserable rations were peppered and no water supplied to quench the resultant thirst, that they were compelled to smear one another with their own excrements, all these things were ancient history and had lost much of their original power to horrify. The really important question was how to obtain the bare necessities of life with a continually dwindling supply of money. The real problem of the masses was not the barbarism of the Nationalists but how to get along without the few pennies which the government had deducted from one's income.

Now and then, in small cafés and restaurants and at the unemployment agencies, Gustav came across the agents of that secret organization of which Georg Teibschitz had spoken. He tried to establish relations with them but was unsuccessful. These people, it was evident, really did not wish to be anything but numbers, as Herr Teibschitz had explained. A man like Gustav had no chance of getting at them.

Once, unexpectedly, in the town of Augsburg, he met Klaus Frischlin. Frischlin did not raise his voice, he did not want to attract attention. That made his words sound all the more curt when he said: "Have you gone mad? What business have you got to be in Germany? How did you get here? I'll make it possible for you to disappear over the frontier again. But I insist that you must be gone within twenty-four hours."

Unforeseen as this encounter was, Gustav had long ago prepared for it. It had been Frischlin who had involved him in this business, it had always been Frischlin, from the moment he had told him on the telephone that he was coming to Berne. Frischlin had been the first to tell him what was happening in Germany. It was owing to Frischlin that Bilfinger had spoken to him. Frischlin had forwarded that card to him, which had reminded him to undertake the task, even if he could never finish it. It was Frischlin, Gustav had long known, who had turned Georg Teibschitz into Number C II 734. So, like a schoolboy voluntarily performing a task which is beyond him but for which he nevertheless expects to be praised on account of his good intentions, with a sly and roguish air, an embarrassed childlike smile spreading over his large, badly shaven face, Gustav imparted his secret to the other. "I hope you have no objection to my being C II 734?" But Frischlin's face hardened. "You are a fool," he said roughly. "What are you thinking of? We can't use you in that way. You'll only make trouble for us." He grew more and more angry. "What are you thinking of, man? What are you up to here? What sort of quixotry is this? Do you think you are a hero in a novel? Whom do you think you are going to make an impression on? The only person you'll impress is yourself. What you are doing will only arouse annoyance, not admiration."

Gustav's face looked dejected. His unshaven cheeks hung loosely, he was an old man. Nevertheless Frischlin's words did not shake his resolution for a moment. Plaintively and stubbornly, like a child misunderstood by adults and still insisting on its original point, he slowly shook his large head. "I thought that you, at least, would understand me, Dr. Frischlin."

Klaus Frischlin had intended to give Gustav a further good, sharp piece of his mind. The fellow was not only injuring himself but everyone else concerned. However, the tone in which Gustav had spoken made it clear to him that there was absolutely nothing to be gained by talking in that way. Suddenly, too, he realized how fond he had become of the slow-going, unpractical fellow with his childlike impetuosity, his gentle stubbornness, and his simplicity, which he had preserved throughout fifty years right into the Germany of today. "I should not like anything to happen to you, Dr. Oppermann," he said. Gustav had never suspected that the man could speak with such warmth and intensity. "You will inevitably be arrested if you go on creeping about here with your seditious talk. I beg of you to leave Germany. I beg of you to hurry and leave. Believe me, our friend Lessing would give you the same advice," he added with a slight smile.

"Our friend Lessing." Gustav was very pleased that Frischlin had said: "Our friend Lessing." "Do you remember," he asked, "the quotation from Lessing I intended using as a text for the Third Book? 'Pursue your inscrutable course, eternal Providence. Let not my faith in you falter because your course is inscrutable. Do not let me despair if your steps seem to retrogress. It is not true that the shortest road is always the straightest. You are confronted by many obstacles along your path, you are obliged to make many detours to avoid them.' You see," he concluded in triumph, "that's why I'm here."

"That's utter madness, my dear man," said Frischlin, again seriously provoked. "That's the very reason you must pack up and leave. What's your idea? To help Providence make a detour? Of course, people are waiting just for you to tell them what's going on. They've known what's been going on for ages. They don't want to know anything more about that. What they do want to know is, what's to be done. Have you any ideas on that subject, Dr. Oppermann? Have you a solution to that problem? But I want you to know that we have one; it is because of this fact that I can permit the people I am in charge of to risk their lives. But I can't allow you to do so," he added sharply.

The two men walked a little distance without speaking. "Are you still angry with me?" asked Gustav at last. He spoke in a pleading, dejected tone, like a boy reprimanded for some escapade, but sure in his heart that he has done the right thing. Frischlin shrugged. "It is too bad about you, Dr. Oppermann," he said. His tone was so like that which Mühlheim had often used toward him that Gustav, in spite of Frischlin's wrath, was pleased they had met.

With quiet obduracy he continued as he had begun. He was now in the neighborhood which had been the scene of Bilfinger's reports. He traveled about the beautiful Swabian countryside. He wished to supplement the material Bilfinger had collected; for the day would come when such material would have more than a merely historical interest. However, these activities also resulted in disappointment. The people who had so far been only names, words, and type, now that they stood before him in the flesh, proved far more shadowy than the shapes of his imagination. There was only one thing that was real about them: their fear, their wretched, intimidated demeanor. At the slightest hint, they grew dumb and showed him the door. He was able to loosen the tongues of some of the eyewitnesses who had no connection with the victims. The faces of the victims themselves, when he mentioned what had happened to them, grew stony in the pretence of having seen nothing and knowing about nothing.

This frozen fear, this deeply embedded horror, filled Gustav with an actual physical compassion. He tried all sorts of means to induce the terrified people to talk. It was not only his desire for material; he believed that the stricken people would more easily rid themselves of the terror, which had ruined their whole lives, if they could speak of it.

One day he was sitting over a pint of wine with a veterinary surgeon, a tradesman, and a mechanic. They became excited when what had happened in their town was mentioned. They let themselves go and used strong language. Gustav did the same. They attracted the attention of the people at the next table; before they were ready to leave the inn, they were arrested.

His papers of identification were examined in the concentration camp at Moosach. Georg Teibschitz, from Charlottenburg in Berlin, 92 Knesebeck Strasse, aged 49, entered for disorderly conduct. His head was shaved; he was made to strip—he reluctantly parted with his gray suit—and was compelled to put on striped clothing. The jacket was too long and the trousers much too tight. Gustav cut a ridiculous figure. If they made him bend his knees, every seam would burst. He thought of Johannes. The idea of the genuflections terrified him, yet he looked forward to them with secret excitement.

He was taken to a courtyard, lined up with five others, and told to stand at attention. Three young mercenaries with stolid, good-natured peasant faces guarded them.

The six men had to stand at attention, nothing more. For the first half hour, the rigid position was not an excessive strain on Gustav. Vaguely, in his heart, he had always been sure that his enterprise would come to such an end as his standing here, his body stiffened, carefully guarded by stupid, good-natured young men. Nevertheless, he had undertaken his task with enthusiasm. Frischlin and young Heinrich might consider it senseless; he knew that it was the right solution for him. Johannes Cohen had been a reproach to him for so long. Johannes, who had stuck it out at his teacher's desk in the midst of riotous Saxon students, Johannes the marionette on his elastic—down on your knees, arm out—the dead Johannes, broken bones, a mutilated mass of flesh in a sealed casket. Johannes had nothing more to reproach him with now. They were quits.

Such were Gustav's thoughts and feelings during the first half hour. From then on he only felt: "I shan't be able to keep this up." They had been given no food at noon. The man next to him had been drooping and getting shaky for some time; a rubber truncheon made him straighten up again. "If only the back of my neck would not ache so," thought Gustav. "Now, I'll shove my right foot forward a little bit. No, my left. They'll hit me if I do it. All the same, I'm going to shove my left foot forward. I must simply lift it up and give it one or two shakes." But he did not do it.

[. . .]

Day after day went by, always in the same torturing monotony and gloom. It was not until the end of the second week that any special incident occurred.

On this occasion an officer of higher rank—one of those with an oak twig—attended the "instructions" of Gustav's section. They had to recite in chorus one of the maxims of the Nationalists: "The State above the people." They recited the sentence and repeated it several times. Suddenly the officer with the oak twig pricked up his ears and interrupted them; asked them to repeat it in groups of four. He arrived at Gustav's group. There—it could be heard quite distinctly—a voice spoke: "Hate above the people." The man with the oak twig made them repeat the sentence again. Again it came: "Hate above the people." It was the half-witted man who had lost his glasses; they all heard the words, they all knew that the poor idiot was reciting them with the best of intentions. He repeated what he had actually understood, what he believed was the idea of the Nationalists. But the half-wit was not officially listed as a half-wit, therefore he must be considered malevolent. He and his entire section were punished by having to forgo alternately their lunch and supper. However, the ringleaders, the group to which Gustav and the man without glasses belonged, were locked up in the coal sheds.

The sheds were situated next to the outhouses. They had at one time been outhouses also, now boards had been nailed across the seats to fit them for their new purpose. Each one was about five foot square and was completely dark. Gustav was locked in one of those sheds for a week, day and night. He was allowed out only for meals. To begin with, he suffered principally from the appalling stench, then he suffered more—increasingly so day by day—from the inability of moving his limbs or stretching himself. His back hurt him most.

There were hours in which Gustav crouched in a sort of doze; there were hours of the most terrible despair, hours of rage, hours of feverish meditation on the possibility of someone trying to do something for him. But there were no longer any hours in which Gustav approved of his destiny. He never thought again: *"Gam su letovo."*

He had been a fool to return to Germany. Those two young men, Heinrich and the other, had been right. The Jews who remained in Germany and held their tongues were right. What an impudent piece of conceit that had been, thinking himself superior to Herr Weinberg. Had Bilfinger ever fixed it up again with his fiancée? That cursed Bilfinger. It was all his fault. He wished he could knock his glasses off his square head for him. No, it was all Johannes Cohen's fault. He was the one who had enticed him here. Johannes had always spoiled everything for him. And he had had an easy time of it with his knee bending. To hop about like a marionette was no art. To stand for two minutes on the tips of your toes is a different proposition, my lad. Especially during movement Number Three.

What were those places called where the Romans used to lock up their slaves? Some ancient writer had described them. Silly of me not to be able to think of the word. I used to believe, in Max Reger Strasse, that I couldn't work unless I had plenty of room to walk up and down. Shall I ask them to dock me another meal and let me out for two hours instead? They wouldn't do it. They have smashed the standards to pieces! Now I have it. Columella was the man who wrote about the slaves, and the places were called *ergastula*. My memory. I still have a decent memory left.

I'm a beast in a cage. It won't help anybody if I perish here in this stench. They were right. There is nothing more ridiculous than a martyr. That Johannes Cohen ought to have been given a punch on the jaw. *De mortuis nil nisi bene.* All the same, he ought to have been given a good punch. Anna should have advised me against this. She should have shut me up in a sanatorium for nervous disorders. And now, I'm really going to give Johannes one right in the middle of his yellow jaw.

He struck out. His fist met the wooden wall of the cell. It had been a weak blow but he was terrified by it. He was afraid someone might have heard it. He sat up erectly and said, "Yes, sir."

One night he, too, was conducted to an "examination." He was classified under the heading of "disorderly conduct." He still belonged to those under "light correction," in spite of the punishment he had undergone. If he was "examined," it was not with any evil end in view but solely because they happened to have nothing else to do. Nevertheless, Gustav returned from this examination in such a state that when they came to fetch him from his cell the next day, he was found there, leaning against the wall in a fainting condition. He was sent to the infirmary barracks for two days. Then he went back to his original room and his days went on as before. Except that the elderly man without glasses had now disappeared, and it was now Gustav who, when he was addressed, held his arm in front of his face and said, "Yes, sir."

[. . .]

Translated by J. Cleugh

Anna Seghers

From
The Seventh Cross

Never perhaps in man's memory were stranger trees felled than the seven plane trees growing the length of Barrack III. Their tops had been clipped before, for a reason that will be explained later. Crossboards had been nailed to the trunks at the height of a man's shoulder, so that at a distance the trees resembled seven crosses.

The camp's new commander, Sommerfeld by name, immediately ordered everything to be cut up into kindling wood. There was quite a difference between him and his predecessor, the gallant Fahrenberg, conqueror of his own home town, Seeligenstadt, where to this day his father runs a humble plumbing shop on Market Square. The new commander had seen service in Africa as a colonial officer before the war, and afterward he had marched upon Hamburg with his old major, Lettow-Vorbeck. All this we learned much later. The old commander had been a fool given to unpredictable fits of cruelty; the new one was a methodical, matter-of-fact fellow whose every action was dictated by cold calculation. Whereas Fahrenberg might suddenly have had us all battered to bits, Sommerfeld would have the men lined up and every fourth one beaten to a pulp. That, too, we did not know as yet. What if we had known it? What would it have amounted to, compared with what we felt when the six trees, and finally the seventh one, were cut down? A small triumph, assuredly, considering our helplessness and our convicts' clothing;

but a triumph nevertheless—how long was it since we had felt the sensation?—which suddenly made us conscious of our own power, that power we had for a long time permitted ourselves to regard as being merely one of the earth's common forces, reckoned in measures and numbers, though it is the only force able suddenly to grow immeasurably and incalculably.

That evening was the first time our barracks were heated. It coincided with a change in the weather. Today I am no longer sure whether the billets we fed to our little castiron stove actually came from that kindling. At the time, we were convinced of it.

We crowded about the stove because our clothes were wet and because our hearts were deeply moved by the unaccustomed sight of an open fire. The SA guard turned his back upon us and looked indifferently toward the barred window. The slight gray drizzle, no more than a fog, had suddenly turned into a sharp rain, hurled against the barrack by gusts of wind. After all, even an SA man, be he ever so hard-boiled, can see autumn's entry but once a year.

The billets crackled. Two little blue flames appeared—the coal had caught fire. We were granted five shovelsful of coal, hardly enough for a few minutes' warmth in the drafty barrack, let alone for drying our things. But we were not thinking of that as yet. We only thought of the wood burning before our eyes. Softly, with an oblique look toward the guard and without moving his lips, Hans said: "Crackling!" Erwin said: "The seventh one!" On every face there was a faint strange smile, a mixture of heterogeneous elements, of hope and scorn, of helplessness and daring. We held our breaths. The rain beat fitfully against the boards and the tin roof. Erich, the youngest of us, glanced out of the corners of his eyes, in which were merged his own inmost thoughts as well as ours, and said: "Where is he now, I wonder!"

[. . .]

George was lying out there under the gray-blue sky in a furrow in the field, about a hundred years from the highway to Oppenheim. Not to get caught now! To be in the city by nightfall! The city! It was like a cave with hiding places and winding passages. From the beginning he had planned to be in Frankfurt by night and to go on at once to the suburbs and Leni. Once with Leni, everything else seemed simple to him. In a case of life and death, an hour and a half on the train shouldn't be an insuperable obstacle. The only trouble was that he was about three hours behind his schedule. True, the sky was still blue, but a haze rising from the river was already invading the fields. Soon the cars on the highway would have to switch on their lamps in spite of the afternoon sun.

Stronger than all fear, stronger than hunger and thirst and the damned throbbing in his hand (blood had long since soaked through the rag), stronger than all this was an overpowering desire to remain lying there, and trust in the approaching night. *Even now the fog is covering you; the sun has already paled behind this haze above your face. During the night they won't be looking for you here. You'll have peace.*

He tried to imagine what Wallau would advise. There was no doubting what he would say: "If you *want* to die, stay where you are. Tear a rag from your jacket for a new bandage. Go on to the city. Anything else is nonsense."

George turned over on his belly. Tears came to his eyes as he pulled the blood-encrusted rag from his hand. He felt nauseated once more when he looked at the stiff, blackish-blue little lump that was his thumb. He rolled over on his back after he had tightened the knot of the new bandage with his teeth. Tomorrow he'd have to find someone to fix up his hand. Suddenly he realized that he was expecting all kinds of things of the morrow, as if time in its flux carried one along automatically.

The denser the haze over the fields became, the stronger grew the blue of the saffron in the meadow. Only now did George notice the flowers. If he didn't succeed in reaching Frankfurt before night, he might send Leni a message. Should he spend on it the mark he'd found in the coat? Since his escape he had not thought of her, except as he thought of some guiding mark in the road, or of that first gray stone. How much energy he'd wasted on dreams, how much precious sleep! Dreams of this girl whom luck had put in his path three weeks to the day before his arrest. "I can't picture her to myself any more," he thought. Wallau, yes, and all the others too. He visualized Wallau clearest of all, but it was the billowing fog that made the others seem blurred.

The first lights were whisking along the highway. George climbed over the ditch. A sudden flash through his mind: "You'll never get me!" The same flash propelled him on to a brewery truck. At first he was dizzy with pain, for he'd had to use his injured hand in jumping. Almost immediately, so it seemed to him, but actually in about fifteen minutes, they drove into a yard on a street in Oppenheim. Only now did the driver notice that he had a passenger. "Beat it!" he growled. Perhaps it was something in George's leap down and his first staggering steps that made the driver turn his head again. "Going to Mainz by any chance?"

"Yes."

"Wait here!"

George had put his injured hand into his coat pocket. So far he had seen the driver only from behind. Even now he couldn't see his face because he was writing something on a pad against the wall. Then the driver walked across the yard and out of the gate.

George waited. The street in front of the gate sloped up gently. There was not fog here as yet; it was as though a summer day were fading out, so soft was the light on the pavement. Across the street was a grocery store, next to it a laundry, and then a butcher's. The bells tinkled as the shop doors opened and closed. There were two women with packages; a boy was biting into a piece of sausage. How in times past he had despised the strength and glamour of everyday life! Now to be able to walk in instead of waiting here, to be the butcher's helper, the grocer's errand boy, a guest in one of these homes! How differently, when he was in Westhofen, had he pictured a street to himself. Then he'd felt that every face and every paving stone reflected shame, that sadness muffled every step and every voice, even the children's games. But this street was quite peaceful, and the people seemed to be in good spirits.

"Hannes! Friedrich!" An old woman in the window above the laundry hailed two SA men who were walking by with their girls. "Come up, I'll make you some coffee."

"All right!" shouted the two couples, after whispering briefly to one another. As they bustled into the house, the woman closed the window with a pleased and contented smile because now she would have good-looking young people around her. George was seized with as strong an attack of sadness as he had even known in his life. He would have wept had not that voice soothed him, the voice that even in our saddest dreams tells us that presently all will be as nothing. "And yet there *is* something," thought George. The driver returned. He was a robust man, with little black birdlike eyes in a fleshy face.

"Get up here," he said curtly. "We're not allowed to pick up riders." He nodded at a sticker which stated tersely MITFAHRER VERBOTEN! "But I'm short a helper on this trip. Here, put on this cap there just in case."

George fumbled in the dashboard compartment and found the uniform cap, marked above the visor GELTZ'S BREWERY. He thought of the street scene. "Not a butcher's or grocer's helper, but a brewer's."

Outside the town, evening had already come. The driver cursed the fog. "What're you going to Mainz for?" he asked suddenly.

"The hospital."

"Which one?"

"The one I was in before."

"You seem to like the stink of chloroform," said the driver. "Me, they couldn't drag me into a hospital with a team of horses. Last February when the roads were icy . . ." They came near bumping into two cars that had been stopped suddenly by the SS patrol. The truck driver slammed on his brake and cursed again. After the SS man had waved the two cars on, he approached the brewery truck. The driver handed down his truck papers.

"And how about you up there?"

"Well, it hasn't been such a bad show," thought George. "I made two mistakes. Too bad one can't practice these things beforehand." He had exactly the same sensation he'd had when he was first arrested, when the house was suddenly surrounded—a quick sorting of all sentiments and thoughts, a lightning jettisoning of all rubbish, a cleancut farewell, and finally . . .

He wore a brown coat of Manchester velvet, there could be no doubt about that. The SS patrol compared descriptions. "It's surprising how many Manchester jackets are to be dug up between Mainz and Worms within three hours," Commissar Fischer had said, when Berger had brought in a velvet-coated fellow a while ago. "This particular type of apparel seems to enjoy a certain popularity among the people of this district." Except for the clothing, the details given in the warrant of arrest were taken from the fugitive's papers when he was admitted in December, 1934. "But for the jacket," mused the patrol, "this man in no way fits the description. This fellow here could be the fugitive's father; the man in the warrant was about his own age, a healthy fellow with a smooth, fresh face. Compare this description with this man's flat, pushed-in mug, with its thick nose and pouting lips!" Then he noticed for the first time the brewer's uniform cap and his preoccupation with Manchester jackets and descriptions that didn't tally faded from his mind. He waved them on. "*Heil Hitler!*"

Without a word, they rolled along for a few minutes at a fifty-mile clip. Suddenly, for the second time, the driver braked on the empty, open road. "Get down," he ordered. George wanted to say something. "Get down," the driver repeated threateningly. His fleshy face grew distorted as George still hesitated. He prepared to throw George out forcibly. George jumped down, bruising his hand again and barely suppressing a howl of pain. He staggered on as the truck speeded up, its lights soon swallowed by the fog that had thickened during the past few minutes. Cars whistled past him at brief intervals, but he dared not hail one. He didn't know whether there were hours of walking ahead of him, or whether he had already been walking for hours. While he was still trying to figure out exactly where he was—he knew he was between Oppenheim and Mainz—he came to a little village with bright lights in the windows. He could not chance asking its name. He heard a tinkling not far ahead and saw tracks that ended in a little square, presumably the village square. Now he was among the people waiting at a streetcar terminus. He spent thirty pfennigs of his mark. At first the car was almost empty, but at the third stop, a factory, a crowd got on, and George kept his eyes down. He looked at nobody, content to give himself up to the warmth and presence of all these people; he felt safe and almost sheltered. But when anyone pushed against him or glanced at him casually, he grew cold.

George got off at Augustinerstrasse, and walked along the rails toward the center of the town. He was suddenly wide awake. But for his hand, he might have felt lighthearted. That was because of the street, the crowd, and the town generally, which leaves nobody to himself, or at least gives that impression. One of these thousands of doors would surely open hospitably, if only he could find it! He bought two rolls in a bakeshop. All this babbling of the women, old and young, around him, about the price of the bread and its quality, about the children and men who would eat it—had it actually gone on uninterruptedly all this time? "What a fancy, George," he said to himself. "It has never ceased, it will never cease." He ate his rolls while he walked, brushed some flour dust from Hellwig's jacket.

Looking through a gate into a yard, he saw some boys drinking water from a fountain there; there was a cup attached to a chain. After he had had a drink, he walked on. Finally he came to a very large square which looked foggy and empty, in spite of lamp posts and the people in it. He would have liked to sit down now, but he didn't dare.

In the meantime, bells had begun to peal, so near and strong that the very wall against which exhaustion had forced him to lean seemed to reverberate. The crowd in the square began to thin. He was certain that the Rhine could not be far distant. The child he questioned answered him briskly: "What's the matter? Do you want to drown yourself tonight?" Only then did he realize that this person, although thin and weakly, was not a child, but a bold and greedy grown woman. She hung around, thinking he might ask her to accompany him down to the river. But nothing was further from his mind; on the contrary, she had made him focus his whirling thoughts and come to a decision: On no account must he cross the river over one of the large bridges; he must spend the night here in the town. Now of all times the bridgeheads were sure to be doubly guarded. To keep on the left bank, though more hazardous, was the more reasonable thing to do. He'd have to find another chance to cross farther downstream. "Don't try to reach your destination by a direct route; make a wide detour!" He looked after the girl blankly.

In the meantime the bells had ceased. The sudden silence in the square and the absence of the reverberation in the wall against which he was once again leaning made him realize how strong and powerful their sound had been. He took a step forward and looked up at the spires, but grew dizzy before he found the highest one. Above the two squat steeples near by a single spire towered into the autumn sky with so effortless a daring and ease that it hurt him. Suddenly it occurred to him that in so vast an edifice there ought to be no dearth of chairs. He looked for the entrance; it was a door, not a gate. Still marveling at actually being able to get in, he collapsed on the nearest end of the nearest bench. "Here," he thought, "I can rest." Only then did he look about him. Not even under the vast expanse of the sky had he felt so tiny. When he saw the three or four women scattered here and there, as tiny as he himself, realized the distance between himself and the nearest pillar, the distance between one pillar and another, and realized too that from where he sat he could see no ending either above or in front of him, but only space and again space, amazement rose within him. And perhaps the most amazing thing of all was that for a moment he forgot his own self.

The sexton, however, quickly put an end to his amazement. Treading firmly—you see, he was used to the place, and besides he was doing what he was supposed to do—he came stalking along between the pillars, announcing in a loud and crusty voice that it was closing time. To the women who seemed unable to tear themselves from their prayers he said—rather as an adviser than a comforter—that the dear Lord at any rate would be there again tomorrow. George jumped up in alarm. The women got up slowly and went past the sexton and through a nearby door. George went back to the door through which he had entered, but it was already closed. He was hurrying across the nave to catch up with the women when a thought flashed through in his mind. He slowed his pace and ducked behind a large baptismal font. The sexton locked the door.

[. . .]

When the doors had been locked and the sexton had gone and the last sound had disintegrated in a distant vault, George realized that he had been granted a reprieve, a respite so tremendous that he almost confused it with actual deliverance. He was filled with a burning sensation of safety for the first time since his flight, even since his imprisonment. This sensation was as violent as it was short-lived. "It's damned cold in this hole," he said to himself.

The twilight was so acute that the colors in the windows grew blurred. It had reached the point when walls recede, vaults lift up, and pillars in endless rows merge into nebulous distances that may be nothing at all, but then again may be infinity. George suddenly felt that someone was watching him. The idea paralyzed him body and soul, and he fought against it. He stuck his head out from under the font, and started to crawl out. When he was sixteen feet away from the next pillar he met the gaze of a man who, with staff and miter, leaned against his sepulchral slab. The twilight dissolved the glory of his billowing vestments, but not of his features. They were clear and innocent, but at the same time threatening; he eyes followed George as he crawled past him.

The twilight did not penetrate from outside, as it usually does. Instead, the cathedral itself seemed to dissolve, to melt. Those vines on the pillars, the distorted faces, and the pierced naked foot over there were just imagination, an illusion. Everything that was stone began to turn into vapor; George alone was stone—petrified with fear. He closed his eyes and drew his breath a few times. And then it was all over, or perhaps the twilight had become a little more acute, and thereby more reassuring. He looked for a hiding place. He darted from one pillar to another, crouching low as if he were still being watched. Against the pillar in front of which he squatted leaned a well-rounded healthy man, who from his marble slab stoically looked beyond George, on his ample face the brazen smile of power. In each hand he held a crown which through eternity he would bestow on two dwarfs, the anti-kings of the Interregnum. With one leap George made the next pillar, as if the intervening spaces were full of eyes. He looked up at a man whose clothes were so ample that he could have wrapped himself in them. He gave a violent start at the face he saw bending over him, full of sadness and compassion. *Why do you struggle on, my son? Resign yourself, for even at the beginning you are at the end. Your heart is throbbing, and your injured hand, too, is throbbing.* George discovered a suitable hiding place, a niche in the wall. Holding his left arm out like a dog with a sore paw, he slid across the aisle, under the eyes of six arch-chancellors of the Holy Roman Empire. He tried to make himself comfortable. He rubbed the joint of his injured hand where it had grown stiff. He rubbed his knees, his ankles, his toes.

He was already feverish. His injured hand must not make any trouble for him before he reached Leni's. Once there, she would bandage it, and he could wash, eat, drink, sleep, and be cured. He started up. In that case he ought to wish that the night, which a moment ago he had desired so ardently, be over as quickly as possible. Again he tried to picture Leni to himself, a conjurer's trick that succeeded at times and failed at others, depending upon place and time. This time he succeeded: a slender nineteen-year-old girl with long slim legs, her blue eyes almost black under their heavy lashes, her face a golden tan. This was the substance of his dream. In the light of remembrance and in the course of their separation this girl, who in reality had impressed him at first as a bit odd because of her long arms and legs that gave her walk a certain awkwardness, had become a fairy creature that occurs only on rare occasions, even in myths. As their separation lengthened, she had become more delicate and more evanescent with every subsequent dream. Even now, as he leaned against the icy wall, he poured out upon her a wealth of endearing terms, partly to keep himself from falling asleep.

Countless similar protestations and any number of unsubstantial adventures had followed the one time they had eventually had together. On the very next day he had to leave town. In his ears rang the assurances, monotonous and desperate: "I'll wait here till you come. If you have to flee I'll go with you."

From his place George could still make out the man at the corner pillar. In spite of the darkness, distance seemed to make the face even clearer. The curved lips seemed to pronounce the last and utmost offer; Peace instead of deathly fear, mercy instead of justice.

The little flat in Niederrad, shared by Leni with an older sister who was away at work most of the time, was favorably located either for a hiding place or for flight. Considerations of this kind had followed him even when he was crossing the threshold of the tiny room, although the room made him forget almost everything else, his past love affairs and long periods of his earlier life. Not even when the walls of the room had merged into one another like impenetrable hedges had the thought ceased to glimmer in his head that this would be a good hideout in an emergency. Once while he was in Westhofen he'd been told there was a visitor to see him, and for a moment he'd been afraid that the authorities had chanced upon Leni. At first he hadn't recognized the woman who confronted him. It might just as well have been any peasant girl, so far from his thoughts was this Elly whom they had brought in.

He must have been on the point of falling asleep when fright woke him up. The cathedral was filled with crashing sounds. A bright light traversed the entire edifice and shone on his extended foot. Should he flee? Was there still time? Where to? All the gates but the one through which the light was coming were locked. Perhaps he could still get to one of the side chapels. He supported himself on his injured hand, stifled a cry of pain, and collapsed.

He no longer dared to crawl across the ribbon of light, for the sexton's voice ran out: "Slovenly womenfolk! If it isn't one thing it's another!" His words resounded like pronouncements of doomsday judgments. An old woman, his mother, called out: "Why, there's your work bag." Another voice, that of the sexton's wife, joined in, reflected by the walls and pillars into a veritable howl of triumph: "I told you, didn't I, that I put it between the benches when I was cleaning?" The two women withdrew. The noise of their footsteps sounded like giantesses dragging their feet. Again the door was locked. Sound was all that remained; it was shattered, re-verberated once more as if it would never subside, died away in the most distant corners, and was still trembling when George had ceased to tremble.

Again he leaned against the wall. His eyelids were heavy. Now it was entirely dark. The flicker of the solitary lamp somewhere in the blackness was so feeble that it no longer lighted up the vault, but only accentuated the all but impenetrable darkness. A moment ago George could have wished for nothing better; but now he breathed heavily and uneasily. "You must take your things off now," Wallau counseled him, "for you will be too weak later." He yielded, as he had always yielded to Wallau and, doing so, was amazed to feel his exhaustion subside.

Wallau had been imprisoned two months later than himself. "So you are George." In these four words, the older man's greeting, George for the first time had sensed his own full worth. Some dis-charged prisoner must have spoken about him outside. While he was being tortured to death at Westhofen, his home village and the towns he'd lived in were forming their judgment of him—an imper-ishable tombstone. Even now, leaning against the ice-cold wall, George thought: "If in all my life I could meet Wallau only in Wes-thofen, I would go through everything again . . ." For the first time, perhaps for the last, a friendship had come into his young life at a moment when it was a matter not of bragging or belittling, or with-holding desperately or giving oneself entirely, but merely of show-ing one's true worth and being loved for it.

The darkness was no longer so dense to his eyes. The plaster on the wall gleamed faintly like newly fallen snow. His whole body seemed to warn him that it stood out darkly. Should he change his place once more? When would they unlock the gates for early mass? There would be countless minutes of safety before morning came. He had as many minutes before him as, let us say, the sexton had weeks. For, after all, even a sexton is not immune to danger all his life.

Far away, toward the main altar, a single pillar was plainly visi-ble as the light played along its grooves. This one illumined pillar seemed to support the entire vault. But how cold it was. An icy world, as though no human hand had ever touched it, like a human thought. As if he had been cast away on a glacier. With his uninjured hand he rubbed his feet and all his joints. In this refuge one might freeze to death.

"A triple somersault! That's the most the human body is capable of." Belloni, the acrobat, his fellow prisoner, had explained it to him minutely. Belloni, whose everyday name was Anton Meier, had been arrested straight from his trapeze because in his luggage a few letters had been found that had come from the artists' lodge in France. How often had Belloni been waked up out of his sleep to do some of his stunts. A dark silent man, a good comrade, but very aloof. "I tell you, there are perhaps only three performers living now who can do that. Oh, well, yes, this one or that may manage it once in a while, but never steadily, one day right after another." Belloni of his own accord had approached Wallau and said that he himself would attempt an escape under any circumstances. They were doomed here anyway. In his flight he relied on his own agility and his friends' readiness to help. He had given George an address where, whatever happened, he would leave some money and clothing for him. A decent fellow most likely, but one could never quite make him out. George didn't care to use the address.

On Thursday morning he would send Leni to some old friends in Frankfurt. If, in addition to his brains, Pelzer had had Belloni's sinews and muscles, he probably would have got away too. Old Aldinger surely had been recaptured by now. He could have been the father of all those blackguards, who even now perhaps were tearing his hair out and spitting into his old peasant face which failed to lose its dignity even when its owner no longer seemed to be in his right mind. The mayor of the neighboring village had denounced him because of an old family feud.

Of the seven, Fuellgrabe had been the only one he had known before. Often, from his till behind the counter, Fuellgrabe had contributed a mark, for his name was on George's collection list. Even in his greatest despair he had never been able to rid himself entirely of a certain resentment. He had just drifted into it, he would grumble; they had persuaded him; he had never been a man to say no.

Albert probably was no longer alive. For weeks he had put up with everything, protesting the trifling nature of his offense—some foreign-currency affair or other—until he had fallen into a frenzy of rage and been transferred to Zillich's punishment squad. How many relentless blows this Albert must have suffered before the last spark had been hammered out of his dulled heart.

"I shall freeze to death here," thought George, "and they will find me. The children will be shown a piece of wall: Here, on an autumn night in those wild days, a fugitive was once found frozen to death." What time was it? Almost midnight. With a new and perfect darkness surrounding him, he thought: "I wonder if anyone still remembers me. My mother? She was forever scolding. On painful feet she used to waddle up and down the street, short and fat, her breasts large and softly swaying. I suppose I'll never see her again, even if I stay alive." As far as her outward appearance was concerned, he had always been conscious only of her eyes, young and brown, but dark with reproach and helplessness. Even now he was ashamed of having been abashed before Elly, who for three months had been his wife, because his mother had such breasts and so funny a Sunday dress.

He thought of his old school chum, Paul Roeder. For ten years they had played marbles in the same street, and soccer for another ten years. Then he had lost sight of him because he himself had become another person, whereas little Roeder had remained the same. He thought now of Paul's round freckled face as of a landscape, beloved and forever barred. . . . Franz came to his mind. "Franz was good to me," thought George, "he took a great deal of pains with me. Thanks, Franz. We had a falling out later. What was it all about? What has become of him? A quiet fellow, decent, loyal."

George held his breath. Across the aisle fell the reflection of a stained-glass window, possibly lighted up by a lamp in one of the houses facing the cathedral square or by a passing car. An immense carpet, glowing with all the colors of the rainbow, suddenly unrolled in the darkness. Vainly and for nobody's benefit it was thrown night after night across the tiles of the empty cathedral, for even here visitors like George did not appear more than once in a thousand years.

While it burned, that light outside, perhaps serving to quiet a sick child or speed a departing man on his way, also served to illumine all the saintly pictures. "Ah," thought George, "these must be the two who were driven from Paradise; these the cattle gazing into the manger that sheltered the Child for whom there was no place anywhere else; there the Supper, when He already knew that He was being betrayed; there the soldier thrusting the spear as He hung on the cross . . ." George had long since forgotten most of the pictures. Many of them he had never known, for in his home such things were given scant attention. Anything that mitigates solitude has the power to comfort. Not only other people's suffering paralleling ours, but also the suffering others have gone through in bygone days.

George listened. A motorcar was going by outside. He heard the squealing and laughter of the men and women who obviously had been squeezed into a car much too small to hold them all. They drove away. Quickly the colors of the window were reflected between the pillars, withdrawn again, farther and farther away from him. His head fell forward upon his chest.

He slept.

When he slumped over on his wounded hand, the pain made him wake up. The deepest part of the night had passed. The plaster on a piece of wall in front of him began to gleam. In an order opposite to that when the evening had come, the darkness at first began to dissolve, then pillars and walls were seized with a ceaseless rippling, as if the cathedral were built of sand, Struck by the feeblest rays of the morning light, the pictures in the windows slowly came to life; they did not flash out, but appeared in dull and somber colors. At the same time the rippling stopped, and everything began to solidify. The vault of the nave became petrified in the immutable laws that had guided the Imperial House of the Hohenstaufens when they had built it, product of individual architects' intelligence and the inexhaustible power of the people. Petrified became the vault into which George had crawled, that vault which in the days of the Hohenstaufens and already been venerable. Petrified likewise the pillars, and all the hideous faces and animal heads in their capitals. Petrified anew on the marble slabs before the pillars the bishops in their stately wakefulness of death, and the kinds of whose coronation they had been so inordinately proud.

"No time to lose," thought George. He crawled out. Of his shirt and other things he had discarded he made a little bundle, drawing it together with his teeth and his uninjured hand. He slid it between

a slab and a pillar. His whole body tense and his eyes shining, he waited for the moment when the sexton would unlock the doors.
[. . .]

George had been successful. No sooner had the cathedral been opened than he assumed the role of early churchgoer. He was one of only a few men among a good many women. Recognizing him from the night before, the sexton thought to himself with a feeling of satisfaction: "Aha, another one who got it just in the nick of time . . ." It took George some little time to stand up straight. Painfully he dragged himself outside. "He won't last more than a few days," thought Dornberger, the sexton. "He'll collapse in the street." George's face was gray, as if he had some fatal disease.

If only his hand were not causing him so much trouble. Why must there always be some tiny bit of nonsense to ruin everything? "When and where did this happen to my hand? On the glass-encrusted wall, about twenty-four hours ago . . ." He felt himself pushed along by the people through the side door of the cathedral and into a short little street, framed by low houses in which the shops were already lighted.

When the cool damp air hit his face, George was done for. His legs slid from under him, and he found himself in a heap on the pavement. Two elderly ladies, spinster sisters, were coming out of the church. One of them forced a five-pfennig piece into his hand. The other scolded! "You know that's forbidden." The donor bit her lips. She had been scolded these fifty years.

In spite of everything, George had to smile. How fond he had been of life! He had loved all of it: the sweet little lumps on the seeded cakes and even the chaff they put into the wartime bread; the cities and the rivers and the country and its people; Elly, his wife; and Lotte and Leni and little Katy and his mother and his little brother; the party slogans to make people come alive; the little songs to the accompaniment of a lute; the sentences Franz used to read to him, which contained great thoughts that upset his whole life; and even the babbling of old women. How good the whole had been; only the single parts were evil.

He pulled himself together and, propped against the wall, looked hungrily and miserably toward the market whose stalls were being put up under the fogbound lanterns. He felt his blood surge to his heart as if, in spite of everything, he were being loved in return, though perhaps for the last time, by all people and by all things, with a painful and helpless love. He stumbled the few steps to a pastry shop. Fifty pfennig he would have to keep as capital. He put a few coins on the counter. The woman poured a plateful of crumbs, broken ends of toast, and burnt edges of cakes on a piece of paper. She glanced briefly at his jacket; it seemed to her much too good for such a purchase.

Her glance brought George fully to his senses. Outside, he stuffed all the crumbs into his mouth. Chewing very slowly, he dragged himself to the edge of the square. The street lights were still lit, but they were useless. The opposite row of houses was already visible through the haze of the autumn morning. George walked on and on through a maze of streets that wound like yarn around the market; he finally emerged again upon it. He noticed a sign: DR. HERBERT LOEWENSTEIN.

"Here's the man who's got to help me," thought George. He walked up the stairs.

For a moment there was silence as he entered the waiting room. Everyone there looked at him briefly. There were two groups of patients. On the sofa near the window sat a woman and a child and a youngish man in a raincoat. At the table, an old peasant and a middle-aged citified man with a boy, and now George.

The peasant was talking. "Now I am here the fifth time. He has not helped me any, but there is a certain relief, yes, a certain relief. I hope it'll last at least until our Martin is home from his military service and gets married." His monotonous voice showed that even talking caused him pain. But he was partly repaid for it by the satisfaction he had in telling his story. "And you?" he added.

"I haven't come here on my own account," said the other drily, "but because of the lad here. He's my only sister's only child. The child's father has forbidden her to send him to Loewenstein. So I just took the boy and brought him myself."

The old man sat clasping his hands round his abdomen, probably the seat of his pain. He said: "As if there were no other doctor to go to."

The other man said quietly: "Well, you yourself come here too."

"I? I've been to all the others too: Dr. Schmidt, Dr. Wagenseil, Dr. Reisinger, and Dr. Hartlaub." Suddenly he turned to George:

"What's the matter with you, eh?"

"My hand."

"Why, this is no doctor for hands, he's internal."

"I have some internal trouble too."

"Automobile accident?"

The waiting-room door opened. Quite overcome by pain, the old peasant leaned on the table and against George's shoulder. It was not only fear that filled George, but a child's irrepressible anxiety in a doctor's waiting room. He remembered having had the same sensation when he was a little boy no older than the jaundiced lad at his side. As in those days, he caught himself continually plucking at the fringes of his chair.

The doorbell rang. George gave a start. But it was only another patient, a half-grown dark girl, who went past the table.

At last he was facing the doctor. Name, address, occupation, please. He said whatever came into his mind. The walls were beginning to sway; he felt himself gliding down an abyss of white and glass and nickel, a meticulously clean abyss. While he was gliding he heard the doctor's voice make obligatory reference to his being a Jew. A smell reminded him of the aftermath of all cross-examinations when iodine and bandages were being applied. "Sit down," said the physician.

On first seeing George, he had thought that this patient made a thoroughly unfavorable impression. He was quite familiar with the symptoms: no gaping wounds, no abscesses, a very delicate, thin shading above and below the eyes—in this case it had already grown into a blackish compact shadow. What could ail the man?

He began to undo the ragged bandage. An accident? Yes. A physician through and through, he was immediately under the spell that every wound and every disease exerted upon him. Yet through it all he was aware of his uneasiness at the mere sight of this man, a feeling that grew stronger when he saw the bandage. From the lining of a jacket? He undid it very slowly. What kind of man was this, anyway? Old? Young? His preoccupation grew.

He looked at the hand which now lay exposed before him. Undoubtedly it was badly messed up, but not so badly as to justify the symptoms displayed on this man's forehead and in his eyes. Why the terrible exhaustion? He had come because of his hand. Without question, perhaps unknown to himself, he was also suffering from some other ailment. The glass splinters had to be removed now. He would have to give the man a hypodermic injection; otherwise he might faint. He had said he was an automobile mechanic.

"In a couple of weeks," said the doctor, "you'll be able to go back to work." The man did not reply. Will he be able to stand the injection? The man's heart, though not entirely sound, was not in a particularly bad condition. What was the matter with him? Why did he not follow his impulse to find out what ailed the man?

And why had the man not gone to the nearest hospital immediately after the accident? The dirt in the wound had certainly been in there at least overnight. He wanted to ask these questions, if for no other reason than to distract the man's attention from his hand.

Now he set to work with the pincers, but the man's eyes restrained him. He stopped short. Again he looked closely at the hand, briefly at the man's face, at his jacket, at his whole person. The man twisted his mouth slightly, gazing at the doctor obliquely but firmly.

Turning away slowly, the physician felt himself go white to his very lips. As he looked at himself in the mirror above the washbasin the dark shadows had spread to his own face. He closed his eyes. He soaped his hands and washed with infinite slowness, letting the water run.

"I have a wife and children. Why does this man have to come and see *me?* . . . To have to tremble every time the bell rings . . . And what I have to go through anyway, day in and day out!"

George looked at the doctor's white back. He thought: "Not you only!"

The physician was holding his hands under the water, making it squirt. "It's unbearable, really, what I have to go through. And now this into the bargain! Why, it's unbearable that anyone should have to suffer so."

George thought again, his brows knit, while the water gushed forth like a spring: "But not you only!"

The doctor turned off the water and dried his hands on a clean towel. For the first time he smelled the chloroform as only his patients usually smelled it. "Why did the man come to me of all people? To me? Why?"

Again he turned on the tap. He washed a second time. "See here, this doesn't concern you at all. It was just a hand that came into your consulting room, a sick hand. Whether it dangles from the sleeve of a scoundrel or from under the wing of an archangel must be a matter of indifference to you." He turned off the water and dried his hands again. Then he adjusted his syringe. Turning George's sleeve back, he noticed that the man was not wearing a shirt. "That does not concern me," he said to himself. "I'm concerned only with the hand."

Later George slid his bandaged hand into his jacket and said: "Thanks very much!" The doctor had meant to ask for some money, but the man had thanked him in a tone that suggested he believed himself treated without charge. Though he reeled a bit when he left, the doctor thought now that after all the chief trouble had been his hand.

As George was going down the stairs, the janitor, a little man in shirt sleeves, planted himself in front of him on the bottom landing. "You coming from the second floor?"

With no time to reflect whether truth or untruth would be wiser, George quickly lied: "From the third."

"Oh, I see," said the little man. "I thought you might have come from Loewenstein's."

[. . .]

George ran on into the evening, so misty and still that it gave him a sense of elusiveness. At every step he told himself that the next step would surely be the last one. Every step, however, was but the next to the last. Shortly after passing through Mombach he had been ordered to get off the market truck. There were no longer any bridges here, but there was a landing place at every village. George had left one after another of them behind him. The moment to cross to the other bank had not yet come. If a man's energies are focused upon one point, everything—instinct as well as reason—will transmit a warning to him.

As on the evening before, he lost his sense of time. Foghorns were sounding from the Rhine. On the highroad which ran beside the river on an embankment, lights were flitting past at ever-increasing intervals. A tree-covered island in the near foreground obstructed his view of the water. Beyond the reeds gleamed the lights of a farm, but they filled him neither with fear nor with confidence. So deserted was this part of the country that they looked like will-o'-the-wisps. The view-obstructing island extended a long distance—perhaps it, too, had already come to an end. The lights might be those of a ship or they might come from the opposite bank which was no longer hidden by a tree-covered island but by the fog. A fellow might perish here in a very ordinary way, a victim of common exhaustion. To have two minutes now of Wallau's company, no matter in what hell. . . .

If Wallau succeeded in getting to a certain Rhenish town, there was hope that he could get out of the country from there. People who had carefully prepared the next stage of his flight were waiting there.

When Wallau was imprisoned the second time, his wife was convinced that she would never see him again. Her requests for a visitor's permit having been denied roughly, even threateningly—she had personally gone to Westhofen from Mannerheim, where she was now living—she had decided to save her husband no matter what cost. She followed up this decision with the uncanny perseverance of a woman whose first step in approaching an impracticable plan is the elimination of her sense of judgment, or at least of that part of it whose function is to pass on the practicability of things. Wallau's wife was guided neither by previous experiences nor by information vouchsafed by those around her, but by two or three legends of successful escapes. For instance, Beimler's from Dachau, Seeger's from Oranienburg. Legends, too, contain certain information and certain experiences. She also knew that her husband, a man of iron determination, had centered all his energies on the burning desire to live, and that he would thus grasp the slightest chance. Her refusal to distinguish in her quest between what was possible and what impossible did not prevent her handling many details skillfully. In the establishment of connections and in the transmission of news she used her two boys, especially the older one. In earlier days he had been well taught by his father and, burning with zeal, he was now in the secret regarding his mother's plans. A dark-eyed, persevering lad in the Hitler Youth uniform, he was burned rather than enlightened by the flame that was almost too much for his heart.

Now, on the evening of the second day, Frau Wallau knew that the jail break itself had been successful. She could not know when her husband would arrive at the bungalow on the allotment garden plot near Worms, where money and clothing were stored for him.

Perhaps he had already passed through there last night. The bunga-low was the property of a family named Bachmann. The man was a streetcar conductor. The two women had gone to school together thirty years before, and their fathers had been friends, as their hus-bands also had been. Both women had shared all the burdens of a common life and, during the past three years, the burdens of an uncommon one as well. Bachmann, to be sure, had been in prison only a short time early in '33. He had been working ever since and had not been molested.

It was this man, the conductor, for whom Frau Bachmann was waiting now, while Wallau's wife was waiting for her husband. Al-though Frau Bachmann knew that it would take her husband ten minutes to get from the car barn to his home, she was greatly dis-turbed, a fact which manifested itself in minute twitching motions of her hands. Perhaps he had had to take another man's place—he would not be home before eleven. Attending to her children, Frau Bachmann grew somewhat calmer.

"Nothing can happen," she said to herself for the thousandth time. "Nothing can be found out. And even if it should be discov-ered, nobody could prove anything against us. He may simply have stolen the money and clothing. We've been living here in the city, and none of us has gone to the bungalow for weeks . . . If one could only go and see whether the things are still there. Ah, this is almost unbearable. I don't see how Frau Wallau can stand the strain."

Frau Bachmann had said to Wallau's wife at the time: "Do you know, Hilde, this thing has changed all the men, ours included?"

Hilde had replied: "Nothing has changed Wallau."

"Ah, if once Death has been so close that one could look him straight in the eye . . ."

Frau Wallau had interrupted her: "Nonsense! How about us? And me? It was nearly all over with me when I had my oldest one. And a year later another."

Frau Bachmann had said: "They know everything about a person."

"'Everything' is saying too much. They know just what one is willing to tell them," Frau Wallau had replied.

Frau Bachmann, sitting quietly and alone, noticed that her hands had begun to twitch again. She got some sewing. That soothed her.

"Nobody can prove anything against us," she said to herself again. "We'd say it was some burglar."

She heaved a sigh of relief when at last she heard her husband's steps on the stairs. She got up to prepare his supper. He entered the kitchen without saying a word. Even before Frau Bachmann had a chance to turn around she felt, not only in her heart but all over her body, as if the temperature of the room had gone down several degrees when her husband came in.

"Anything the matter?" she asked when she saw his face. He did not reply. She put the full plate of soup between his elbows. The steam from it went up into his face. "Otto," she asked, "are you ill?" Still he did not answer.

The woman became mortally afraid. "But," she thought, "it can't have anything to do with the bungalow, for after all he is here. The thing must be weighing on his mind. I wish it were all over."

"Don't you want to eat?" The man did not reply. "You mustn't always think of it," said his wife. "If we always have it on our mind we'll go mad." From the man's partly closed eyes veritable rays of agony were darting. Frau Bachmann had again taken up her sewing. When she looked up she saw that her husband had closed his eyes. "What is the matter with you? Do tell me!"

"Nothing!" But how he said it! As if his wife had asked him whether there was nothing in the world left for him, and he had truthfully answered: "Nothing!"

"Otto," she said, sewing, "perhaps there is something, is there?"

But the man replied vacantly and quietly: "Nothing, nothing at all!" When she looked into his face, quickly raising her eyes to his from her sewing, she knew that there truly was nothing at all. All that he had ever had was lost.

The woman felt cold as ice. She hunched her shoulders and turned her body away, as if it were not her husband sitting at the head of the table but . . . She sewed on and on. She did not think; she asked no question, for fear that the answer might destroy her whole life.

And what a life! An ordinary life, surely, with the usual struggle for one's daily bread and stockings for the children. But at the same time a bold, strong life, with a burning interest in everything that was worthy to be experienced. Add to it what they—she and the Wallau woman—had heard their fathers say when they were still two little pig-tailed girls who lived on the same street, and there was nothing that had not resounded within their four walls: struggles for the ten-hour day, for the nine-hour day, the eight-hour day; speeches that were read even to the women as they bent over the truly fiendish holes in the stockings; speeches from Bebel to Liebknecht, and from Liebknecht to Dimitroff. Even their grandfathers, the children were told proudly, had been imprisoned because they had taken part in strikes and demonstrations. Ah, to be sure, in those days no one had been murdered and tortured for such misdeeds. What a straightforward life? And now that a single question, a thought even, had the power to undo it all! But here it was already, the thought. What ailed her husband? Frau Bachmann, a simple woman, was fond of her husband. Lovers once, they had been together now for many years. She was not like the Wallau woman who had managed to add a good deal to her knowledge. Ah, but the man at the end of the table was not her husband at all. He was an unbidden guest, strange and sinister.

Where had the man come from? Why had he been so late? While he had been a different man for a long time, now he seemed utterly destroyed. Ever since he had suddenly been discharged from prison that day, he had been a changed man. Though his wife had been glad and shouted with joy, his face had remained vacant and tired. A voice within her whispered: "Would you actually want him to share Wallau's fate?" The woman wanted to answer: "No! No!" But a voice, far older than she and at the same time much younger, had already replied: "Yes, it would be better." "I can't stand the sight of his face," Frau Bachmann thought. As if she'd spoken aloud, the man got up and walked to the window, his back to the room, although the shade was drawn.

[. . .]

Much later, someone telling about that morning said: "The bringing in of Wallau made upon us prisoners about the same impression as the fall of Barcelona or Franco's entry into Madrid or some other event that showed clearly that the enemy had all the power in the world on his side. The flight of the seven men had the most catastrophic consequences for all of us. Nevertheless, with equanimity and at times even with scorn, everyone bore being deprived of food and blankets, the increased hardness of the work, and the hours of being grilled to the accompaniment of blows and threats. Our atti-

tude, which we seemed unable to hide, incensed our tormentors all the more. So strongly did most of us consider these fugitives to be part of ourselves that we felt as though they were our emissaries. Although we had known nothing of the plan, we had the sensation of having succeeded in some rare undertaking. To many of us the enemy had seemed all-powerful. The strong can afford to be wrong at times without loss of prestige, because even the most powerful are after all only human—yes, their mistakes make them all the more human—but he who claims omnipotence must never be wrong because there can be no alternative to omnipotence except insignificance. If one stroke, no matter how tiny, proved successful against the enemy's alleged omnipotence, everything was won. This feeling soon gave way to terror and even despair when one after another was brought back comparatively quickly and, so it seemed to us, with scornfully little effort. During the first two days and nights we asked ourselves whether they'd ever get Wallau. We hardly knew him. After his admission he had been with us for a few hours, but he had soon been taken off again for a grilling. Two or three times after being questioned we had seen him led away reeling, one hand pressed to his abdomen; but with the other he made a tiny motion toward us as if he wanted to tell us that all this was of no conclusive importance and that we must be of good cheer. Now that Wallau himself had been caught and brought back, we bawled as if we had been little children. We were all of us lost now, we thought. Wallau would be murdered, as all the others before him had been murdered. In the very first month of the Hitler régime hundreds of our leaders had been murdered in every part of the country, and every month more were murdered. Some were executed publicly, others were tortured to death in the concentration camps. A whole generation had to be annihilated. These were our thoughts on that terrible morning; then for the first time we voiced our conviction that if we were to be destroyed on that scale, all would perish because there would be none to come after us. The almost unprecedented in history, the most terrible thing that could happen to a people, was now to be our fate: a no-man's-land was to be established between the generations, which old experiences would not be able to traverse. If we fight and fall, and another takes up the flag and fights and falls too, and the next one grasps it and he too falls—that is natural, for nothing can be gained without sac-

rifice. But what if there is no longer anyone to take up the flag, simply because he does not know its meaning? It was then that we felt sorry for the fellows who were lined up for Wallau's reception, to stare at him and spit on him. The best that grew in the land was being torn out by the roots because the children had been taught to regard it as weeds. All those lads and girls out there, once they had gone through the Hitler Youth, the Work Service, and the Army, would be like the fabled children nurtured by animals who finally tore their own mothers to pieces.

[. . .]

George took another car to Niederrad. The nearer he came to his goal, the stronger grew the impression that he was being awaited, that his bed was now being made, his dinner prepared. At this very moment his girl would be listening for a sound on the stairs. When he got off the car, he was filled with a tension akin to despair; as if his heart struggled against actually taking the way he had walked countless times in his dreams.

He passed through a few quiet streets with front gardens as one strolls through memories. Consciousness of the present was erased within him, and with it consciousness of danger. He not the dry leaves at the roadside rustled that day? he asked himself, not aware that his own shoe was disturbing the leaves. How his heart struggled against entering the house! This was no longer a pounding, it was a furious rattling! He leaned out of a window on the stairs. The gardens and courtyards of many houses came together here. The tops of walls and balconies were thickly covered with the endlessly falling leaves of a mighty chestnut tree. A few of the windows were already lighted. This sight so calmed him that he was able to continue his climb. Hanging at the door was still the old sign bearing the name of Leni's sister, and below it a new one, a little intarsia work, with a strange name. Should he ring or knock? Didn't that use to be a children's game? He knocked softly. "Yes?" said a young woman in a striped sleeved apron. She only opened the door a crack.

"Is Miss Leni at home?" asked George, less softly than he had intended, because his voice was hoarse. The woman stared at him, and into her healthy face and her round blue eyes, sparkling like glass marbles, came an expression of alarm. She tried to shut the door, but he put his foot in it. 'Miss Leni at home?"

"No one here by that name," said the woman hoarsely. "See that you get out of here immediately."

"Leni," he said calmly and firmly, as if he wanted to implore his own Leni of the past to leave for his sake the body of the buxom, prosaic, aproned woman into which she had been bewitched. It was in vain. The woman kept staring at him with the unabashed fear of a person bewitched who stares at those who have remained unchanged. Quickly he pushed open the door, elbowed the woman back into the hall, and closed the door behind him. The woman went back toward the open kitchen door. She held a shoebrush in her hand. "Why, Leni, listen to me. It is I. Don't you know me?"

"No, I don't," said the woman.

"Why were you startled then?"

"If you don't get out of this flat at once—" all of a sudden she was bold and saucy—"you'll get all you're looking for. My husband will be here any moment."

"Is that him?" asked George. On a little bench stood a pair of highly polished black top boots, beside them a pair of woman's low shoes. There was also an open tin of shoe polish and a few rags.

"Yes, it is." Now she had barricaded herself behind the kitchen table. "I'll count three," she said. "By three you'll be gone or else . . ."

George laughed. "Or else what?" He pulled the sock from his hand, a filthy black sock he had found somewhere on the way and pulled on glovelike to hide his bandage. She watched him with open mouth. He circled the table. She shielded her face with her arm. With one hand he grabbed her by the hair, with the other he jerked down her arm. In a voice one might use to speak to a toad which one knew had once been a human being, he said: "Stop it, Leni, and recognize me. I am George."

Her eyes became saucers. He held her fast, endeavoring at the same time to wrest the shoebrush from her hand, disregarding the pain in his own injured hand. Imploringly, she said: "But I don't know you."

He let go of her and took a step backward. "Very well," he said. "Just give me the money and the clothes."

For a moment she was silent; then, again quite bold and with renewed sauciness, she answered: "We give nothing to strangers. Only directly to the winter aid."

He stared at her, but in another way than before. The pain in his hand subsided, and with it the consciousness that all this was happening to him. He felt only faintly that his hand had begun to bleed again.

The blue-checked tablecloth on the kitchen table was set for two. Clumsy little swastikas were carved in the wooden napkin rings, an amateurish job. Slices of sausage, radishes and cheese were neatly decorated with parsley. A couple of open boxes contained pumpernickel and Swedish toast. He thrust his uninjured hand here and there on the table, stuffing in his pocket whatever came into his grasp. The glass-marble eyes followed his movements.

His hand on the latch, he turned round once more.

"You wouldn't make me a fresh bandage, would you?" She shook her head twice, quite seriously.

Going down the stairs, he leaned against the same window. He crooked his elbow and drew the sock back over his hand. "She won't say anything to her husband because she is afraid. She must never have known me. Almost all the windows are lighted now. Just look at all these leaves from the chestnut tree." As if autumn itself were dwelling in this tree, powerful enough to cover the whole city with foliage.

Slowly he shuffled on along the edge of the pavement. He wanted to make himself believe that another Leni with long swinging steps was coming to meet him from the other end of the street. Suddenly he became aware that never again would he be able to go to Leni and, what was infinitely worse, that he could never again even dream he was going to Leni. That dream was now utterly destroyed. He sat down on a bench and, without a thought, began to munch a slice of toast. As it had become cool and dusky and was much too conspicuous to keep on sitting there, he got up presently and trudged on, following the rails, for he no longer had the price of carfare. Where to go now, before nightfall?

Overkamp closed the door to have a few minutes' solitude before Wallau's questioning. He arranged his slips of paper, looked over his notes, sorted them, underscored words, and connected various items by a certain system of lines. His questionings were famous. Fischer had once said that Overkamp could get information from a corpse. His notes for an examination were comparable only to intricate musical scores.

Beyond the door, Overkamp could hear the scraping jerky sound that accompanies a military salute. Fischer came in and closed the door behind him. In his face, anger and amusement struggled for supremacy. He immediately sat down close to Overkamp. With only a lift of his eyebrows the latter warned him of the guard's presence beyond the door and of the partly open window. "Anything else the matter?"

In a low voice Fischer said: "This affair has affected Fahrenberg's brain. He'll certainly go insane over it. Perhaps he is already. He'll be fired anyway. We'll put some steam behind that. Just listen to what he's been up to again.

"We can't have three separate steel chambers built expressly for these three captured fugitives, can we? We made an agreement with the fellow, didn't we, that the three men were not to be touched until we had all of them safely back again? After that he can make sausage meat of them, as far as we are concerned. He had the three men brought before him once more. There are some trees standing in front of his quarters—I mean the things that used to be trees—he had them all trimmed this morning. Well, as I was going to say, he had the three men stood against the trees, so—" here Fischer spread out his arms— "after he'd had the trunks studded with nails so that the men couldn't lean against them. He had all the prisoners line up and made them a speech. You should have heard it, Overkamp. He took an oath that every one of the seven trees would have its occupant before the new week began. And do you know what he said to me? 'You see, I'm keeping my word—not a blow.'"

"How long is he going to keep them standing that way?"

"That's what caused all the rumpus. Will the men be fit for questioning after an hour or an hour and a half? Well, all right. He'd only exhibit the men to the camp once a day. That'll be his last fun in Westhofen. He thinks if he gets all seven back, he'll be allowed to stay."

"Even if this fellow Fahrenberg falls down the ladder now, he'll land at the bottom with such a bounce that it'll land him several rungs up another ladder," said Overkamp.

"As for this Wallau," continued Fischer, "I plucked him from Fahrenberg's third tree." He got up suddenly and opened the window. "Here they come. You'll excuse me, won't you, Overkamp, for giving you some advice now?"

"Which is?"

"Have them bring you a raw beefsteak from the canteen."

"What for?"

"Because you'll sooner knock a deposition out of that beefsteak than out of the man they're bringing in here now."

Fischer was right. Overkamp knew it as soon as he saw the man. He might just as well have torn up the slips of paper on his table. This fortress was impregnable. What Overkamp saw was an exhausted little man with an ugly little face, dark hair coming to a point on his forehead, heavy brows, and between them a furrow cleaving the forehead. Inflammation had made the eyes look smaller; the nose was broad and somewhat bulbous; the lower lip was bitten through and through.

Overkamp fastened his eyes on that face, the scene of the approaching action. This was the fortress which he was now to penetrate. If, as was alleged, it was impervious to fear and threats, there were other means of taking a fortress unawares, provide it was famished and weakened by exhaustion. Overkamp was familiar with all these means and he knew how to use them. He'd start with asking questions. In an effort to ascertain the weak points of the fortress he'd begin with the simplest of questions. He would ask for the date of birth and at once be informed of the star under which the man was born. Overkamp watched the prisoner's face as an officer watches a terrain. He had already forgotten his first sensation at Wallau's entrance. He had returned to his fundamental principle: there are no impregnable fortresses. Taking his eyes off the man's face, he looked at one of his slips. With his pencil he stabbed a little point behind a word and gazed back at Wallau. Politely he asked: "Your name is Ernst Wallau?"

Wallau replied: "I shall from now on refuse to answer any question."

To which Overkamp said: "So your name is Wallau. Let me point out to you that your silence will be interpreted as affirmation. You were born in Mannheim, on October 8, 1894."

Wallau remained silent. He had spoken his last words. If a mirror were held to his lips, not a breath would cloud it.

Overkamp did not take his eyes of Wallau. He was almost as motionless as the prisoner himself. Wallau's face had become a shade paler, the line cleaving the forehead a little blacker. The man's gaze was directed straight ahead, right through the affairs of a world that had suddenly become glassy and transparent, right through Overkamp and the board partition and the guard posted outside, right through to the core that is impenetrable and able to withstand the gaze of the dying. Fischer, a similarly motionless witness of the questioning, turned his head in the direction of Wallau's gaze. All he could see was the luscious everyday world that is not transparent and without core.

"Your father's name was Franz Wallau; your mother's Elisabeth Wallau, maiden name Enders."

Instead of an answer, silence came from the bitten-through lips. Once there had been a man named Ernst Wallau. That man was dead. Hadn't we just witnessed his last words? He had had parents whose names were as cited. One might as well place beside his father's tombstone that of his son. *If it is true that you can get depositions out of a corpse, I'm deader than all your dead.*

"Your mother lives in Manheim, Mariengaesschen 8, with her daughter Margarete Wolf, maiden name Wallau. No, stop: used to live . . . This morning she was transferred to the Home for the Aged at An der Bleiche 6. Following the arrest of her daughter and her son-in-law because they are suspected of having aided your escape, the flat at Mariengaesschen 8 was sealed."

When I was still alive I had a mother and a sister. Later I had a friend who married my sister. As long as a man lives he has all kinds of connections and family ties. But this man is dead. And no matter what strange things happen to these people in this strange world after my death, they need no longer concern me.

"You have a wife, Hilde Wallau, maiden name Berger. The fruit of this marriage was two children, Karl and Hans. Let me point out to you again that I am taking your silence to mean Yes." Fischer stretched out his hand, shifting the shade of the 100-watt lamp so that the light fell full in Wallau's face. Still the face remained as it had been, steeped in a dull evening light. No even a 1000-watt lamp can reveal traces of torment and fear or hope in the hopeless finality of dead men's faces. Fischer pushed the shade back again.

When I was still alive I also had a wife. We even had children. We raised them in our common belief. What a joy it was for husband and wife to see the teachings take root. How sturdily the little legs swung at their first political demonstration! The pride in the little faces, and the anxiety lest the heavy flags in their fists tip over! When I was still alive during the first years of the Hitler régime, when I was still doing all the things that meant life to me, I could without fear reveal my hiding places to these boys, at a time when other sons were betraying their fathers and teachers. Now I am dead. Let the mother worry about providing for the fatherless waifs.

"Your wife was arrested yesterday with your sister for having aided in your escape. Your sons were handed over to the Educational Institute at Oberndorf, to be brought up in the spirit of the National Socialist State."

When the man whose sons were now mentioned was still alive, he tried in his way to take care of his family. Now it would soon become apparent what the care was worth. Others who were far stronger than two foolish children have given way. And the lies are so luscious, and the truth so dry! Strong men have sworn their lives away. *Bachmann has betrayed me. But two young boys—that, too, is said to happen occasionally—will not deviate a hair's-breadth from the way of truth. My fatherhood, at any rate, has come to an end, no matter what the final outcome may be.*

"You fought in the World War as a soldier at the front."

When I was still alive I went to war. I was wounded three times—at the Somme, in Rumania, and in the Carpathian Mountains. My wounds healed, and I was sound when I came home. Even though I am dead now, at least I did not fall in the World War.

"You joined the Spartakus League in the month it was founded."

The man, while he was still alive in October 1918, joined the Spartakus League. But what of that now? They might as well summon Karl Liebknecht to be questioned; he would answer as much and as loudly. Let the dead bury their dead.

"Look here, Wallau, do you still cling to your old ideas?"

They should have asked me that yesterday. Today I am no longer able to answer. Yesterday I should have been compelled to shout Yes! Today I keep silent. Today others are answering in my stead; the songs of my people, the judgment of posterity . . .

It was growing cool around him. Fischer was feeling chilly. He would have liked to tell Overkamp to have done with this useless questioning.

"And so you were hatching plans for an escape, weren't you, Wallau? Ever since you were assigned to the special work squad?"

Several times in my life I was compelled to flee from my enemies. At times the flight was successful; at others it miscarried. Once, for instance, it ended badly. That was when I wanted to escape from Westhofen. Now I have been successful. I have escaped. In vain do the dogs sniff at my trail, it has been lost in infinity.

"And then, first of all, you told your friend George Heisler about your plan, didn't you?"

When I was still a living man, in the life I used to live, I met a young fellow named George at the very last. He was much younger than I. I became attached to him. We shared our sorrows and joys. Everything in this young man was dear to me. Everything in life that was dear to me I found again in him. Now he has no more to do with me than any living man has with a corpse. May he remember me occasionally, if he finds time for it. I know that life is busy and crowded.

"You made Heisler's acquaintance only at the camp?"

No flood of words, but an icy flood of silence came from the lips of the man. Even the guards listening at the door shrugged their shoulders uneasily. Was this a questioning? Were there still three of them in there?—The man's face was no longer pale, but alight. Overkamp suddenly turned away. He made a dot with his pencil and broke the point.

"You'll have yourself to blame for the consequences, Wallau."

What consequences could there be for a dead man who was being thrown from one grave into another? Not even the towering monument of the final grave is of any consequence to the dead.

Wallau was taken away. Within the four walls the silence held; it would not depart. Fischer, sitting motionless on his chair as if the prisoner were still there, looked steadfastly at the place where Wallau had been standing. Overkamp sharpened his pencil.

[. . .]

George put his thumb on the doorbell. Not even in Westhofen had he ever been seized with so poignant a feeling of homesickness. He withdrew his hand. How could he enter here, where they would welcome him innocently without any suspicion? Could not a single pressure on this bell disperse the family inside like chaff before the wind? Bring in its wake imprisonment, torment, and death?

George's mind was filled with a piercing light. "My exhaustion was to blame," he said to himself, "for having suggested the idea to me." Had he not been convinced, no less than half an hour ago, that he was being followed? Did he really think that a man like himself could shake off his shadowers so easily?

George shrugged his shoulders and descended a few steps. At that moment somebody came in from the street. His face turned toward the wall, George let Paul Roeder pass him going upstairs. He dragged himself to the nearest stair window and leaned against it, listening.

Roeder, however, instead of entering his flat, also stopped and listened. Suddenly he turned and walked downstairs. George went down another few steps. Roeder leaned over the banister. "George!" he called. Without answering, George went on downstairs. Roeder, at his side in two leaps, again said: "George!" He grabbed him by the arm. "Is it you, or isn't it?"

Paul laughed and shook his head. "Were you up at our place? Didn't you recognize me just now? I thought to myself: 'Good Lord, isn't that George?' But you're changed, man . . ." Suddenly he sounded hurt: "It has taken you three years to remember Paul again. Oh, well—come along anyhow."

Without saying a single word to all this, George followed his friend. Now they were standing at the large stair window. Roeder gave George an upward glance. No matter what Paul was thinking, his face was too thickly freckled to allow any suspicion of a gloomy expression.

"Well," said Paul, "you look a bit green about the gills. Tell me, are you still the George I used to know?" George moved his parched lips. "You are, aren't you?" Roeder asked quite seriously. George laughed shortly. "Come on, man, come on!" said Roeder. "It's really surprising that I recognized you on the stairs."

"I was ill a long time," said George quietly. "My hand hasn't healed yet."

"Any fingers missing?"

"No. I was lucky."

"Where did that happen? Have you been around here all this time?"

"I was a chauffeur in Kassel," said George. In a few calm sentences he described the place and the circumstances as he recalled them from a fellow prisoner's tale.

"Now we'll have some fun," said Paul. "Liesel's face'll be a study." He pressed the doorbell. Even while the fine piercing sound of the bell still echoed, there came a thunderstorm of banged doors, children's loud voices, and Liesel's "Well, I'll be darned!" Clouds of flowered dresses and wallpaper were swirling, intermingled with pictures and faces with thousands of freckles and frightened little eyes—then darkness and quiet.

The first thing George was conscious of was Roeder's voice ordering angrily: "Coffee! Coffee! Do you hear? Not dishwater!" George sat up on the sofa. With a tremendous effort he came back from his unconsciousness, in which he had felt so secure, into Roeder's kitchen. "That still happens now and then," he explained. "Nothing serious. Liesel needn't bother about coffee."

George stretched his legs under the kitchen table. He put his bandaged hand on the oilcloth between the plates. Liesel Roeder had grown into a stout woman who would no longer look so well in a page's breeches. The warm, rather heavy gaze of her brown eyes rested briefly on George's face.

"All right," she said. "The best thing you can do now is eat. We'll have the coffee later." She set the table and prepared the meal.

Roeder got his three oldest children seated around the table. "Wait, I'll cut it for you, George. Can you spare it all right? I hope you don't mind our simple fare. Do you want some mustard? Some salt? He who eats well and drinks well keeps body and soul together."

"What day is today?" asked George.

The Roeders laughed. "Thursday."

"Why, Liesel, you've given me your own two sausages," said George, who was using every ounce of his will power to fit himself into an ordinary evening, he who had had to fit himself into utmost danger. As he was eating with his uninjured hand and the others were eating, he caught brief looks, now from Liesel and now from Paul, which made him feel that he was fond of them and that they, too, were still fond of him.

Suddenly he heard somebody coming up the stairs—higher and higher. He listened. "What are you listening to?" asked Paul. The steps grew fainter. On the oilcloth near his injured hand was a faded circle that had probably been made by a hot plate. George pressed his beer glass on the faded spot like a stamp: "Let things take their course!" Paul, interpreting George's motion in his own way, poured some more beer in the glass. Slowly they finished the meal.

"Are you staying with your parents again?" asked Paul.

"Temporarily."

"How about Elly?"

"We don't see each other any more . . ." George pulled himself together. He looked about him, at all the curious little eyes. "Well," he said, "you seem to have accomplished quite a lot in the meantime."

"Why, don't you know that the German nation must quadruple?" asked Paul, his eyes dancing. "You apparently don't listen to the *Führer's* speeches."

"Oh, yes, I do, but I never heard him say that little Paul Roeder of Bockenheim must do the job all by himself."

"Well, it isn't so difficult nowadays to have children," said Liesel Roeder.

"It never was."

"Oh, George," Liesel laughed, "now you're getting back into your stride again."

"No, I meant it. There were four of us at home. Fritz, Ernst, myself, and Heinie. And you, Paul?"

"I was one of five . . ."

Liesel interrupted him: "Nobody ever cared a straw about us; but now, at last, things are different."

Paul said laughing: "Liesel got an official message of congratulation . . ."

"I certainly did. Yes, sir!"

"Well, but how about Paul? Shouldn't he have been congratulated on his fine performance?"

"Joking apart, George, look at all the allowances and the extra pay. Seven pfennigs an hour is not to be sneezed at. Then there's the exemption from wage deductions and the free supply of diapers. As if the Social Welfare knew that a succession of three little behinds would completely wear out the old ones."

"Don't listen to him," said Liesel. "He's quite satisfied with things as they are. Last August on our vacation he was as spry as on his honeymoon . . ."

"Where'd you go?"

"To Thuringia. We went to the Wartburg, and Martin Luther, and the Contest of Minnesingers, and the Venusberg. That, too, was a kind of official reward. I tell you, never before in all history has anything like it been tried."

"Never," said George. He thought to himself: "Such wholesale trickery? No, never!" Aloud he said: "And you, Paul? How are you getting along? Are you satisfied?"

"Oh, I can't complain," answered Paul. "Two hundred and ten marks a month. That's fifteen marks more than I got in '29; that was the best year since the war, and then I only got it for two months. But this time it'll last . . ."

"Why," said George, "it's obvious even on the street that everything's going full blast." His throat grew ever more constricted; his heart felt heavy.

"Well," said Paul, "what do you want? That's the war."

"Isn't that a funny feeling?" mused George.

"What?"

"What you said. Just think that you are manufacturing the things that'll kill thousands of others over there."

"Oh, well," Paul replied, "what's an owl to one is a nightingale to another. If we're going to worry our heads over such things . . . Ah, there you are, Liesel! Now for our coffee. George will have to come again soon and have another fainting spell."

"This is the best coffee I've had in three years," said George. He patted Liesel's hand. He thought: "Out of here—but where?"

"You always were given to brooding, Georgie, weren't you?" Paul said, "And what's it got you? Now, I suppose, you've settled down. Before, you would have told me exactly everything I had on my conscience." He gave a short laugh. "Do you remember, George, how you came to see me once and you were all in a stew? I was out of work, but nothing would do—I had to buy something from you—something Chinese. I, of all men—a little booklet— from the Chinese, of all people! . . . And don't start telling me about your Spaniards either," he said harshly, although George had remained silent. "Don't do it. They don't need Paul Roeder's help to settle their hash. They offered resistance, didn't they? And now they are licked. My few little percussion caps won't make any difference." George still said nothing. "You always used to start the damnedest arguments—about the most farfetched things."

"As long as you admit making the caps, it isn't so farfetched, is it?" asked George.

In the meantime Liesel had cleared the table and got all the children ready for bed. "Say good night to Father. Say good night to George."

"I'll put the children to bed," said Liesel. "You don't need a light yet for your arguing."

George thought: "What else is there for me to do? I have no other choice." "I say, Paul," he said casually, "can you put me up for tonight? Do you mind if I stay?"

Roeder, somewhat surprised, said: "Why, no! Why should I mind?"

"You see, I had a row at home, and I want to let it blow over."

"Stay here as long as you want," said Roeder.

Resting his elbows on the table, George covered his face with his hands. He looked at Roeder between his fingers. Paul would have looked serious if his face weren't so merrily freckled.

"Are you still getting into rows about one thing or another?" asked Paul. "What schemes and plans you used to have! Even then, if you remember, I used to say to you, 'Leave me out of it, George. I have no use for futile dreams. I'd rather be sure of my bread and sausage.' And those Spaniards, they're a bunch of Georges too. I mean as you were before, George. Now, it seems, you're taking it easier. Look at your Russia, what a mess they've made of things! At first it looked like the real thing, and a fellow was tempted to think: 'Perhaps—who knows?' Now . . . ."

"Now?" George urged him on.

Although he covered his eyes quickly, Paul had been struck by one of the piercing looks that darted between George's fingers. He faltered. "Now . . . Well, you know. . . ."

"What?"

"How topsy-turvy everything is over there. One 'liquidation' on top of another."

"Who, for instance?"

"Oh, I don't know . . . I can't remember those jawbreaking names."

Liesel came back into the room. "You'd better go to bed now, Paul. Don't be angry, George, but—"

"George wants to stay here tonight, Liesel. He had a row at home."

"You're a fine one," she said. "What's happened?"

"Oh, that's a long story. I'll tell you all about it tomorrow," evaded George.

"All right! Enough talking for one evening, though. Paul will be knocked out tomorrow."

"I can well imagine," said George, "that they don't handle him with kid gloves."

"Better to be driven hard and earn a few extra marks," replied Paul. "I'd rather work overtime any day than do air-raid practice."

"And how about growing old more quickly?" asked George.

"You'll have a chance for that as soon as the next war comes. And besides, George, the whole thing isn't so wonderful that you'd want to look forward to it forever and ever. I'm coming, Liesel." He looked around and said: "The only thing, George, what'll we give you for a blanket?"

"Just give me my overcoat, Paul."

"What a funny coat you've got, George. Put that rug under your feet, so's you won't dirty Liesel's roses." Suddenly he asked: "By the way, just between ourselves, what was the row about? Girl?"

"Oh, because . . ." floundered George, "because . . . because of the little one, Heinie. You know how fond of me he always used to be."

"Oh, by the way, I met that Heinie of yours the other day. I suppose he's about sixteen—seventeen, eh? All you Heislers were good-looking fellows, but Heinie beats you all. I hear they put a bug in his ear about joining the SS later."

"What, Heinie?"

"Well, I suppose you know more about it than I do," said Roeder. In spite of Liesel, he had sat down again at the kitchen table. Seeing George's face again squarely before his own, the same foolish thought that he'd had on the stairs flashed through his mind again: "Is that really George?" George's face had suddenly changed again. Roeder would have been at a loss to describe the nature of the change in a face that had remained so still. But that's exactly what it was: the change in a clock that stops suddenly. "There used to be rows with your family because Heinie stuck to you, and now . . ."

"Is that really true about Heinie?" asked George.

"How come you don't know anything about it? Haven't you been home?" asked Roeder.

Suddenly little Roeder's heart began to beat furiously. He scolded: "That's the limit. You've been telling me stories. Three years you don't come to see me, and now you tell me stories! You always were that way—you still are. Telling stories to your Paul! Aren't you ashamed of yourself? What have you been up to? Must have been something. Don't take me for an absolute fool. So you haven't been home! Where have you been all the time? You seem to be in a fine mess. Ran away? What's the matter with you anyway?"

"Perhaps you can spare me a few marks," said George. "I've got to get away from here right away. Don't let Liesel notice anything."

"What's the matter with you?"

"You have no radio?"

"No," said Roeder, "seeing what a fine voice Liesel's got, and all the noise in the house anyway—"

"Well, I'm big news on the radio," said George. "I escaped." He looked squarely into Roeder's eyes.

Paul had suddenly grown pale, so pale that his freckles seemed to glisten. "Where did you escape from, George?"

"From Westhofen. I . . . I . . ."

"From Westhofen? You? Have you been up there all this time? You're a fine one, I must say. They'll kill you if they catch you."

"That's right," said George.

"And in the face of that you want to leave here? You must be out of your mind, man!"

George was still looking into Roeder's face. Sprinkled with stars, it looked like Heaven itself to him. "My dear, dear Paul!" he said quietly. "I can't, don't you see? You and your whole family . . . Here you are all happy, and I . . . Do you realize what you're saying? If they should come up here—perhaps they are on my trail as it is."

Roeder said: "Then it's too late anyway. If they come I'll say I didn't know anything. These last few sentences have never been spoken. Do you understand? The words were never spoken. An old friend has a right to turn up unexpectedly, hasn't he? How was I to know what you've been up to in the meantime?"

"When did we see each other the last time?" George asked.

"The last time you were at the flat was in December '32, on Christmas Day. I remember you ate up all our cinnamon stars."

George warned him: "They'll question you and question you. You don't know what new tricks they've invented." In his eyes flashed the tiny pointed sparks which Franz had been so afraid of as a child.

"Don't talk of the devil or he'll appear. Why should they hit on our flat? They didn't see you come in, or they'd have been here long ago. You'd better think of the future, and of how you're going to get away from here . . . You'll excuse my saying so, George, but I like you better outside the place than in."

"I've got to get out of town, out of the country. I have to find my friends."

Paul laughed. "Your friends! First you'd better find the holes they've crawled into."

George said: "Later, when there is more time, I'll tell you about some of the holes they've crawled into. For instance, out there in Westhofen there are a few dozen men whom no one knows anything about. . . . Oh, I can tell you about it . . . that is, if by that time we ourselves, you and I, haven't crawled into some of those holes ourselves."

"See here, George," said Paul. "I've been thinking of one particular fellow: Karl Hahn of Eschersheim. At that time he—"

George interrupted him: "Never mind!" He too was thinking of one particular man. Was Wallau already dead? Dead, in a world whirling on all the more madly the more inert he lay there? Once more he could hear him say "George!"—a single word that had traversed not only space but also time.

"George!" It came from little Roeder.

George gave a start. Paul watched him anxiously. For a moment, George's face had been strange to him again. His voice strange too, he asked: "Yes, Paul?"

Paul said: "I could go and see these people tomorrow, so's to get rid of you."

"Let me think once more who's living in the city," answered George. "It's been more than two years, you know."

"You wouldn't have got yourself into this jam," said Paul, "if you hadn't been so taken up with that fellow Franz. Do you remember? It was him that got you in properly, for before that . . . Well, we all used to go to a meeting once in a while or take part in a demonstration. We'd all been worked up now and then. And hopeful too. But that Franz of yours, he was the real article."

"It wasn't Franz," said George. "'It was something that was stronger than everything else . . .'"

"What do you mean, stronger? Stronger than what?" asked Paul, while he opened the footboard of the kitchen sofa to make George comfortable for the night.

[. . .]

Fahrenberg received the report: Sixth fugitive found. Found dead. How? That no longer concerned Westhofen. That was the Good Lord's affair and the affair of the Wertheim officials, the peasant officials of Aldinger's district, and the local Burgomaster. Fahrenberg then went to the square that was known as the Dancing Ground. The SA and SS who were detailed to this particular service were already lined up. Commands grated. Deathly tired, heavy with dirt and despair, the column of prisoners still moved quickly and softly like a wind made by departed souls. The two plane trees left intact at the right of the door to the commander's barrack were resplendent in their autumn red and the sun's last rays; for the day was declining, and from the boggy country the fog was rolling up to the accursed place. Cherub-faced Bunsen was standing in front of his SS squad as if he were awaiting his Creator's orders. Of the dozen or so plane trees that had stood to the left of the door, all but the seven that were needed had been cut down yesterday. Zillich, commanding the SA, ordered the four recaptured fugitives to be tied to the trees. Every evening when this command was given a tremor passed through the ranks of the prisoners, feebly and inwardly, like the last shiver before rigidity sets in, for the vigilant SS would permit no one to move as much as a finger.

The four who were tied to the trees did not tremble. Not even Fuellgrabe trembled. His mouth open, he stared straight ahead as if Death himself had commanded him to behave decently at the last. On his face too there was a gleam of that light compared with which Overkamp's torture lamp was but a miserable contraption. Pelzer had closed his eyes; his face had lost all its delicacy, all its timidity and weakness; it had grown bold and sharp. His thoughts were collected; they did not dwell on doubts and evasions, but on the comprehension of the inevitable. He felt Wallau's presence at his side.

On Wallau's other side was that man Buetler who had been recaptured immediately after the escape. At Overkamp's instructions he had been patched up again, though only superficially. He too did not tremble; he too had long since ceased to do so. Eight months ago, when his coat had been lined with foreign currency, he had betrayed himself at the border by his trembling. Now he was hanging suspended rather than standing on his strange place of honor at Wallau's right, which even his wildest imagination could never have pictured to him. His camp face was spotted with light. Of all the men's eyes, only Wallau's were purposeful. Whenever Wallau was led up to the crosses, his almost petrified heart gave a new leap. Would George be one of them? What he was staring at now was not death but the column of prisoners. He could even discover a new face among the familiar ones—Schenk's who had been in the hospital. Schenk to whose house Roeder had gone that very morning to obtain shelter for George.

Fahrenberg advanced. He ordered Zillich to draw the nails out from one of two trees. Bare and empty stood the two trees, two veritable crosses for graves. Now there was but one unoccupied studded tree, the one at the extreme left, at Fuellgrabe's side.

"The sixth fugitive found!" announced Fahrenberg. "August Aldinger. Dead, as you see. He has only himself to blame for his death. As for the seventh, we won't have to wait long for him, for he is on his way. The National Socialist State relentlessly prosecutes anyone who transgresses against the national community. It protects those who deserve protection, it punishes where punishment is due, and it destroys what ought to be destroyed. No longer does our country offer a haven for fugitive criminals. Our people is healthy; it shakes off the diseased and kills the insane. No more than five days have elapsed since the escape. Here—open your eyes wide, and impress this on your minds!"

This said, Fahrenberg returned to his barrack, and Bunsen ordered the column of prisoners to advance two yards. Now only a narrow space separated the trees and the first line. During Fahrenberg's speech and the commands that followed it, daylight had completely vanished. On its right and left the column was firmly hemmed in by the SA and SS. Above and beyond lay the fog. It was the hour when all gave themselves up for lost. Those among the prisoners who believed in God knew He had forsaken them. Those who believed in nothing at all let their souls decay; for decay can set in while the body is still alive. Those who believed in nothing but the strength inherent in man thought that this strength lived only in their bodies, that their sacrifice had been in vain, and that their people had forgotten them.

Fahrenberg sat down behind his table. What day was today? True, the day was practically over, but there were still three days left of the time he had set himself. If six could be found in four days, one must be found in three. Besides, this one was already surrounded and wouldn't have another minute's sleep; neither, unfortunately, would Fahrenberg.

It was almost dark in the barrack, and Fahrenberg switched on the light. This light shining from his window made the shadows of the trees reach the front line of the column. How long had the men been standing there? Was it night already? And still no command came, and the tied-up men's sinews were burning. Suddenly a man in the next to the last row of the column screamed. At the scream the four crucified ones gave a violent start that thrust them against the nails. The man pitched forward, brought the man in front down with him, and rolled screaming on the ground, blows and kicks already raining on him. The SA swarmed everywhere.

At that moment, from the center of the camp, came the two commissars, Overkamp and Fischer, hatted and raincoated, briefcases under their arms, and accompanied by an orderly with their bags. Overkamp's activity at Westhofen had come to its end. The hunt for Heisler had nothing to do with his further presence there.

The two men went into the commander's barracks and came out again presently and again walked down the line. This time, Overkamps' gaze rested briefly on the trees. Wallau's eyes met his. Overkamp hung back almost imperceptibly. Into his face came an expression, a mixture of recognition, of "Sorry!," of "It's your own fault!" Perhaps in this mixture there was even a little kernel of respect.

Overkamp knew that as soon as he had left the camp these four men were lost. At best they might be kept alive until the seventh man was brought in—unless, of course, someone bungled or lost his patience.

When the motor started, it could be heard on the Dancing Ground, a sound that made hearts turn over. Of the four tied-up men, only Wallau was able to realize clearly that now they were doomed. But what of George? Had he been found? Was he on his way here?

"This fellow Wallau will be the first to bite the dust," said Fischer. Overkamp nodded. He had known Fischer a long time. They were nationally-minded men with a profusion of war decorations. Even under the System they had occasionally worked together. In his profession, Overkamp was in the habit of following the usual police methods. Grueling questionings, when harsh means were called for, were for him all in the day's work; they did not amuse him one whit, nor did he have any predilection for them. To him, the men he had to prosecute were always enemies of order, according to his own conception of order. Thus far everything was quite clear. Things grew muddled only when he started reflecting for whom he was working.

Overkamp forced his thoughts away from Westhofen. There was still that Heisler case. He looked at his watch. He and Fischer were expected in Frankfurt in an hour and twenty minutes. The fog kept the speed of their car down to twenty-five miles. Overkamp wiped the window.

[. . .]

Every enclosed space being odious to him, he went to the window. He saw the white road that bisected the settlement. Beyond it—the settlement resembled an all-too-clean village—he could see parks and forests.

He was overcome by a feeling of abject homelessness that was almost immediately followed by a feeling of pride. Was there any man who could look with the same eyes at the wide steel-blue sky and the road which, for him only, led into a perfect wilderness? He contemplated the people who were passing—people in their Sunday clothes accompanied by children and old women and strange packages; a motorcyclist with a girl on the seat behind him; two youths; a man with a folding-boat sack on his back; an SA man leading a child; a young woman carrying a bunch of asters.

Presently the doorbell rang. "Never mind," said George to himself. "I suppose there are any number of rings here in the course of the day." House and street remained quiet. Kress came up the stairs. "Come out on the landing a minute." With knitted brows George looked at the young woman with the asters who was suddenly standing there in Kress's house, three steps below him.

"I am to hand you something," she said, "and in addition I am to tell you that tomorrow morning at half-past five you are to be at the Kastella Bridge landing in Mainz. The ship's name is *Wilhelmine*. You are expected."

"Good!" said George, but he didn't budge.

Without letting go of her flowers, the woman unbuttoned the pocket of her jacket. She handed George a thick envelope. "Now I have delivered this envelope to you." From her attitude it could be assumed that she took George for a comrade who had to hide, but that she did not know his identity.

"All right!" said George.

[. . .]

A hard rain struck his face. At last the houses retreated. The city across the river was hidden behind a curtain of rain. Against the immeasurable dull sky the city seemed bereft of all reality—one of those cities one fashions in one's sleep for the length of a dream, and that doesn't last even that long. And yet it has withstood the rush of two thousand years.

George reached the Kastella bridgehead. The guard challenged him, and he showed his passport. When he was on the bridge, he realized that his heart had not beaten any faster. He could have passed ten other bridgeheads without trouble—one gets accustomed even to that. He felt that his heart was now proof not only against fear and danger, but also perhaps against happiness. He walked a bit slower so as not to be a minute early. Looking down, he saw his tugboat, the *Wilhelmine*, with her green load line mirrored in the water. She lay quite near the bridgehead, unfortunately not touching the bank but alongside another vessel. George was less concerned about the guard at the Mainz bridgehead than about how he would get across the strange boat. He need not have worried. He was still twenty paces from the landing place when the globular, almost neckless head of a man popped over the *Wilhelmine's* gunwale. George had obviously been expected by the man with the round, fattish face, whose wide nostrils and deep-set eyes gave it a rather sinister look. It was precisely the right kind of face for an upright man who was willing to run considerable risk.

On Monday evening, the seven trees in Westhofen were cut down. Everything had happened very quickly. The new commander had assumed his duties before the change had become generally known. Presumably he was the right man to straighten out a camp in which such things had happened. Instead of roaring, he spoke in an ordinary tone of voice, but he left not the slightest doubt in our minds that at the least provocation we would be shot down like so many wild beasts. He ordered the crosses to be dismantled at once, for they were not what he went in for. Rumor had it that Fahrenberg had gone to Mainz that same Monday. He was said to have taken lodgings at the Fuerstenberger Hof and to have put a bullet through his brain—but that was only rumor. It didn't quite fit him. Perhaps it was someone else who, because of debts or a love affair, shot himself through the head that night at the Fuerstenberger Hof. Or perhaps Fahrenberg has bounced up another ladder and is now wielding even greater power.

We didn't know any of this as yet then. So many things happened later that nothing that could be learned could be believed implicitly. True, we had thought that it was impossible to experience more than we had already experienced; but once outside, we found out how much there still was to be experienced.

But on that evening when the prisoners' barrack was heated for the first time, and we watched the flames of the kindling wood that we thought had come from the seven trees, we felt nearer to life than at any time later—much nearer, too, than all the others who are under the impression that they are alive.

The SA guard had stopped to wonder how long the rain would keep up. He turned around suddenly to surprise us at something that was forbidden; he roared at us and, for good measure, distributed a few penalties. Ten minutes later we were lying in our bunks. The last little spark in the stove had gone out. We had a foreboding of the nights that were in store for us. The damp autumn cold struck through our covers, our shirts, and our skin. All of us felt how ruthlessly and fearfully outward powers could strike to the very core of man, but at the same time we felt that at the very core there was something that was unassailable and inviolable.

Translated by James A. Galston

Excursion of the Dead Girls

"No, from much further away. From Europe." The man looked at me with a smile, as though I had answered, "From the moon." He was the landlord of the *pulqueria* at the entrance to the village. He stepped back from the table and began, leaning motionless against the wall, to study me, as though searching for signs of my fantastic origins.

It suddenly seemed just as fantastic to me as to him that I had drifted from Europe to Mexico. The village was like a fortress, surrounded by organ-cactuses as though by a palisade. Through a chink I could see into the gray-brown mountain slopes, the mere sight of which—bleak and wild like a lunar landscape—averted any suspicion that they had ever had anything to do with life. Two pepper trees glowed on the edge of a completely barren ravine. These trees too seemed to be burning rather than blossoming. The innkeeper had squatted on the floor, under the vast shadow of his hat. He had stopped looking at me; he was attracted neither by the village nor the mountains; he was staring motionless at the only thing that presented him with measureless, insoluble riddles: total nothingness.

I leant against the wall in the narrow shadows. The refuge I had found in this land was too dubious and too uncertain to be called salvation. Just behind me I had months of illness that had overtaken me here, although the manifold dangers of the war had been unable to touch me. Although my eyes were burning with heat and fatigue, I could follow the part of the road that led out of the village into the desert. The road was so white that it seemed to be engraved on the inner side of my eyelids as soon as I shut my eyes.

I also saw on the brink of the ravine the corner of the white wall that had caught my eye from the roof of my lodging in the large village higher up, from which I had come down. I had immediately enquired about the wall and ranch, or whatever it was, with its single light fallen from the night sky, but no one had been able to give me any information. I had set out along the road. In spite of the weakness and weariness which had compelled me to stop for a breather, I had to find out for myself about the house. This idle curiosity was the only remnant of my old urge to travel, an impulse springing from the compulsion of habit. As soon as it was satisfied I would climb up back to my prescribed residence. The bench on which I was now resting was up to now the last point of my journey, actually the most westerly point to which I had even been on earth. The desire for the bizarre, extravagant enterprises, which in the past used to make me restless, had long since been stilled, had reached satiety. There was only one enterprise that could spur me on: the journey home.

The ranch, like the mountains themselves, lay in a shimmering haze; I did not know whether this consisted of particles of dust in the sunlight or was the product of my own fatigue, which made everything hazy, so that the nearby faded away and the distance became as clear as a mirage. I stood up, because my own weariness was already repugnant to me, and as a result the haze before my eyes cleared slightly.

I walked through the opening in the palisade of cactuses and then round the dog that was sleeping like a carcass, completely motionless and covered in dust, in the road, with outstretched legs. It was shortly before the rainy season. The exposed roots of bare, twisted trees clung to the mountainside in the process of fossilizing. The white wall drew nearer. The cloud of dust or of fatigue which had become a little thinner, grew denser; in the spaces between the mountains it was not dark as clouds usually are but glittering and shimmering. I would have put it down to my fever, if a light, hot gust of wind had not wafted the clouds away like shreds of mist toward other slopes.

There was a shimmer of green behind the long white wall. Probably there was a spring there or a diverted stream that irrigated the ranch more than the village. At the same time it looked uninhabited with the low house which was windowless on the side facing the road. The single light yesterday evening had probably, if it had not been an illusion, belonged to the watchman. The lattice-work, long since superfluous and rotten, had broken out of the gateway. But the arch over the entrance still showed the last remains of a coat of arms washed out by countless rainy seasons. The remnants of the coat of arms struck me as familiar, like the stone half-shell within which they lay, I stepped into the empty gateway. Now I heard inside, to my astonishment, a slight regular creaking. I took another step forward. Now I could smell the greenery in the garden, which grew fresher and more luxuriant the longer I peered in. The creaking soon became clearer and I saw among the shrubs, which became continually denser and lusher, the regular rise and fall of a swing or a seesaw. Now my curiosity was aroused, so that I ran through the gateway toward the seesaw. At the same moment someone called out, "Netty!"

No one had called me by this name since my school days. I had learned to listen to all the good and bad names by which friends and enemies were accustomed to call me, the names I had been given in the course of many years in streets, meetings, festivities, night-time rooms, police interrogations, book titles, newspaper reports, records and passports. While I lay, sick and unconscious, I had actually often hoped for that old, early name, but the name remained lost which I believed in self-deception could make me well again, young, gay, ready for old life with the old companions, who were irretrievably lost. At the sound of my old name I was so taken aback. Although I had always been laughed at for this movement in class, I clutched with both fists at my plaits. I was surprised that I was able to grasp the two thick plaits. So they hadn't cut them off in the hospital.

The tree stump to which the seesaw was nailed also seemed at first to be standing in a dense cloud, but he cloud immediately parted and cleared into a lot of dogrose bushes. Soon the first isolated buttercups gleamed in the vapor rising from the soil through the tall, thick grass; the vapor drew back until dandelions and crane's bill stood there individually. In between there were also brownish-pink tufts of quaking-grass that trembled as soon as I looked at it.

At each end of the seesaw there rode girls, my two best school friends. Leni was pushing herself off vigorously with her big feet shod in angular button-boots. It occurred to me that she always inherited the boots of an elder brother. The brother, of course, had died already in autumn 1914 in the First World War. At the same time I wondered how it was that Leni's face showed no trace of the grim events which had ruined her life. Her face was as smooth and shiny as a fresh apple; it showed not the slightest residue, not the slightest scar from the blows which the Gestapo had struck her when they arrested her and she refused to give information about her husband. Her thick Mozart plait stood out strongly from the back of her neck as she seesawed. With her thick brows knit, her round face wore the resolute, rather forceful expression which ever since she was little she had always assumed when engaged in any difficult undertaking. I knew the furrow in her brow, if her otherwise mirror-smooth and round apple face, from all sorts of occasions, from difficult ball games and swimming races and school essays and later too during excited meetings and while distributing leaflets.

I had last seen the same furrow between her brows when in Hitler's time, shortly before my final flight, I had met my friends for the last time in my home town. Before that she had had this furrow on her forehead when her husband failed to appear at the agreed place at the agreed time, from which it was clear that he had been arrested by the Nazis at the illegal printing press. No doubt she had also wrinkled up her brows and her mouth when, immediately afterward, she was arrested herself. The furrow in her forehead, which previously came into being only on special occasions, became a constant characteristic when she was slowly but surely done to death by hunger in the women's concentration camp in the second winter of this war. I wondered how I had in the meantime been able to forget her head, which was shadowed by the broad ribbon round the Mozart plait, when I was sure that she had retained her apple face with the grooved forehead even in death.

At the other end of the seesaw sat Marianne, the prettiest girl in the class, her long, thin legs crossed in front of her on the plank. Her ash-blond plaits were pinned up over her ears. In her face, as nobly and regularly carved as the faces of the medieval stone figures of girls in Marburg Cathedral, there was nothing to be seen but gaiety and charm. She showed no sign any more than a flower does—of heartlessness, of guilt or coldness or conscience. I myself at once forgot everything I knew about her and was glad to see her. A jerk ran through her straight lean body each time she intensified the movement of the seesaw without pushing off. She looked as if she could easily fly away, with the carnation between her teeth and her firm little breast in the washed-out green linen overall.

I recognized the voice of the elderly teacher, Fräulein Mees, looking for us just behind the low wall which separated the courtyard with the seesaw from the cafe terrace. "Leni! Marianne! Netty!" This time I did not clutch hold of my plaits with surprise. The teacher could not have called me along with the others by any other name. Marianne took her legs from the seesaw, and as soon as the plank went down on Leni's side, set her feet firmly on the ground, so that Leni could get off in comfort. Then she put one arm around Leni's neck and carefully plucked blades of grass out of her hair.

All the things that had been told and written to me about the two of them now seemed impossible to me. If Marianne so carefully held the seesaw still for Leni and pulled the grass out of her hair with so much friendship and so much consideration and actually put her arm round Leni's neck, she could not possibly later on have brusquely refused with cold words to render Leni a service of friendship. She could not possibly have retorted that she could not be bothered with a girl who sometime, somewhere had happened to be in her class. Every penny spent on Leni and her family was thrown away, fraud against the State. The Gestapo officials who had arrested the two parents one after the other, declared to neighbors that Leni's child, left unprotected, would now go straight into a National Socialist educational institution. Thereupon the neighbors fetched the child from the playground and kept her hidden so that she could go to relations of the father in Berlin. They went to borrow the fare from Marianne whom they had often seen in the past arm in arm with Leni. But Marianne refused and added that her own husband was a highly placed Nazi official, and Leni and her husband had been justly arrested because they had committed a crime against Hitler. The women were afraid they themselves would be denounced to the Gestapo.

It flashed through my mind to wonder whether Leni's little daughter had had the same grooved forehead as her mother when they did after all take her away to undergo forced education.

How the two girls, Marianne and Leni, one of whom had lost her child through the other's fault, came from the seesaw garden with their arms round each other's neck, temple to temple. I was just feeling a little sad, excluded from the shared play and heartfelt friendship of the others, as easily happened during our school days, when the two of them stopped again and took me in between them.

Like three ducklings behind the duck we walked along behind Fräulein Mees on to the café terrace. Fräulein Mees limped slightly, which, together with her large behind, made her all the more like a duck. On her bosom, in the opening of her blouse, hung a big black cross. I would have had to suppress a smile, like Leni and Marianne, but amusement at her comical appearance was mitigated by a respect that was not easily combined with it. Later she never removed the clumsy black cross from the opening in her dress. Openly and fearlessly she had gone around wearing this same cross, instead of a swastika, after attending the banned church services.

The café terrace by the Rhine was planted with rose trees. By comparison with the girls they seemed as regular, as stiff and erect, as well cared for as garden flowers beside wild flowers. The smell of coffee penetrated enticingly through the smell of water and garden. From the tables with their red and white checked cloths in front of the long, low inn came the buzz of young voices like a swarm of bees. First I was drawn closer to the riverbank, to breathe in the limitless sunny expanse of the landscape. I dragged the other two, Leni and Marianne, to the garden fence, where we stood gazing down at the river that flowed gray-blue and glittering past the inn. The villages and hills on the other bank were reflected with their fields and woods in a network of ripples flashing in the sunlight. The more and longer I looked round, the more freely I could breathe, the more quickly my heart was filled with gaiety. For the heavy pressure of dejection, which had lain upon every breath, almost imperceptibly vanished. The mere sight of the soft, hilly landscape made joie de vivre and gaiety, instead of melancholy, spring up out of our very blood, like a particular grain out of a particular air and soil.

A Dutch steamer pulling a train of eight barges sailed through the hills reflected in the water. They were carrying timber. The skipper's wife was just sweeping the deck, her little dog jumping up and down around her. We girls waited until the white wake behind the chain of timber barges had disappeared from the Rhine and there was nothing else to be seen in the water but the reflection of the opposite bank, which collided with the reflection of our garden on this side. We turned back to the cafe tables, led by our wobbling Fräulein Mees, who no longer looked to me funny at all with the equally wobbling cross on her bosom, which had suddenly become for me important and irrefutable and as solemn as an emblem.

Perhaps there were also sullen and mean ones among the school girls. In their bright summer dresses, with their hopping plaits and jolly ringlets, they all looked fresh and festive. Because most of the places were occupied, Marianne and Leni shared a chair and a coffee cup. Little snub-nosed Nora with a thin voice and two plaits wound round her head, in a check dress was self-confidently pouring out coffee and distributing sugar as though she owned the cafe. Marianne, who was generally in the habit of forgetting her former fellow pupils, clearly remembered this outing when Nora, who had become the leader of the National Socialist Women's Club, greeted her there as a comrade and former schoolfellow.

The blue cloud of vapor that came out of the Rhine or was still coming from my own overtired eyes misted over all the tables occupied by the girls, so that I could no longer clearly distinguish the individual faces of Nora and Leni and Marianne and the rest of them, just as no single blossom stands out in a confusion of wild flowers. I listened for a while to the argument as to where it would be best for the younger teacher, Fräulein Sichel, who had just come out of the inn, to sit. The cloud of vapor vanished from before my eyes, so that I clearly distinguished Fräulein Sichel, who was approaching, dressed in fresh, light-colored clothes like her pupils.

She sat down close beside me; the alert Nora poured out coffee for her, the favorite teacher. In her eagerness to be obliging she had even placed a few jasmine twigs round Fräulein Sichel's place.

If her memory had not become as thin as her voice, Nora would certainly have regretted this later, as leader of our town's National Socialist Women's Club. Now she watched with pride and almost with love as Fräulein Sichel put a few of these jasmine twigs in the buttonhole of her jacket. During the First World War she would still be glad that in a section of the Women's Service which provided food and drink for soldiers passing through the town, she had the same hours of duty as Fräulein Sichel. But later she hounded this same teacher, who by then was shaky with old age, with coarse words from a bench by the Rhine because she was about to sit on a bench which Jews were forbidden to use.

The thought flashed through my mind, as I sat close beside her, like a serious omission in my memory—as though I had the higher duty to notice the slightest details and retain them forever—that Fräulein Sichel's hair had by no means always been snow-white, as I remembered it, but at the time of our school outing was brown and silky, apart from a few white strands by her temples. Now she had so few white hairs that you could count them, but they dismayed me, as though today and here I had come upon a sign of age. All the other girls at the table were delighted, like Nora, by the proximity of the young teacher, unaware that later they would spit on Fräulein Sichel and mock her as a "Jewish cow."

The oldest of us all, Lore—she wore a skirt and blouse, had reddish waved hair, had long since begun to have genuine love affairs—had meanwhile gone from table to table distributing homemade cakes. In this girl there were united all sorts of valuable gifts, relating partly to the art of love and partly to the art of cooking. Lore was always gay and pleasant and ready for playful jokes and pranks. The frivolous way of life she had embarked upon unusually early, and for which she was stringently reproved by the teachers, did not lead to marriage or even to any serious love affair, so that when most of the girls had long since become dignified mothers she still looked the same as today, a school girl with a short skirt and a big, red mouth with sweet teeth. How could she have met such a gloomy end? A voluntary death from a tube of sleeping powder. An angry Nazi lover had threatened her with a concentration camp, because her infidelity meant "dishonoring the race." He had long been spying on her in vain in the hope of surprising her with her lover who was forbidden by law. But for all his jealousy and desire to punish, he had not been able to obtain proof until shortly before this war, during a practice air raid warning, when the air raid warden forced all the occupants of the house to leave their rooms and beds and go down into the basement, including Lore with her prescribed sweetheart.

She now secretly, but not unnoticed by us, gave a leftover cinnamon star to the likewise strikingly pretty, artful Ida with her wealth of natural curls. She was her only friend in the class, since Lore was looked at somewhat askance on account of her gay life. We whispered a great deal about the merry goings on of Ida and Lore and also about their joint visits to swimming pools to meet agile bathing companions. I don't know why Ida, who was surreptitiously chewing the cinnamon star, was never the target of the secret society of mothers and daughters—perhaps because she was a teacher's daughter and Lore the daughter of a hairdresser.

Ida brought her loose life to an end in time, but she did not marry either, because her fiance was killed at Verdun. This sorrow drove her into nursing, so that at least she might be useful to the wounded. Since she did not wish to give up her profession with the 1918 Armistice, she joined the Deaconess. Her loveliness was already slightly faded, her curls already slightly gray, as though strewn with ash, when she became an official of the National Socialist nurses, and even if she had no fiance in this war, her desire for revenge, her bitterness were still alive. She impressed upon the younger nurses the State regulations forbidding conversation and false acts of compassion when nursing prisoners of war. But her order to use the newly arrived muslin solely for their compatriots proved totally abortive. For the site of her new activity, the hospital far behind the front, was struck by a bomb that shattered friend and foe and naturally also her curly head, over which Lore now once again ran five manicured fingers, such as she alone possessed in all the class.

At the same time Fräulein Mees tapped with her spoon on her coffee cup and ordered us to throw our contribution to the cost of the coffee into onion-pattern plates which she was just sending round the tables with her favorite pupil. With just the same briskness and spirit she later collected for her church, banned by the Nazis, of which finally, being used to such duties, the became treasurer, a post that was not without danger, but she collected the mites just as gaily and naturally. Her favorite pupil, Gerda, rattled the collection plate merrily and then took it to the proprietress. Gerda, without being beautiful, was captivating and deft, with a head like a mare's with coarse, shaggy hair, strong teeth and beautiful loyal brown eyes under gently arched brows, eyes that were also like a horse's. She came running straight back from the proprietress—she was also like a colt in that she was always galloping to ask permission to separate from the class and return on the next ship. She had learnt at the inn that the proprietress's child was seriously ill. Since there was no one else to look after her, Gerda wanted to nurse her. Fräulein Mees overcame all Fräulein Sichel's objections and Gerda galloped off to her nursing as though to a feast.

She was born to tend the sick and love mankind, to the profession of teacher in a sense that has almost vanished from the world as it is today, as though she were chosen to seek everywhere for children who needed her and always and everywhere she found those who needed help. Even if finally her life ended unregarded and senselessly, yet nothing in it was lost, not even the most modest of her helpful acts. Her life itself was more easily wiped out than the traces of her life, which exist in the memory of many whom she once happened to help. But who was there to help her when her own husband, flouting her prohibition and her threat, hung out a swastika flag on the First of May, as the new State demanded because otherwise he would have lost his job? There was no one there to calm her down in time when she came back from the market, saw the horribly beflagged apartment, ran upstairs, filled with shame and despair and turned on the gas tap. No one stood by her. She remained at that moment hopelessly alone, no matter how many people she herself had stood by.

A steamer hooted from the Rhine. We craned our necks. On its white hull there stood in gold letters *Remagen*. Although it was drifting along far down below I had no difficulty in deciphering the name with my sick eyes. I saw the curl of smoke above the funnel and the hatches of the cabin. I followed the steamer's wake, which was continually smoothed out and produced afresh. My eyes had meanwhile grown accustomed to the old familar world, and I saw everything even more clearly than when the Dutch tug sailed past. There clung to this little steamer *Remagen* on the wide, still river, gliding over villages and ranges of hills and stretches of cloud, a clarity which nothing had diminished, which nothing could diminish, which nothing in the world could dim. I myself had already discerned on the steamers' deck and in the portholes the familiar faces which the girls were now shouting out: "Teacher Schenk! Teacher Reiss! Otto Helmholtz! Eugen Lutgens! Fritz Muller!"

All the girls were calling out together, "It's the grammar school! It's the lower sixth!" Was this class, which, like us, was on an outing, going to stop here at the next steamship station? After a brief consultation, Fräulein Sichel and Fräulein Mees ordered the girls to form fours, since at all costs they wished to prevent the two classes from meeting. Marianne, whose plaits had come undone while she was on the seesaw, began to rearrange the coils over her ears, because her friend Leni, with whom she had been sharing a chair since they had seesawed together, observed with better eyes that Otto Fresenius was on board, Marianne's favorite suitor and dancing partner. Furthermore, Leni whispered to her: "They're getting off here; he's signaling with his hand."

Fresenius, a dark-blond, loose-limbed lad of seventeen, who had been stubbornly waving to us from the ship for a long time already, would have swum across to us in order to be united with his girl. Marianne put her arm firmly round Leni's neck; the friend whom later she refused to remember at all, when she was asked for help, was like a real sister to her, in the joys and distresses of love a faithful confidant, who conscientiously carried letters and arranged secret meetings. Marianne, who was always a beautiful, healthy girl, became through the mere proximity of her boyfriend such a miracle of tenderness and charm that she stood out like a child of legend from all the schoolgirls. Otto Fresenius had already revealed his predilection to his mother, with whom he shared secrets. Since his mother herself was delighted by the happy choice, she thought that later, if they waited long enough, nothing would stand in the way of a marriage. Their engagement was indeed celebrated, but not their marriage, for the fiancé was killed in 1914 in the students' battalion in the Argonne.

The steamship *Remagen* now veered round toward the landing stage. Our two teachers, who had to wait for the ship going in the opposite direction to take the girls home, immediately began to count us. Leni and Marianne gazed tensely at the steamer. Leni turned her head as curiously as though she could feel that the course of her own destiny too depended upon the uniting or parting of the lovers. If it had rested solely with Leni, instead of with Kaiser's mobilization and later with the French snipers, the two of them would certainly have become a couple. She felt just how well the two young people suited each other body and soul. Then Marianne would never have refused later to look after Leni's child. Even before that Otto Fresenius might have found means of helping Leni to flee. He would probably have gradually imparted to the gentle, beautiful face of his wife Marianne such an expression of the love of justice, of respect for human dignity, as would have prevented her from denying her school friend.

Now Otto Fresenius, whose belly was to be ripped open by a bullet in the First World War, spurred on by his love, was the first to cross the landing stage and made for the inn garden. Marianne, who never took her other hand from Leni's shoulder, gave him her free hand and left it to him. It was clear not only to Leni and me, but to all us children, that these two were a loving couple. They gave us for the first time, not dreamed, not read in poetry or fairy stories or classical dramas, but authentic and real, the right idea of a loving couple such as Nature herself had planned and joined together.

One finger still linked with his, Marianne's face wore an expression of total surrender, which now became an expression of ever-lasting fidelity to the tall, lean, dark-blond boy for whom when her Army Postal Service letters came back marked KILLED IN ACTION she would mourn like a widow in black. During those difficult days, when Marianne—whom in the past I had seen worshipping life with its great and small joys, whether it was a question of her love or of a seesaw—despaired of life altogether, her friend Leni, round whose shoulders she now kept her arm, met Fritz, a soldier on leave and a member of a railway worker's family in our town. While Marianne was for a long time enveloped in a black cloud, in despairing charm, in deeply sorrowful loveliness, Leni was the ripest, rosiest apple.

For a time the two friends were estranged in the usual human way in which suffering and happiness are estranged. After the period of mourning was over, Marianne, after a few encounters in cafés on the banks of the Rhine, with intertwined fingers and the same expression of eternal fidelity as now, would choose a new relationship with a certain Gustav Liebig, who had come through the First World War unscathed and was later to become an SS Sturmbannführer in our town. This Otto Fresenius would never have become, even if he had returned safe and sound from the war, either an SS Sturmbannführer or a man in the confidence of the provincial government. The respect for justice and the law that was already visible in his boyish features rendered him unsuited for such a career and such a profession.

Leni was only relieved when she heard that her school friend to whom at that time she clung as to a sister, had found her way into a fresh, new destiny that promised joy. Just as now she was far too light-minded to have any idea that the fates of boys and girls together make up the fate of the homeland, the fate of the nation, and that therefore in the short or the long term the sorrow or happiness of her school friend could throw shadow or sunshine on herself. I did not fail to see, any more than Leni, the silent inextinguishable vow in Marianne's face, which rested lightly as though by chance against her friend's arm, the guarantee of everlasting togetherness. Leni drew a deep breath, as though it was a special joy for her to be the witness of such a love. Before they, Leni and her husband, were arrested by the Gestapo, Marianne was to hear from her new husband Liebig—to whom she had also vowed everlasting fidelity—so many contemptuous words about her school friend's husband that she soon relinquished her friendship with a girl who was held to be so contemptible. Leni's husband had struggled with every possible means against joining the SA or the SS. Marianne's husband, who was proud of rank and order, would have been his superior—in the SS. When he noticed that Leni's husband despised entry into this organization, which he regarded as so honorable, he drew the attention of the authorities in the little town to the neglectful citizen.

Gradually, the whole of the boys' class with their two teachers had landed. A certain Herr Neeb, a young teacher with a little blond moustache, after a bow to our two teachers, ran his sharp gaze over us girls and noted that Gerda, for whom he was involuntarily looking, was not there. Gerda was still nursing and washing the proprietress's sick child in the inn and had no idea about the influx of boys into the garden outside, nor that the teacher Neeb whose attention she had already attracted on other occasions by her brown eyes and helpfulness—had already noted her absence. It was not until after 1918, after the end of the First World War, when Gerda herself was already a teacher and both of them supported the educational improvements of the Weimar Republic, were they both to meet at last in the recently founded Association of Resolute School Reformers. But Gerda remained truer to their old wishes and aims than he. After he had finally married the girl, whom he had chosen because of her convictions, he soon set a higher value on their life together in peace and prosperity than on their convictions. Therefore, he hung the Swastika flag from his living room window, because the law threatened that if he did not he would lose his job and thereby bread for his family.

I was not the only one to notice Neeb's disappointment at not seeing among us the girl Gerda, whom he was later so unerringly to find and make his own, that he became partially responsible for her death. Else, I believe, was the youngest of us all, a rotund girl with thick plaits and a round, cherry red mouth. She remarked, apparently casually, calmly, that one of us, Gerda, had stayed in the inn to care for a sick child. Else, whom I and everyone else quickly forgot in her smallness and inconspicuousness, just as in any bunch of flowers one forgets a particular fat bud, had not yet had any love affairs of her own, but liked to discover other people's and to poke about in them. Now the gleam in Herr Neeb's eye told her that she had guessed right. She added, apparently casually, "The sickroom is just behind the kitchen."

While Else was thus testing outer craftiness—and she could decipher Neeb's thoughts far better with her glittering child's eyes than with grown-up eyes dimmed by experience—she was to wait a long time for her own love. For her future husband, the joiner Ebi, went to war first. Even then he already had a pointed beard and a paunch and was much older than she. When, after that particular Armistice, he made the still round and snub-nosed Else mistress of his joinery shop, it was useful to him in the business that she had meanwhile learned bookkeeping at the commercial college. For both of them the important things were the workshop and their three children. The joiner was later in the habit of saying that his trade ran just the same whether there were Grand-ducal or Social Democratic cabinets in Darmstadt, the provincial capital. Hitler's power and the outbreak of the new war he also looked upon as a kind of evil natural event, like a thunderstorm or a blizzard. He was elderly by then. Else's bushy plaits also contained several gray strands. He probably had no time to change his opinion when, within five minutes of the launching of British air raid on Mainz, his wife Else, he himself, his children and his journeymen lost their lives, while his house and workshop were transformed into splinters and rubble.

While Else, firm and round as a dumpling and looking as though nothing short of a bomb could shatter her, sprang into her row of girls, Marianne took up her position in the farthest corner of the back row, where Otto could still stand beside her, her hand in his. They looked over the fence into the water, where their shadow mingled with the reflections of the mountains and clouds and the white walls of the inn. They did not speak to each other; they were sure that nothing could part them, no rows of girls and no steamer trip, not even, later, death together in peaceful old age among a horde of children.

The older teacher of the boys' class—he shuffled and cleared his throat and he was called by the boys the "Old Man"—came across the landing stage into the garden, surrounded by his boys. They sat down swiftly and greedily at the table that we girls had just left, and the proprietress, who was glad that her sick child was still being tended by Gerda, brought her fresh blue and white onion-pattern crockery. The boys' form master Herr Reiss, began to lap up his coffee. It sounded as though a bearded giant were lapping it up.

The reverse of the usual order of events, the teacher watched his young pupils die in the following and in the present war, in black, white, and red and in Swastika regiments. But he survived it all unharmed. For he gradually became too old for struggle and even for utterances that might have put him in prison or in a concentration camp.

While the boys hanging round the Old Man, some of them well-behaved, some of them rowdy, resembled cohorts of the legend, the swarm of girls down below in the garden were squeaky and elfin. When we were counted, a few girls were found to be missing. Lore was sitting among the boys' class, for she always remained as long as possible, today as throughout her whole life which a Nazi's jealousy brought to a bad end, in male company. Besides her giggled a certain Elli, who had suddenly discovered her friend from the dancing class, Walter, a fat-cheeked little boy. Now his trousers—to his distress still short—were too light over his solid bottom; later, already an elderly, but still very fine looking SS man, he was to be in charge of the transport which carried Leni's arrested husband away forever. Leni was still carefully standing at an angle, so that Marianne could exchange final words with her beloved, unaware by how many future hostilities she was surrounded here in the garden. Ida, the future Deaconess, trotted down to us whistling and with comical dance steps. The round saucer eyes of the little boys and the slanting, comfortable eyes of the old coffee sipper rested delightedly on her curly head, round which a velvet band was twisted. One day in the Russian winter of 1943, when her hospital was under fire, she will think of the velvet band round her hair and the white, sunny inn and the garden by the Rhine and of the boys who were arriving and the girls who were leaving.

Marianne had let go of her Otto Fresenius's hand. Nor did she any longer have her arm on Leni's shoulder; she stood in her row of girls alone and abandoned to her meditations on love. In spite of this most earthly of all states of mind she stood out from the other girls by an almost supernatural beauty. Otto Fresenius returned to the boys' table, side by side with the yong teacher Neeb. The latter displayed no mockery and asked no questions, like a good comrade, because he was looking for a girl in the same class and because even in the very youngest he respected enterprises of love. Since death was to tear this boy Otto away from his loved one so much quicker than the older teacher, fidelity was preserved for him throughout his short life and he was spared all the evil, all the temptations, all the meanness and shame, to which the older man fell victim when he tried to save a State post and salary for himself and Gerda.

Fräulein Mees, with the mighty, indestructible cross on her bosom, watched carefully over us girls, so that none of us should run off to her dancing class friend before the arrival of the steamer. Fräulein Sichel had gone in search of a certain Sophie Meier and finally found her on the seesaw with a boy called Herbert Becker, who just like her was thin and bespectacled, so that they looked more like brother and sister than lovers. Herbert Becker ran away at the sight of the teacher. I often used to see him later running through our town, grinning and making faces. He still had the same bespectacled, wide-awake boy's face when I met him again a few years ago in France, after he had just got back from the Spanish Civil War. Sophie was scolded by Fräulein Sichel for gadding about, so that she had to polish her tear-wet glasses. Not only the teacher's hair, which now too I again discovered to my surprise to be mingled with gray strands, but also the hair of her pupil Sophie—which was now as black as ebony like the hair of Snow White—was to be white all over when they were deported to Poland together by the Nazis in a truck that was crammed full and sealed. Sophie was actually completely wizened and senile when she died, surprisingly, in Fräulein Sichel's arms like a sister of the same age.

We were comforting Sophie and wiping her glasses as Fräulein Mees clapped her hands for us to go down to the steamer station. We felt ashamed because the boys' class was watching us being made to march in line and because they all made fun of our teacher's crooked, waddling duck's walk. In me alone mockery was mitigated by respect for the unchanging firmness of her attitude, which even an appearance before the People's Court, called into being by Hitler, with a threat of imprisonment, could do nothing to alter. We all waited together on the landing stage, until our steamer cast its mooring rope ashore. The catching of the rope by the boatman, the winding of the rope round the bollard, the lowering of the gangplank seemed to me extraordinarily dexterous, the welcome of a new world, the guarantee of our trip by water, so that all voyages over unending seas from one continent to another paled and became fantastic as children's dreams. They were not nearly so exciting, so true to nature in the smell of timber and water, in the slight swaying of the gangplank, in the creaking of the rope as the commencement of the twenty-minute trip down the Rhine to my home town.

I jumped on to the deck in order to sit near the wheel. The ship's bell rang, the rope was hauled in, the steamer put about. Its white, glittering arc of foam buried itself in the river. I thought of all the white grooves of foam that all possible ships had furrowed in the seas at all possible degrees of latitude. The fleetingness and the immutability of a voyage, the bottomlessness and the attainability of water never again impressed themselves so powerfully upon me. Then Fräulein Sichel was suddenly standing in front of me. In the sunshine she looked very young in her spotted dress with her firm little bosom. She told me with shining gray eyes that because I liked traveling and because I liked writing essays, I should write a description of the school outing for the next German lesson.

All the girls in the class who preferred to deck over the cabin threw themselves on the benches around me. From the garden the boys were waving and whistling. Lore whistled shrilly back; she was vigorously scolded for it by Fräulein Mees, while the boys on the bank continued to whistle in unison. Marianne leaned far over the rail and did not let Otto out of her sight, as though this parting might be forever, like the one later in 1914. When she could no longer make out her friend, she put one arm around me and one round Leni. At the same time as the tenderness of her thin, bare arm I felt the sun shining on my neck. I too now looked back at Otto Fresenius, who was still gazing after his girl, as though he could keep her in sight and, as she now leaned her head on Leni, and remind her forever of inviolable love.

We three looked upriver in a close embrace. The slanting afternoon sun on the hills and vineyards ruffled the white and pink blossoms of fruit trees. In the late sunshine a few windows were gleaming as though aflame. The villages seemed to grow the closer we came to them, and no sooner had we passed than they shriveled up again. We felt the inborn desire for travel that can never be stilled because always one only brushes against things in passing. We sailed on under the Rhine bridges, across which, in the First World War, military trains were to pass carrying all the boys who were now drinking their coffee in the garden and all the pupils of all the schools. When this war ended, the soldiers of the Allies crossed the same bridge and later Hitler crossed it with his young army that was reoccupying the Rhineland, until the new military trains carried all the boys of the nation to death in the new world war. Our steamer sailed past the Petersau on which one of the bridge piers stood. We all waved to the three little white houses that had been familiar to us since childhood as though from picture books with fairy tales about witches. The little houses and a fisherman were mirrored in the water and with them the village on the other bank which rose in a Gothic triangle with its fields of rape and corn through a border of pink apple trees in a squat swarm of interlocking gabled roofs to the little church steeple on the mountainside.

The late light shone now into the crack of a valley with traces of a railway, now into an out-of-the-way chapel, and everything looked out once more from the Rhine before vanishing in the dusk.

In the silent light we had all become silent, so that we heard the cawing of a few birds and the howling of the factory at Amoneburg. Even Lore had fallen completely silent. Marianne and Leni and I had all three linked our arms in an alliance that was simply part of the great alliance of everything earthly under the sun. Marianne's head was still resting against Leni's head. How was it that later a deception, an insane idea managed to creep into her thoughts—that she and her husband were the only people who loved this land and therefore had a perfect right to despise and denounce the girl against whom she was now leaning. No one, while there was still time, ever reminded us of this voyage in common. However, many essays were written about the homeland and the history of the homeland and love of the homeland, no one ever mentioned that our swarm of girls leaning against each other as they sailed upstream in the slanting afternoon light were especially a part of this homeland.

One arm of the river was already branching off to the raft harbor, from which the freshly felled, cut, and rafted timber was taken to Holland. The town seemed to me still sufficiently far away never to be able to compel me to disembark and remain, although its raft harbor, the rows of plane trees and warehouses on the bank were much more familiar to me than any of the entrances into foreign towns that have forced me to stay. Bit by bit I recognized already familiar streets and rooftops and church towers, undamaged and familiar, like long since vanished places in fairy tales and songs. The one day's school outing seemed at the same time to have taken everything away from me and to have given it back.

As the steamer now veered round to moor and children and vagabonds pushed their way idly over to watch our arrival, we seemed to be coming home not from an outing, but from a voyage that had lasted for years. There was no gap, no fire damage in this familiar winding, teeming town, so that my uneasiness passed and I felt at home.

Lotte was the first to say good-bye, the moment the ropes had been thrown out. She wanted to get to evening mass in the cathedral, whose bells were already ringing as far as the floating bridge. Lotte ended up later in the convent on the Rhine island of Nonnenworth, from where she was taken across the Dutch frontier with a troop of nuns; but Fate came after her.

The class said good-bye to the teachers. Fräulein Sichel reminded me again of the essay; her gray eyes flashed like finely polished flints. Then our class divided up into single groups according to the direction in which their homes lay.

Leni and Marianne walked along arm in arm toward the Rheinstrasse. Marianne still had a red carnation between her teeth. She had put a similar carnation in the ribbon round Leni's Mozart plait. I see Marianne still with the red carnation between her teeth even when she returned an angry answer to Leni's neighbors, even when she lay with a half-charred body and smoking rags of clothing among the ashes of her parent's house. For the fire brigade arrived too late to save Marianne, when the fire from the air raid spread from the houses that had suffered direct hits to the Rheinstrasse, where she was visiting her parents. She had no easier death than Leni, whom she had denied and who died of hunger and disease in the concentration camp. But through her denial Leni's child survived the bombing. For it was taken by the Gestapo to a remote Nazi educational institution.

I trotted along with a few pupils in the direction of the Chrissthofstrasse. At first I felt frightened. As we turned in from the Rhine toward the inner town I felt a weight on my heart, as though something senseless, something evil lay ahead of me, perhaps bad news or a disaster that I had frivolously forgotten during the sunny outing. Then I realized clearly that the Christhofskirche could not possibly have been destroyed by a night air raid, because we could hear its evening bells. I had shuddered unnecessarily at the prospect of going home along this road, because I had got it firmly into my memory that this central area of the town had been totally destroyed by bombs. It also passed through my head that that newspaper photograph might have been mistaken on which all the streets and squares were razed to the ground or destroyed. I thought at first that perhaps on orders from Goebbels, in order to misrepresent the scale of the attack, a fake town had been thrown up with all speed in which no stone stood upon the other as it had done, but which nevertheless looked quite compact and pleasant. We had all long since grown accustomed to such tricks and deceptions, no only in relation to air raids but also in connection with other events that were difficult to see through.

But the houses, the steps, the fountain stood as always, including Braun's wallpaper shop, which was to be burned along with the family in this war. In the first war, the shop window was merely smashed in by a piece of shrapnel, showing the flowered and striped wallpapers on display, so that Marie Braun, who had just been walking along with me, ran into her father's shop. The next one among us homecomers, Katherine, ran to her tiny little sister Toni, who was playing under the plane trees on a stone step in front of the fountain. The fountain and all the plane trees had long ago been blown to bits, but the children did not miss the things they had used for their games, for their last hour too had struck in the basements of the surrounding houses. Toni also died then in the house which she had inherited from her father, with a little daughter, as tiny as she was today as she spurted the water out of fat cheeks. Katherine, the big sister, who now grabbed her by the pigtail, and her mother and her aunt who greeted them both with kisses in the open door of the house—all of them were to die together in the cellar of her father's house. Katherine's husband, a paperhanger, her father's successor, was meanwhile helping to occupy France. With his short moustache and his paperhanger's thumb, he thought himself a member of a nation that was stronger than other nations—until the news came to him that his house and his family had been smashed to pieces. The little sister turned round once again and spattered me too with the last drop of water she had stored up in her cheeks.

I ran the rest of the way alone. In the Flachsmarktstrasse I met the pale Liese Mobius, also a girl from my class, who because of an attack of pneumonia had not been able to go on any outings for the last two months. Now the evening bells of the Christhofskirche had lured her away from home. She raced past me with her two long brown plaits dangling and a pince-nez on her small face, as nimbly as though she were running to a playground instead of to evening mass. She later begged her parents to let her go with Lotte into the convent at Nonnenworth. When Lotte alone was given permission, Liese became a teacher in a primary school in our town. I still used to see her sometimes running to mass with her pale, pointed little face, as now with the pince-nez clipped on to it. She was treated contemptuously by the Nazi authorities because of her loyalty to her faith, but even her transfer to a school for the educationally sub-normal—which, under Hitler, was considered a light work— did not disturb her, because through her faith she was used to persecutions of all kinds. Moreover, the most rabid Nazi women, the most malicious scornful neighbors, grew gentle and mild when they sat around Liese in the cellar during air raids. It passed through the minds of the older ones that they had already sat with the same neighbor Liese in the same cellar in the first war when the first shots rang out. Now they moved up close to the despised little teacher, as though she had already mollified death once by her faith and her calm. The most impudent and mocking were actually inclined to take on something of the faith of the little teacher Liese, who in their eyes had always been shy and timid, but who now sat confidently among all the gray-white faces in the artificial light of the cellar during the bombing, which this time almost completely destroyed the town, including herself and her believing, unbelieving neighbors.

The shops had just been shut. I ran down the Flachsmarktstrasse, through a seething mass of people on their way home. They were glad that the day was at an end and a restful night lay ahead of them. Just as their houses were still undamaged by gunfire, by the first great test of 1914 to 1918 and by the most recent direct hit, so their comfortable, utterly familiar, thin and fat, mustached or full-bearded, warty and smooth faces were undamaged by guilt, by watching and tolerating this guilt out of cowardice, out of fear of the might of the State. Yet they were soon to have enough of puffed-up State power, of grandiose orders. Or had they developed a taste for it, this baker with the twirled mustache and the round little tummy, on the corner of the Flachsmarkt, where we always bought the yeast cake, or the tram conductor who was just tinkling past us? Or was there something repellent to all the children about this evening with the hurried footsteps of the homecomers, the pealing of the bells, the knocking-off sirens from distant factories, which I was now enjoying like a boon—so that they soon absorbed the war reports of their fathers and longed to get out of their floury or dusty overalls and into uniform?

I felt another spasm of fear at the prospect of turning into my own street, as though I had a premonition that it had been destroyed. The premonition soon vanished. For along the last stretch of the Bahnhofstrasse I was already able to take my favorite way home, under the two tall ash trees that spanned the street from left and right like a triumphal arch, touching each other, undestroyed, indestructible. I could also already see the white red and blue circle of flowerbeds filled with geraniums and begonias in the lawn that crossed my street. As I approached, an evening breeze, stronger than I had ever before felt it on my temples, blew a cloud of petals from the hawthorn trees which at first seemed to have the sun shining on them, but in reality were themselves sun-red in color. I felt as I always did after day excursions as though it had been a long time since I last heard the soughing of the wind from the Rhine caught in my own street. I was utterly exhausted, so that I was glad at last to be standing in front of my house. Only it seemed to me an intolerable effort to climb the stairs. I looked up at the second floor, on which our flat lay. My mother was already standing on the little verandah decorated with geraniums in window boxes above the street. She was already waiting for me. How young my mother looked, much younger than I. How dark her smooth hair was, compared with mine. Mine very soon turned gray, whereas not a single visible gray strand yet ran through hers. She stood there merry and erect, intended for a busy family life, with the usual joys and burdens of everyday living, not for an agonizing, dreadful end in a remote village, to which she was banished by Hitler. Now she caught sigh of me and waved, as though I had been away on a journey. This was the way she always laughed and waved after outings. I ran to the staircase as fast as I could.

I hesitated before the first step. I was suddenly far too tired to climb fast, as just before I had wanted to do. The gray-blue mist of fatigue enveloped everything. And yet it was all bright and hot around me, not twilight as on most staircases. I forced myself to climb up to my mother; the stairs, lost in a haze, seemed to me unattainably high, insurmountably steep, as though they ran up a mountainside. Perhaps my mother had already gone into the hall and was waiting for me in the door to the stairs. But my legs failed me. Only as a very small child had I felt a similar anxiety that some disaster might prevent me from seeing her again. I imagined her waiting for me in vain, only a few stairs away. Then it occurred to me as a consolation that if I were to break down from exhaustion here, my father could find me at once. He wasn't dead at all, because he would be home in a moment, work was over for the day. It was only that he liked to chat with his neighbors on the street corner longer than my mother liked him to.

They were already rattling the plates for supper. Behind all the doors I heard the slapping of hands on dough in the familiar rhythm. I was put off by this way of making pancakes, slapping the ropy mass flat between the hands instead of rolling it out. At the same time I heard from the yard the unrestrained screeching of turkeys, and wondered why people were suddenly keeping turkeys in the yard. I wanted to look round, but at first I was dazzled by the excessively bright light from the yard windows. The stairs were swimming in a haze, the staircase stretched out to an impenetrable depth, like an abyss. Then clouds gathered in the window recesses that pretty quickly filled the abyss. I thought weakly: what a pity, I should so much have liked to be embraced by my mother. If I'm too tired to climb up, where shall I find the strength to reach the village higher up the mountain whence I came and where they are waiting for me by night? The sun was still burning strongly, its light never burned more cuttingly than when it came down at an angle. As always I found it strange that there was no dusk here, but always a swift transition from day to night. I pulled myself together and stepped out more strongly, although the ascent was lost in an impenetrable abyss. The banisters twisted and arched into a vast state-like fence of organ cactuses. I could no longer make out which were mountain ranges and which chains of clouds.

I found my way to the inn where I had sat after my descent from the village higher up the mountain. The dog had run away. Two turkeys, which had not been there before, were now feeding on the roadway. My innkeeper was still sitting in front of the house, and beside him sat a friend or a relation, just like him, rigid with meditation or with nothing at all. At their feet, in harmony, sat the shadows of their hats. My innkeeper made no move as I came back; I wasn't worth it, I had already taken my place among the ordinary sensory impressions. I was too tired now to take so much as one more step; I sat down at my old table. I wanted to get back into the mountains, as soon as I had recovered my breath a little. I asked myself how I was to pass the time, today and tomorrow, here and there, for I could now feel an immeasurable river of time, as indomitable as the air. We have been taught from childhood, instead of surrendering ourselves humbly to time, to overcome it in some way or other. I suddenly remembered my teacher's request that I should carefully describe the school outing. I wanted to carry out her instructions tomorrow, or even this evening, as soon as my tiredness had worn off.

Translated by Michael Bullock

The Authors

ALFRED DÖBLIN was born in Stettin in 1878. After his father emigrated to America with a young girl in 1888, the family moved to Berlin, where they were supported by a relative. Döblin managed to attend prep school and completed his education there despite his discontent with his teachers, and in 1905 earned a degree in medicine specializing in neurology and psychiatry. He devoted himself to scientific studies while a resident physician in various mental institutions, and starting in 1912 he ran his own practice in a working-class district of Berlin. He had begun to write while still a student at the gymnasium, and his first success as a writer came in 1912 when he published a volume of short stories, *Die Ermordung einer Butterblume* (*The Murder of a Buttercup*, 1972). Together with Herwarth Walden, his friend for many years, Döblin helped found the Expressionist association Der Sturm. Döblin's first major novel, *Die drei Sprünge des Wang-lun* (1915; The three leaps of Wang-Lun) was awarded the Fontane Prize; in *Wallenstein* (1920) he used the example of the Thirty Years War to show his response to World War I, in which he had served as a military doctor. The essay collection *Der deutsche Maskenball* (1921; The German masked ball) reflects his disappointment at the outcome of the 1918–19 revolution and is critical of the young Weimar Republic. In a series of more-or-less leftwing organizations, including the German Writers Union (Schutzverband deutscher Schriftsteller) of which he became chair in 1924, Döblin committed himself to defending freedom of speech, which he saw threatened by the so-called Harmful and Obscene Publications Acts, legal charges brought against artists, and the banning of books. In his futuristic novel *Berge, Meere und Giganten* (1924; Mountains, seas, and giants) Döblin decried a form of nature mysticism that is opposed to modern technology. *Reise in Polen* (1925; *Journey to Poland),* a report on what he regarded as the unspoiled life of Eastern European Jews, was published in the U.S. in 1991; the big-city novel *Berlin Alexanderplatz,* a classic of Expressionist prose that treats many of Döblin's central themes, quickly became an international success. Shortly after Hitler came to power, Döblin, who once called himself a "revolutionary of the mind," fled to France, and in 1940 he escaped to the United States via Lisbon. Döblin felt relatively at home in Paris, where in 1940 he worked under Jean Giraudoux in France's ministry of information. One of his sons, who fought in the French army against Germany, committed suicide when threatened with capture and a second son went missing in action for a time. Once in America Döblin began a rapid decline into isolation, poverty, and loss of success as a writer. In 1934, Amsterdam's exile-publishing house, Querido, brought out his novel *Babylonische Wandrung oder Hochmut kommt vor dem Fall* (Babylonian wandering; or, pride goes before a fall), followed a year later by *Pardon wird nicht gegeben* (1935; *Men without Mercy,* 1937), a warning against National Socialism, and in 1937–38 the first part of what later became his South American trilogy, *Das Land ohne Tod* (Land without death). Other projects were never completed, or failed for a long time to find a publisher, including *November 1918* (1938/1949), *Schicksalsreise* (1949; Fatal journey), and, after the war, *Hamlet oder Die lange Nacht nimmt ein Ende* (1956; Hamlet; or, the long night comes to an end). Döblin's conversion to Catholicism while in exile in Los Angeles was not understood by many of his Jewish friends. One of the first exiles to return to West Germany in 1945, he worked there as a cultural attaché for the French occupation forces and founded the magazine *Das goldene Tor* (1946–51), but quickly realized that his previous fame as a Weimar author no longer counted for much. Disappointed by the lack of response to his work and disillusioned by the restoration of conservative forces in West Germany, Döblin returned to France, and after a long, severe illness he died in 1937 while at a health resort in his German homeland.

LION FEUCHTWANGER was born in Munich in 1884, the son of margarine manufacturer Sigmund Aaron Meir Feuchtwanger and his wife Johanna. He studied German literature, philosophy, and anthropology in Berlin and then in Munich, where he earned his doctorate in 1907 with a dissertation on Heinrich Heine's fragmentary work *Der Rabbi von Bacherach*. He wrote scores of dramas and theater reviews until the publication of his first successful novel, *Jud Süss* (*Jew Süss*, 1926) in 1925. With his wife Marta, he made long trips to the Mediterranean region. Poor health exempted him from military service in World War I. Feuchtwanger's lifelong friendship and collaboration with Bertolt Brecht, who like him witnessed the revolutionary events in southern Germany, began in 1919. From the mid-1920s onward, Feuchtwanger enjoyed wide success both in Germany and abroad for his thoroughly researched but popularly written historical novels including *Jud Süss*, the Josephus trilogy (1932–42), *Der falsche Nero* (1936; *The Pretender*, 1937), and *Goya* (1951; *This Is the Hour*, 1951). At the same time, he explored the political conflicts of his age and the increasingly open anti-Semitism in Germany through plays and novels such as *Drei angelsächsische Stücke*, (1927; *Three Plays*, 1934), *Erfolg* (1930; *Success*, 1930), *Die Geschwister Oppenheim*, (1933; *The Oppermanns*, 1933), and *Exil* (1940; *Paris Gazette*, 1940). When Hitler came to power in 1933, Feuchtwanger went on a lecture tour and did not return to Germany, settling instead in Sanary-sur-Mer on the French Mediterranean coast. His home in Berlin was seized by the Nazis and his books publicly burned. His travel report, *Moskau 1937* (1937; *Moscow, 1937*, 1937), in which he gave a positive portrait of Stalin and did not unequivocally condemn the tyrant's show trials, aroused hostility that dogged Feuchtwanger until his death. After his internment in Les Milles camp and a hazardous escape from France that he describes in his novel *Unholdes Frankreich* (1942; *The Devil in France*, 1941), he arrived in the U.S. in 1940 and bought a villa in Pacific Palisades, California. During and after the war years, he produced not only historical novels such as *Die Brüder Lautensack* (1943; *Double, Double, Toil and Trouble*, 1943), *Die Jüdin von Toledo* (1955; *Raquel, the Jewess of Toledo*, 1955) and *Jefta und seine Tochter* (1957; *Jephtha and His Daughter*, 1957) but also a novel about America, *Waffen für Amerika* (1947–48; *Proud Destiny*, 1947) and a play in which he adapted early American history to explore the anticommunist atmosphere in the U.S. at the start of the cold war (*Wahn oder Der Teufel in*

Boston, 1948; Delusion; or, the devil in Boston). The German Democratic Republic, which printed and reprinted his books faster, and more often than the Federal Republic, awarded Feuchtwanger a national prize in 1953, and in 1954 gave him an honorary doctorate from Humboldt University. He remained in the United States until his death in 1958. His international fame assured him a comfortable standard of living even in exile. Feuchtwanger did not dare to revisit Europe since the FBI maintained an intensive surveillance on the suspected Communist fellow-traveler, and he feared that he would be refused a visa to reenter the United States, as happened to his friend Charlie Chaplin. Villa Aurora, his house perched above the Pacific coast, was converted into a meeting place for European and American artists after the death of Marta Feuchtwanger in 1987.

ANNA SEGHERS was born in Mainz in 1900 as the daughter of Jewish art dealer Isidor Reiling and his wife Hedwig. After a sheltered childhood, she commenced in 1919 to major in art history and in 1924 earned her degree at Heidelberg University with a dissertation on Jews and Judaism in the work of Rembrandt. In Heidelberg she met the Hungarian Communist, Laszlo Radvanyi, whom she married in 1925. They had two children. She began her career as a writer in 1924 with the story "Die Toten auf der Insel Djal" (The dead on Djal Island), which she published under the pseudonym Antje Seghers. In 1928, now under the name Anna Seghers, she was awarded the Kleist Prize for "Grubetsch" and *Aufstand der Fischer von St. Barbara* (1928; *The Revolt of the Fishermen*, 1930). In the same year she joined the German Communist Party, the KPD, and shortly after the Union of Proletarian Revolutionary Writers. A year following publication of her novel *Die Gefährten* (1932; The companions), she fled the Nazis coming to Paris, where she wrote the novels *Der Kopflohn* (1933; A price on his head), *Der Weg durch den Februar* (1935; The way through February), *Die Rettung* (1937; Rescue), and *Das siebte Kreuz* (1942; *The Seventh Cross*, 1942). In September, 1940, she again ran from the German troops, first into unoccupied southern France, then, after her husband's release from the Le Vernet camp, to New York, where she and her family were denied entry, and finally to Mexico. While the success of *The Seventh Cross* in the United States brought her fame and income, in Mexico Seghers involved herself in Communist-leaning organizations such as the Heinrich Heine Club, the Free Germany Movement, and the publishing house El Libro Libre. A novel about her flight through France, *Transit* (1944; *Transit,* 1948), and the story "Der Ausflug der toten Mädchen" (1946; "Excursion of the Dead Girls") were published in America either in English translation or in German alone. In spring 1947, Seghers returned to Berlin with a manuscript about Germany since World War I, *Die Toten bleiben jung* (1949; *The Dead Stay Young,* 1950), and there produced two novels dedicated to the building of socialism in the GDR, *Die Entscheidung* (1959; The decision) and *Das Vertrauen* (1968; Trust). As chairperson of the East German Writers Union and recipient of numerous national awards, Seghers belongs to the generation of authors that rebuilt cultural life in Germany after 1945 but that, although revered, steadily lost their literary influence. Until her death in Berlin in 1983, Seghers was noted for her public appearances on behalf of the peace movement, for her speeches at writers' conferences, for incessant travels, and for cautious efforts to exert a moderating influence on the dogmatic forces in East Germany's Socialist Unity Party, the SED. Now suffering from frequent illnesses, Seghers returned in later years to her favorite literary genre, the short story, in volumes such as *Überfahrt* (1971; The crossing) and *Sonderbare Begegnung* (1973; Strange encounter).

ARNOLD ZWEIG was born in 1887 in Glogau in Silesia, the son of shipping agent and harness maker Adolf Zweig, and his wife Bianca. After graduating from a science-oriented secondary school in Katowice, Zweig studied various branches of the humanities at a series of universities from 1907 to 1914. His first literary success was *Novellen um Claudia* in 1912 (*Claudia,* 1930). That same year, stimulated by the writings of Martin Buber, Zweig began studying the problems of East European Jews. In 1915, he won the Kleist Prize for his drama *Ritualmord in Ungarn* (Ritual murder in Hungary). His unhappy experiences in World War I, first at Verdun and then on the Eastern front, formed the basis for his popular novel *Der Streit um den Sergeanten Grischa* (1927; *The Case of Sergeant Grischa,* 1927). In 1916 Zweig married his cousin Beatrice, and from the end of the war he worked as a freelance writer, contributing to journals like *Weltbühne* and editing the magazine *Jüdische*

Rundschau. In the following years, he became a Zionist and also supported the revolutionary developments in Russia. In the mid-1920s, Zweig, a friend of Sigmund Freud, underwent his first course of psychoanalysis. From then on, a severe eye disorder forced Zweig to dictate his texts to a secretary. By 1933, when he fled from the Nazis to Haifa, Zweig had published a number of works including the novels *Junge Frau von 1914* (1931; *Young Woman of 1914*, 1932) and *De Vriendt kehrt heim* (1932; *De Vriendt Goes Home*, 1933). In his first years of exile Querido Verlag, in Amsterdam, printed what Zweig called "an essay," *Bilanz der deutschen Judenheit 1933* (1934; Survey of German Jews in 1933) and two more novels from the monumental cycle about World War I called The Great War of White Men (*Der große Krieg der weißen Männer*): *Erziehung vor Verdun* (1935; *Education before Verdun*, 1938) and *Einsetzung eines Königs* (1937; *The Crowning of a King*, 1938). In 1942, Zweig founded in Haifa the German-language exile magazine *Orient*, which aroused the hostility of Zionist extremists and ceased publication in 1943. *Das Beil von Wandsbek* (1943; *The Axe of Wandsbek*, 1947), a novel about the effects of a judicial murder in Hamburg, was published in Hebrew in 1943, followed by a German edition published in Stockholm in 1947. In 1948, Zweig responded to an invitation from colleagues by settling in East Berlin. For the next two decades, he committed himself to working for the cultural growth of the GDR, which awarded him a national prize in 1950. That same year, Zweig, who since 1949 had served in the lower house of the East German Parliament as a deputy for the League of Culture, became president of the German Academy of Arts in Berlin. In 1958, he received the Peace Prize in Moscow. Among the literary works he produced in the GDR were two more books about World War I, *Die Feuerpause* (1954; Temporary ceasefire) and *Die Zeit ist reif* (1957; The time is ripe), as well as a World War II novel about the Greek resistance against German occupation in the period 1941–42, *Traum ist teuer* (1962; Expensive dreams). Zweig died in Berlin in 1968 and like Anna Seghers is buried in the Dorotheenstadt Cemetery.

Translated by Jan van Heurck

Acknowledgments

Every reasonable effort has been made to locate the owners of rights to previously published works and translations printed here. We gratefully acknowledge permission to reprint the following material:

From THE CASE OF SERGEANT GRISCHA by Arnold Zweig, translated by Eric Sutton, copyright 1927 by Gustav Kiepenheuer Verlag. Translation © 1928 by Viking Press, Inc., renewed 1955. Used by permission of Viking Penguin, a division of Penguin Putnam Inc.

Lion Feuchtwanger, JUD SÜSS © Aufbau-Verlag Berlin and Weimar 1984 and DIE GESCHWISTER OPPERMANN © Aufbau-Verlag Berlin 1956.

From THE OPPERMANNS by Lion Feuchtwanger, translated by J. Cleugh, copyright 1933 by The Viking Press, Inc. Renewed Copyright © 1962 by The Viking Press, Inc. Used by permission of Viking Penguin, a division of Penguin Putnam Inc.

Anna Seghers, DAS SIEBTE KREUZ © Aufbau-Verlag GmbH, Berlin 1946.

Anna Seghers, "Excursion of the Dead Girls" ("The Outing of the Dead Girls") from 3 GERMAN STORIES, translated by Michael Bullock, copyright © 1968 by The African Education Press. Used by permission of African Education Press. (Title change by permission.)

Author Listing
in The German Library
by Volume Number

Titles Available in
The German Library

*All titles available at your bookstore or
from Continuum International
370 Lexington Avenue, New York, NY 10017
www.continuumbooks.com*

Titles Available in The German Library

Titles Available in The German Library

Titles Available in The German Library